D1544838

REASON'S DEBT TO FREEDOM

REASON'S DEBT TO FREEDOM

Normative Appraisals, Reasons, and Free Will

Ishtiyaque Haji

OXFORD
UNIVERSITY PRESS

OXFORD

UNIVERSITY PRESS

Oxford University Press, Inc., publishes works that further
Oxford University's objective of excellence
in research, scholarship, and education.

Oxford   New York
Auckland   Cape Town   Dar es Salaam   Hong Kong   Karachi
Kuala Lumpur   Madrid   Melbourne   Mexico City   Nairobi
New Delhi   Shanghai   Taipei   Toronto

With offices in
Argentina   Austria   Brazil   Chile   Czech Republic   France   Greece
Guatemala   Hungary   Italy   Japan   Poland   Portugal   Singapore
South Korea   Switzerland   Thailand   Turkey   Ukraine   Vietnam

Copyright © 2012 Oxford University Press

Published by Oxford University Press, Inc.
198 Madison Avenue, New York, New York 10016

www.oup.com

Oxford is a registered trademark of Oxford University Press

Library of Congress Cataloging-in-Publication Data
Haji, Ishtiyaque.
Reason's debt to freedom: normative appraisals, reasons, and free will / Ishtiyaque Haji.
     p.   cm.
ISBN 978-0-19-989920-3 (alk. paper)
1. Responsibility. 2. Free will and determinism. 3. Frankfurt, Harry G., 1929–I. Title.
BJ1451.H353   2012
123'.5—fdc23   2011039184

1 3 5 7 9 8 6 4 2

Printed in the United States of America
on acid-free paper

CONTENTS

REASON'S DEBT TO FREEDOM

Chapter 1

Freedom, Normative Judgments, and Reason

1.1. FREEDOM AND NORMATIVE JUDGMENTS: THE BASIC ISSUES

Various normative judgments are conceptually tied to freedom. For instance, we are at home with the view that moral responsibility requires control. More exactly, there is widespread concurrence that the following principle captures an essential metaphysical element of responsibility: one is morally praiseworthy or blameworthy for doing something only if one can do it. Alternatively, we could express this association between judgments of moral responsibility and freedom in this way: one is either morally praiseworthy or blameworthy for doing something only if one has control regarding or one is free in doing it.[1] This sort of conceptual connection also holds between morally deontic judgments—judgments of overall moral right, wrong, and obligation—and freedom.[2] We are, for example, familiar with the dictum—*Kant's Law*—that "ought" implies "can": if one morally ought to do something, then one can do it; or, then again, if one morally ought to do something, one has control regarding or is free in doing it. Still further, and not surprisingly, we find this same sort of conceptual association between freedom and judgments of prudential obligation.

While this connection between such judgments and freedom is frequently acknowledged, there is a great deal of debate about the precise nature of the control or freedom that the truth of, for example, responsibility judgments, morally deontic judgments, or prudential judgments presupposes. To appreciate some of the relevant disagreement, introducing some key concepts and drawing some preliminary distinctions will prove useful. The *free will thesis* affirms that with respect to some acts, we have both the ability to perform and the ability to refrain from performing them. This thesis entails that for something we did do "of our own free will," we were at some time prior to our doing it able to refrain from doing it (van Inwagen 2008, 329). Our having free will with respect to doing something—making a decision or performing some overt action, for instance—entails our having the power to refrain from doing what we did.

Determinism is the view that there is at any instant exactly one physically possible future (van Inwagen 1983, 3). If the world is deterministic, then a complete description of the total state of the world at any given time, conjoined with a complete statement of the laws of nature, entails every truth about how the world is at every other time. On this view, given the laws of nature, how the world is at any time completely determines how it is at any other time.

Incompatibilism with respect to free will is the view that determinism is incompatible with our having free will; it is incompatible with our being able to do otherwise, or, if one wants, it is incompatible with our having access to alternatives. Analogously, incompatibilism with respect to moral responsibility (or moral or prudential obligation) is the view that determinism is incompatible with moral responsibility (or moral or prudential obligation). Compatibilism is the denial of incompatibilism.[3] So, for example, compatibilism with respect to free will entails that determinism is indeed compatible with our being able to do otherwise. Libertarians concerning moral responsibility affirm that incompatibilism with respect to free will is true, and that at least some of us, at times, perform (free) actions for which we are morally responsible.

Some compatibilists—"traditional compatibilists"—and some incompatibilists—"traditional incompatibilists"—regarding moral responsibility affirm that the truth of responsibility judgments entails our having free will; they concur that responsibility requires our having alternative possibilities. On this view, to incur responsibility we must have different pathways into the future, and it must be up to us on which of these we tread. But these theorists differ on their conception of alternatives. Traditional incompatibilists—but not traditional compatibilists—hold that the alternatives responsibility requires are nonexistent in a world at which determinism obtains. Here, it will help to distinguish between strong and weak alternatives (or between a strong sense of "can" and a weak sense of "can"). Assuming agent S does action A at time t in world w, S has a strong alternative at t if the combination of w's past and w's laws of nature is consistent with S's not A-ing at t. Determinism effaces strong alternatives; no one has such alternatives in a deterministic world, or at least it is customarily acknowledged that this is so. Weak alternatives are alternatives one can have despite determinism's obtaining. On one conception of weak alternatives, for instance, although an agent does one thing—she donates to a good charity, say—she would have refrained from donating had she wanted, tried, intended, or chosen not to donate. Traditional compatibilists can be understood as proposing that responsibility requires our having weak alternatives; traditional incompatibilists can be thought of as endorsing the view that responsibility requires our having strong alternatives. Both these traditional sorts of theorists, however, do not deny the association between the truth of responsibility judgments and freedom. (They may, of course, deny that this association is conceptual.) These parties may take a similar stance on the truth of morally deontic judgments, agreeing that the truth of such judgments is conceptually linked to freedom but differing on how they construe this freedom.

Other compatibilists—"nontraditional compatibilists"—regarding moral responsibility claim that the truth of responsibility judgments does not presuppose our having access to alternatives. In their view, although having free will or "two-way" control is not required for being morally responsible, responsibility does entail having control but only "one-way" control. The first but not the second half of this view stands opposed to the view of traditional incompatibilists. And, again, nontraditional compatibilists may opt for a similar position regarding morally deontic judgments.

Whereas a number of normative judgments are similar in that the truth of each is associated with freedom in the manner in which I have claimed, the diverse views regarding freedom held by nontraditional compatibilists regarding moral obligation and traditional incompatibilists regarding such obligation may suggest that there is no further feature pertaining to freedom—a "freedom-relevant feature"—that these judgments share; there is no "deep" freedom-relevant feature that "unifies" these judgments. A primary objective of this work argues that this view is false; the elements of a significant set of such judgments do in fact exemplify a freedom-relevant feature they have in common.

To sketch this feature, we need to introduce yet another species of normative judgment, the truth of which is also conceptually tied to freedom. These are judgments of practical reason of the sort such statements as "reason requires that one do something," or "reason forbids that one to do something," or "reason permits that one to do something" roughly capture. "Reason," however, is multiply ambiguous, the ambiguity deriving partly because there are different sorts of practical reason. For instance, Davidsonian reasons are complexes of desires and beliefs. Suffering from an injury, you believe that taking some medicine will help to alleviate your pain. This belief, together with your desire to rid yourself of the pain, constitutes a Davidsonian reason of yours to take the medicine. One may provisionally think of such reasons as "internal" since they are constituted by "internal" mental states (or, perhaps, their physical realizers[4]) of the agent whose Davidsonian reasons they are. In contrast, "external" or "objective" reasons (I use these labels interchangeably) are, roughly, facts dissociated from internal states of the agent. Something's being intrinsically good or one's recognizing that something is intrinsically good, for instance, is an objective reason for one to desire or pursue it. *Pro tanto* reasons are reasons that other reasons can outweigh, as opposed to all-things considered reasons (or "oughts") which cannot be outweighed. *Al* has a *pro tanto* reason to spend the evening shooting pool because he has been working so hard, but all things considered, he should finish yet another paper, which he has promised to submit by the following morning.

This book motivates the view that our having objective *pro tanto* reasons entails our having free will. No one, for example, can have such a reason to do something unless one can refrain from doing it. This is *practical reason's debt to free will*. Further, members of a set of normative judgments—morally deontic judgments, prudential judgments, various axiological judgments concerning intrinsic value, and perhaps some aretaic judgments—are conceptually or logically tied to our having objective *pro tanto* reasons. As an illustration, an act cannot be overall morally obligatory for one unless one has an objective *pro tanto* reason to do it. It follows that the truth of the members of this set of normative judgments presupposes our having free will. The normative judgments in this set exemplify a freedom-relevant "unifying" feature via their association with practical reason.

I hope that at least some interested parties will concur that undertaking this project of exposing reason's debt to freedom is philosophically worthwhile. First, the project is of intrinsic interest. Here, an analogy may prove fruitful. Some people are of the mind that showing that determinism is incompatible with our having free will has significance only because, as a well entrenched although controversial view affirms, moral responsibility requires our having free will; so if determinism expunges free will, it expunges responsibility as well. But I share with others the thought that establishing, if it is indeed so, that determinism is incompatible with our having free will is of intrinsic appeal. Similarly, showing, if it is indeed the case that our having objective *pro tanto* reasons requires our having alternatives is of intrinsic relevance.

Second, an incompatibilist theme of ascending popularity in the literature on free will is that being deprived of free will is not of momentous consequence. On this view, no judgments of moral responsibility are true in a world devoid of free will. However, being without free will does not compromise the truth of important varieties of *other* normative judgments, such as morally deontic judgments or axiological judgments concerning intrinsic value; thus, living without free will is not a big deal. Although intriguing, I believe that noteworthy elements of this theme are not sustainable and argue that being bereft of free will *is* a big deal: living without free will does have telling costs.

Third, the project is noteworthy because some of its findings bear on important, controversial issues in free will, moral obligation, and axiology. With respect to the first, so called "semi-compatibilists" have proposed that although determinism may undermine our having free will, it does not undermine the sort of control that moral responsibility requires because this control is "one-way"—it does not require our having access to alternatives—as opposed to "two-way." Semi-compatibilists have relied heavily, although not solely, on famous Frankfurt examples to galvanize semi-compatibilism. These examples, directed against the principle of alternative possibilities concerning responsibility (*PAP-R*)—the principle that persons are morally responsible for having done something *only* if they could have done otherwise—purport to show that a person can be morally praiseworthy, for example, for doing something despite not being able to do otherwise; this is so as long as the conditions that render her unable to do otherwise play no role in bringing about her action (Frankfurt 1969). Although semi-compatibilists deny that moral responsibility requires our having free will, they do not deny the association between moral responsibility, on the one hand, and our having reasons, on the other. Indeed, they wholeheartedly embrace the position that our being morally responsible presupposes our having reasons. They do so because they endorse the view that being responsible for making a decision, for instance, requires that our reason states nondeviantly cause this mental action. In their view, the control that responsibility demands consists largely in our having reasons appropriately causing our choices, actions, and so forth. It seems that at least some major semi-compatibilist contenders are most plausible when the reasons in question are objective *pro tanto*. But then, against these versions of semi-compatibilism, it turns out that appeal to alternative possibilities cannot, after all, be eschewed wholesale because one cannot have an objective *pro tanto* reason to do something unless one could have done otherwise.

Regarding moral obligation, as an illustration of a provocative and central issue on which the findings of this project have relevance, just as some believe that Frankfurt examples undermine the principle of alternative possibilities concerning responsibility (*PAP-R*), so, they believe, such examples should, with appropriate revision, be equally effective against the principle of alternative possibilities concerning obligation (*PAP-O*): a person is morally obligated to do something only if she could have done otherwise. Undermining *PAP-R* facilitates defense of the part of semi-compatibilism that affirms that determinism is compatible with moral responsibility. Analogously, it might be thought that undermining *PAP-O* should make it easier to defend the view that determinism is compatible with moral obligation. John Martin Fischer writes that he has "sought to argue that causal determinism is compatible with moral responsibility [partly by invoking Frankfurt examples]. . . . This result would be considerably less interesting if causal determinism were nevertheless incompatible with the central judgments of deontic morality" [that is, judgments of moral right, wrong, and obligation] (2006, 217). Again, *PAP-O* cannot be so easily dismissed if moral obligation is tied to our having objective *pro tanto* reasons, and there is an alternative possibilities requirement for the truth of judgments of such reasons.

Concerning axiology, as an example of a focal issue that would benefit from the explorations of this work, if the principle, in roughly hewn strokes, that something is intrinsically good only if one has a reason to want or pursue it is true, then intrinsic goodness presupposes our having alternatives provided, again, that the pertinent reasons, as I will argue, are objective *pro tanto*.

1.2. A BRIEF OUTLINE

The book is divided into two parts. In the first part, a primary goal is to establish that there is an alternative possibilities requirement for the truth of judgments of objective *pro tanto* reasons (chap. 2). I remain neutral, in this part, on whether the alternatives are weak (compatibilist) or strong (incompatibilist) alternatives; and I deliberately avoid taking a stance on whether determinism precludes the truth of various normative judgments by precluding the truth of judgments of objective *pro tanto* reasons. I then argue that, necessarily, moral obligation is tied to our having alternative possibilities as is prudential obligation because both these varieties of obligation are conceptually coupled with our having objective *pro tanto* reasons (chap. 3). Next, I propose that a class of judgments of intrinsic value is logically associated with our having alternatives, again, via a necessary link between having such judgments and having objective *pro tanto* reasons (chap. 4); and that several moral sentiments are, likewise, allied with our having alternatives as well (chap. 5). In brief, I show that a number of normative judgments or, more generally, many things we value, are tied to our having reasons of a certain sort—objective *pro tanto reasons*—but there is a requirement of alternative possibilities for our having such reasons.

In the second part, I address directly the issue of whether determinism is indeed a threat to a cluster of normative appraisals. First, I argue that if one is an incompatibilist who believes the alternatives that the truth of judgments of objective reasons presupposes are strong alternatives, then determinism precludes a significant slate of normative judgments. And that from such an incompatibilist perspective, determinism threatens the rationality of a range of moral sentiments (chap. 6). Next, I argue that if one is a compatibilist who opts for the view that the truth of judgments of objective *pro tanto* reasons presupposes one's having only weak alternatives, then quite a few versions of semi-compatibilism are not sustainable. For instance, semi-compatibilism with respect to moral obligation—the thesis that although determinism may preclude free will, it does not preclude moral obligation because there is no requirement of alternative possibilities for moral obligation—is false (chap. 6). Finally, I argue that an alternative possibilities requirement for the truth of judgments of objective *pro tanto* reasons threatens a variety of prominent compatibilist approaches, such as versions of a Frankfurtian, a Strawsonian, and a reasons-responsiveness approach, to moral responsibility (chap. 7). In this second part, in effect I defend the view that if various things we value are conceptually tied to our having reasons of a certain sort (as I argue in the first part), and our having such reasons requires that we could have done otherwise, then depending upon how we understand "could have done otherwise," determinism may well imperil these things. The book closes with a summary of its principal argument and some general conclusions (chap. 8).

NOTES

1. Some philosophers deny the association of responsibility and freedom. See, for e.g., Schlossberger 1992, 4–7, 117–18; Adams 1994; Arpaly 2003, 149–77; Smith 2005.
2. I use "permissible" and "right" interchangeably, as I do "impermissible" and "wrong."
3. Kadri Vihvelin (2008a) suggests that we take compatibilism and incompatibilism (with respect to free will) to be contraries rather than contradictories. She defines the free will thesis as the thesis that at least one non-godlike creature has free will, and free will worlds are those in which the free will thesis is true. She proposes that impossibilism is the thesis that there are *no* free will worlds. Incompatibilism is the thesis that there are free will worlds, but no deterministic world is a free will world. Compatibilism is the thesis that there are free will worlds and free will worlds include deterministic worlds. Nothing substantial in this work turns on whether one opts for the traditional twofold or Vihvelin's threefold classification.
4. Hereafter, this qualification will be assumed but frequently suppressed.

Chapter 2

Reasons and Alternative Possibilities

2.1. INTRODUCTION

Practical reasons are reasons to have our desires and goals, make decisions, form intentions, and perform actions. I do not have an account of practical reasons. Fortunately, such an account is not essential to achieving the objectives of this work (I say more on this later). We should, however, distinguish among different sorts of practical reasons (sec. 2.2). In the remaining sections I argue that the truth of judgments of certain sorts of reasons—objective *pro tanto* reasons—requires alternatives.

2.2. TYPES OF REASONS

I confine discussion to types of reasons that are germane to the primary concerns to be addressed in this work. I begin with the distinction between objective (or external) and Davidsonian reasons. Davidsonian reasons are complexes of desires and beliefs; typically, they are desire/belief pairs (Davidson 1963). Such reasons are frequently, or by the lights of some, always cited in an explanation of intentional action. Fred opened the window because he wanted to let in some fresh air, and he believed that by opening the window he would do so. His desire to let in some air, and his belief that opening the window would allow some air into the room, are constituents of his Davidsonian reason for opening the window.

Some may take Davidsonian reasons to be merely explanatory. In this view, to say that a person has a Davidsonian reason to do something is not to say that she ought, from reason's standpoint, to do it. Rather, it is simply to say that she acted for a reason—there is a desire/belief pair that provides a rationalizing explanation for what she did. But we may conceive of Davidsonian reasons more broadly. In this more expansive view, some Davidsonian reasons can be normative and not merely explanatory. For example, suppose you desire to help a friend and believe that you can do so by lending her some money. You believe, too, that you morally ought to help her. This desire, together with these beliefs, may constitute a normative (or justifying) reason for you to help: from reason's perspective, you ought to help. When it matters, I will use the label "normative Davidsonian reasons" to refer to Davidsonian reasons of this sort.

In contrast, as a first stab, external reasons are facts dissociated from the agent's desires or attitudes with "built in" motivation. Jack has no desires that would be thwarted by his drinking at one go all the whiskey in the newly opened bottle. The fact that drinking that amount of alcohol would make him sick is an external reason for Jack not to drink it, and this would be so even if he, unusually, has no desires that would be frustrated by his being very sick (cf. Mele 2003, 79). We may get more precise. Alfred Mele recommends that we understand something's being a strictly external reason in this way:

Strictly External Reason: If R is a strictly external reason for S to A, R is not an attitude of S, does not have an attitude of S as a constituent; and is not, even in part, a fact, truth, proposition, or the like about any actual attitude of S. (Mele 2003, 77)

Plausible examples of such reasons are the fact that something is intrinsically good, or the fact that some action is morally obligatory for one. What, however, about a fact that is a reason, highlighted in italics, such as the following: One forgives because *one ceases to regard the wrong done to one as a reason to terminate some relationship*? An agent's ceasing to regard something as such and such on a broad reading of "attitude" may be taken to be an attitude of that agent. This attitude would appear to be a constituent of the reason (expressed by the proposition in italics), and so this reason, one may worry, would not qualify as a strictly external one. It does, however, seem that an agent can have such a reason without having a desire to cease to regard the wrong done as a reason to end the relationship. Use "motivating desire" to refer to attitudinal states of mind (or their neural realizers) that are, constitute, or include motivation. (Mele 2003, 14–15 uses "motivation-encompassing attitude" to refer to such states). What we ordinarily take to be a desire, such as Bob's desire to eat ice cream, qualifies as a motivating desire. A belief, on a customary understanding of "belief," is not a motivating desire. We may now introduce another term of art, a "partially external reason":

> *Partially External Reason*: If R is a partially external reason for S to A, R is not a motivating desire of S, does not have a motivating desire as a constituent; and is not, even in part, a fact, truth, proposition, or the like about any actual motivating desire of S.

Suppose that an agent's ceasing to regard a wrong done to her as a reason to terminate some friendship is the reason why she forgives on a certain occasion when she forgives. And suppose that on this occasion she lacks the desire to cease to regard the wrong done as a reason to end the friendship. The reason for which she forgives on this occasion is a partially external reason for this agent.

One may, nevertheless, have certain qualms about this limited characterization of a partially external reason. Imagine that Ralph intentionally does wrong, and takes himself to be doing wrong: he breaks a promise. Suppose his intentional wrongdoing is a reason for him to apologize. This reason is a partially external reason even if Ralph's doing the wrong that he did is explained partly by a desire to hurt his friend, an antecedent motivating desire of his. There is, of course, a sense in which this motivating desire is a constituent, an indirect one, of the reason he has—intentionally doing wrong—to apologize. But it is not a constituent in the way in which Fred's motivating desire to let in some fresh air is a constituent of his Davidsonian reason for opening the window. In this latter case, Fred's motivating desire is part of the Davidsonian cluster that rationalizes his intentional action. Similarly, in Ralph's case, his motivating desire to hurt his friend is a constituent of the Davidsonian cluster (we may suppose) of his breaking the promise. But this motivating desire is not a "proper" constituent of the reason he has to apologize. Here, I will not try to refine the distinction between a motivating desire's being a proper constituent of a reason or a motivating desire's being an indirect constituent of a reason; but the distinction, I believe, is real and is fairly transparent. I rest content with the proposal that if R is a partially external reason for an agent to do something, R does not have a motivating desire as a proper constituent.

Finally, we may coin another semi-technical term:

> *External Reason*: An external reason for S to A is a reason that is either a strictly external reason for S to A or a partially external reason for S to A.

In brief, external (that is, objective) reasons are, roughly, facts disso-ciated from internal states of the agent; they are screened off from the agent's motivating desires.

Objective reasons, just like Davidsonian ones, may enter into an explanation of intentional action. Mele gives the following sort of example. An agent has an intrinsic desire for something if and only if the agent desires that thing for its own sake and not instrumen-tally. Someone may hold that some things are intrinsically good, that something is intrinsically good is an external reason to desire and pursue it, and that x is intrinsically good, or an agent's appre-hension of this fact, may contribute causally to this agent's acquiring an intrinsic desire for x. This desire, in conjunction with an appro-priate belief, may be cited in a reasons explanation of why this agent pursued x (Mele 2003, 81).

Next, contrast subjective reasons with objective ones. Subjec-tive reasons are beliefs concerning objective reasons: an agent has such a reason to do something if and only if the agent believes, truly or falsely, that she has an objective reason to do it. To bring out the distinction between objective reasons and subjective reasons, ima-gine that Fred, on the advice of his medical team, nonculpably believes that he has the most reason to take some pills that are in the experimental stage of development. His doctors have informed him that it is highly likely that the pills will assuage his pain. But in fact he has no reason to take these pills because, unbeknown to the doc-tors, taking the pills will kill him. Although he has no such objective reasons, Fred has subjective reason to take the pills.

I said that subjective reasons are beliefs concerning objective ones. Our mundane view of beliefs suggests that subjective reasons have no desire component. Consequently, they may be thought of as "stand alone" reasons—reasons without a desire or desirelike constituent. Some might be drawn to the opposed view. It may be that if subjective reasons were "stand alone," one would be committed to what is the untenable position, for instance, that if an agent believes falsely that taking a vitamin would make her more healthy (this agent believes that she has an objective reason to take the vitamin), then she has a reason to take the vitamin despite having no motivating desire to be more healthy because she is already healthy. Rather, it might be suggested, contrary to being stand alone, subjective reasons are either the belief components of Davidsonian reasons or, perhaps, they may be conceived as having a "built in" desire-like or motivational constituent. Fred is sick and he wants to get well. He believes, on credible evidence, that taking medicine M will cure his malady. But he has no objective reason to take M because taking M will in fact make him worse. His belief that he has an objective reason to take M is a subjective reason of his. On one option, this belief, together with Fred's desire to be cured, constitutes a Davidsonian reason of Fred to take M. In a second option, this belief itself has a built in desire-like motivational component with appropriate representational content.

Others, however, might see nothing amiss with the idea that if Fred believes he has an objective reason to take the vitamin pill, he has a reason to take the pill despite his having no motivating desire to be healthier because he is already optimally healthy.

The distinction between "stand alone" subjective reasons and essentially desire-linked subjective reasons will assume some importance in a later discussion. The contrast between *pro tanto* reasons—reasons that can be outweighed by other reasons—and all things considered reasons (or "oughts"), which cannot be outweighed, is significant. If the term "reason" means *pro tanto* reason, each reason has a certain weight. On a particular occasion, suppose you have several different alternatives, and your *pro tanto* reasons to act in some way are stronger than your reasons to act in any other way.

Then you have the most reason to act in this way. We may say that acting in this way is reasons-wise obligatory for you; you reasons-wise *ought* to act in this way. In more common parlance, we might say that you have decisive reason to act in this way. On a different occasion, suppose you have sufficient or enough *pro tanto* reason to act in two or more ways, and no better reason to act in any other way. Then we may say that it is reasons-wise permissible (or reasons-wise right) for you to act in either of these ways. Finally, suppose you have most *pro tanto* reason not to act in a certain way. Then we may say that acting in this way is reasons-wise wrong (that is, impermissible) for you or you have decisive reason not to act in this way.[1]

One may have a *pro tanto* reason to do something, the doing of which would fulfill, for instance, some moral or prudential obligation, although one may have an all-things-considered reason not to do it.

2.3. A REQUIREMENT OF ALTERNATIVE POSSIBILITIES FOR OBJECTIVE *PRO TANTO* REASONS

I now argue for the view that there is requirement of alternative possibilities for the truth of judgments of objective *pro tanto* reasons; one cannot have such a reason to do something if one could not have done otherwise. Unless otherwise specified or the context makes clear, "a reason" refers to an objective *pro tanto* reason.

Overall Summary

If one ought to do something from the perspective of objective reasons, then one can do it; the "ought" of objective reasons implies "can." This is a control or freedom requirement of reasons-wise "ought." But if reasons-wise "ought" implies "can," then so do reasons-wise "wrong" and reasons-wise "right" because the fundamental freedom requirements of obligation, wrong, and right are symmetric. Consequently, we may reason as follows: If you reasons-wise ought not to do something, it is wrong for you to do it. If it's reasons-wise wrong for you to do something, you can do it. So, if you reasons-wise ought not to do something, you can do it. It is also true, however, that if you reasons-wise ought not to do something, you can refrain from doing it. Hence, there is an alternative possibilities requirement for reasons-wise "ought." Similarly, we can derive the conclusion that there is such a requirement for reasons-wise "wrong" and "right" too.

Details

If you have most moral reason to do something, and, thus, if morality *requires* that you do it, then you can do it. In other words, the moral "ought" implies "can." I have referred to this principle as *Kant's Law*. Suppose, now, that you have *most practical reason* to do something; you ought to do it from the point of view of reason. Then it seems that you *can* do it. You cannot have an "obligation"—it cannot be necessary—from reason's perspective, for you to do something if you cannot do it.

Imagine that you are in western Canada in Vancouver. You don't know how to swim, and you don't believe that there is child drowning in the ocean off the Australian coast at the time you are enjoying your morning coffee. It turns out, however, that at this time a child *is* just about to drown off this coast. Had this child lived, she would have transformed the world from the predominantly horrible place it is into a blissful one. At the time you are sipping your coffee, how can you have a reason to save this child? For that matter, if the child were drowning before you started drinking coffee, how could it be that at the time you were having your coffee, you have a reason to save the child? If it is false that you could have a reason, at the time you were having the coffee, to save the child, it is also false that, at this time, you could have most reason to save the child.

One may object that in cases involving an action one can perform only if one does something that it is physically or nomologically impossible for one to perform, or one does something that necessitates acquiring beliefs that one cannot in one's circumstances acquire, one *does* have a standing reason to perform the relevant action. It is just that other reasons override this reason. For instance, even if it is physically impossible for you to save the child, you have a standing reason to do so, but this reason is overridden by another reason you have: the fact that you cannot physically save the child.

No argument has been given for the view that one can have a (standing) reason to do something even if one cannot do it. Rather, what we have in the previous paragraph is an appeal to intuition: Some may think it is at least intuitively plausible, for example, that while you are relishing your coffee you have a reason to save the child although you cannot then do so. So, I will, initially, reply in kind by giving intuitive considerations to support the contrary position. Notice, first, that even when physical or nomological impossibility is involved, still the following principle seems to be true: If one has a reason for doing something that is not overridden by any others, then one can do it. Second, the alleged overriding reason that you have for not saving the child is revealing. If you think the nonpractical reason why your standing reason to save the child is overridden is because it is physically or nomologically impossible for you to save the child, why suppose you have the standing reason at all? Third, I believe that there are no unowned practical reasons: necessarily, if something is a practical reason, then it is a reason for someone (Dancy 2005, 42; Schroeder 2007; Rønnow-Rasmussen 2009, 230). Imagine that there is a reason to save the child in the example introduced. If there are no unowned reasons, whose reason is it? Surely, it isn't a reason for *all* persons. But then why believe it is a reason for you, the coffee drinker, especially when you are in no position to effect a rescue? This brings me to the fourth point: I don't see what, in the first place, motivates the view that one can or does have a standing reason to save the child or, say, the Brazilian rain forest, even if it is physically or nomologically impossible for one to do so, or even if saving the child or the rain forest would necessitate acquiring beliefs that you cannot acquire.

Aside from these preliminary observations, some general considerations—clearly not decisive—support the view that one cannot have a reason to do something that one cannot do. First, the view has implications that are hard to swallow. It is pretty far-fetched to suppose that you can now have a reason to prevent Neil Armstrong from having landed on the moon in 1969; or that you have a reason, while in solitary confinement, to save the children in the village that your platoon has been ordered to destroy. It seems that the simplest and least ad hoc explanation, as Bart Streumer proposes (Streumer 2007a, 358–59), of the nonexistence of such reasons (and relevantly similar ones) is that you can't now do what you allegedly have reasons to do. Second, practical reasoning has a purpose (or purposes): among other things, it provides guidance regarding what to do (see, e.g., Copp 1997; 2003; Streumer 2007a; 2010). How can practical deliberation, however, provide such guidance if its prescriptions recommend we do things that, for instance, it is physically or nomologically impossible for us to do?

It seems that just as there is an association between the "ought" of morality and "can," there is a similar association between the "ought" of reason and "can." The "can" here is the relevant personal sense of "can" or "control" we have in mind, for instance, when we say that responsibility or moral obligation require control. Precisely what this sense of "can" is turns out to be tricky; it is something I have discussed elsewhere (Haji 2002). Here, I simply note the following. First, the "can" in the moral or the reasons-wise "ought" implies "can" principle is stronger than the "logical can." You can't save the drowning child if you are tethered to your seat although there is some distant world in which you free yourself and rescue the child. Second, "can" (in these principles) does not imply your having a dual ability to do what you do *and* to refrain from doing what you do as Frankfurt examples (Frankfurt 1969) strongly suggest. It seems that having this dual ability would suffice for having the sort of personal control at issue. Third, in at least one sense of "ability," "can" (in these principles) does not imply having this ability. If Jim doesn't know the combination of the safe, in this sense of ability Jim lacks the ability to open the safe although he can, in the personal sense of "can" we are discussing, open the safe: he can dial the right combination. And, fourth, "can" (in these principles) does not imply that the agent can intentionally do what he does. Suppose Ted ought to turn on the furnace. To turn on the furnace, he simply flicks a switch on a side of the furnace to the "on" position. When he flicks the switch to this position, he initiates a series of events, including activating various mechanisms within the furnace. He knows nothing whatsoever about these mechanisms; he has no idea that turning the furnace on consists, partly, in his activating them. Their activation is something he can bring about but presumably not intentionally because he is totally unaware of them or their role in the workings of the furnace. Their activation, however, is a prerequisite to executing his obligation to turn on the furnace. Hence, if he ought to turn on the furnace, he ought, also, to see to it that these mechanisms are activated, despite his so seeing not being an intentional action.

Indeed, the moral "ought" implies "can" principle appears just to be a more restricted version of the following general principle that if you have most reason to do something, you can do it:

> *Reasons-Wise "Ought" Implies "Can" (Reason Ought/Can):* If *S* has most reason to do something, *A*, and, thus, if *S* reasons-wise ought to do *A*, then *S* can do *A*.

2.3.1. *"Wrong" Implies "Can"*

I now argue for the view that "wrong," just like "ought," implies "can." As "wrong" or "ought not" also implies "can refrain from," there is an alternative possibilities requirement for "wrong."

If reasons-wise "ought" implies "can," I see no reason to deny that reasons-wise "wrong" (and reasons-wise "right") imply "can" as well. As a preliminary remark regarding what may be provided as support for this view, the moral "ought" implies "can" principle, where "ought" expresses all in moral obligation as opposed to merely *prima facie* obligation, can more fully be thought of as the principle that if you morally ought to do something, you can do it; and if you morally ought not to do something, you can refrain from doing it:

> *Kant's Law:* If it is overall (as opposed to merely *prima facie*) morally obligatory for *S* to do something, *A*, then *S* can do *A*; and if it is overall morally obligatory for *S* to refrain from doing *A*, then *S* can refrain from doing *A*.[2]

It has been emphasized that moral *responsibility* requires control; if one is morally praiseworthy or blameworthy for an action, one has responsibility-relevant control in performing it. Likewise, think of *Kant's Law* as a control principle for moral *obligation*: if one has a moral obligation to perform an action, one has obligation-relevant control in performing it. Obligation, just like responsibility, requires control.

If we conceive of *Kant's Law* as a principle of control, then barring persuasive reasons to believe otherwise, there is little reason not to assume, too, that moral "wrong" and moral "right" imply "can." I advance, specifically, three considerations in favor of this view. First, and most basic, just as moral praiseworthiness and moral blameworthiness require control or freedom, so do moral obligation, wrong, and right. The control requirements of blameworthiness, unless we have sound reason to believe the contrary, mirror those of praiseworthiness—both have the same freedom requirements. An essential element of the freedom requirement of these responsibility appraisals, as noted previously, is captured by this principle: One is morally praiseworthy or blameworthy (whatever the case may be) for doing something only if one *could have* done it. This principle highlights a link between moral responsibility and freedom that holds of conceptual necessity. Again, the link is simply that praiseworthiness and blameworthiness both require control. Furthermore, if we think that praiseworthiness requires a certain variety of control, then without good reason to believe the contrary, blameworthiness, also requires this variety of control. Similarly, it would seem that the control or freedom requirements of moral obligation, *unless we have strong reason to think otherwise* (and I know of no such reason), should also be the very ones of moral wrong and moral right. If *Kant's Law* expresses just one more incarnation of the association between morality and freedom, then, again, in the absence of special reason to believe otherwise, it should also be the case that the principle that each of "wrong" and "right" implies "can" expresses two other instances of this association. In brief, if obligation requires control, so do right and wrong; and if obligation requires a certain sort of control—that we can do the thing we are obligated to do—right and wrong require this sort of control as well.

Second, a powerful *analysis* of the concept of moral obligation informed largely by Fred Feldman's (1986) and Michael Zimmerman's (1996; 2008) work on the morally deontic "ought" validates the symmetry I propose in the freedom requirements of obligation, wrong, and right. The analysis provides a plausible treatment of a wide array of deontic puzzles, sometimes partly in virtue of implying that "wrong" implies "can." The account builds on the idea that at each time of moral choice, there are several possible worlds accessible to a person as of that time: there are, at the time, various ways in which a person might live out her life. For each of these complete "life histories," there is a possible world—the one that would exist if she were to live out her life in that way. Roughly, a possible world is accessible to a person at a time if and only if it is still possible, at that time, for the person to see to the occurrence of that world. Accessibility can be thought of as being a relatively weak version of "can do." You don't for example make the sun rise; the sunrise isn't something you do at all. Still, the *sun's rising* occurs in a world now accessible to you. (In contrast, if some state of affairs, q, is impossible for you as of now, and if q's impossibility is metaphysical or merely physical, then no q-world is accessible to you as of now. At any time, there is no world accessible to you in which you run faster than the speed of light.) Or suppose I can't alone push my car to the edge of the block, but you and I together can do so. If right now I can persuade you to help me to move the car, then, as of now there is a world accessible to me in which my car is pushed to the edge of the block. Again, the root idea is that a world is accessible to a person at a time if and only if it is still possible, at that time, for the person to see to it that the world is actual.[3] A world may be accessible to a person at a time, but once the person behaves in some way other than the way in which he behaves in that world, it is no longer accessible—it has been "bypassed." Once bypassed, that world never again becomes accessible. As a person moves through life, she inexorably pares down the stock of worlds accessible to her. Making use of the notion of accessibility, we can say that a state of affairs is possible for a person at a time if and only if it occurs in some world still accessible to the person at that time.

On this analysis, actions are morally judged not by appeal to the value of their outcomes but by appeal to the values of the accessible possible worlds in which they are performed. Worlds may be ranked in accordance to a value-relation; each world is as good as, or better than, or worse than, each other world. A world is best if no world is better than it is. For purposes of "value-wise" ranking worlds, one can supply one's favorite axiology. I simply label the relevant value "deontic value." Some may opt for the view that deontic value consists in intrinsic value; others might resist this view and propose, instead, that deontic value consists in maximizing compliance with God's commands or with some principle of rationality. The analysis can now be stated in this way:

> (MO): A person, S, ought, as of t, to see to the occurrence of a state of affairs, p, if and only if p occurs in some world, w, accessible to S at t, and it's not the case that p's negation (not-p) occurs in any accessible world deontically as good as or deontically better than w (see, e.g., Feldman 1986, 37).[4]

More intuitively, and simplifying somewhat, according to *MO*, as of some time, an act is *morally obligatory* for you if and only if you can do it, and it occurs in all the best worlds accessible to you at this time. In all your best life histories, you perform this act at the relevant time. As of some time, an act is morally permissible for you if and only if you can do it and it occurs in some but not all the best worlds accessible to you at this time. And, as of some time, an act is wrong for you if and only if you can do it and it does not occur in any of the best worlds accessible to you at this time. According to *MO*, on each occasion, one ought to do the best one can.

MO verifies a version of *Kant's Law*. If, as of some time, you ought to do something that occurs in all the best worlds accessible to you at this time, and accessible-to-you worlds are worlds you can make actual, then you can do that thing. Put a bit more formally, let $K_{s,t,p}$ abbreviate "there is a world accessible to *s* as of *t* in which state of affairs *p* occurs." $K_{s,t,p}$ is equivalent to "as of *t*, *s* can still see to the occurrence of *p*." Allowing *K* to stand for the relevant sort of possibility *Kant's Law* expresses, this implication relation can be stated as follows: $MO_{s,t,p}$ implies $K_{s,t,p}$. $MO_{s,t,p}$ means that there is an accessible *p*-world such that there is no as good accessible not-*p* world. Hence, there is an accessible *p*-world. It follows that $K_{s,t,p}$ is true as well. Similarly, *MO* entails that, if, at some time, *p* is wrong for you, *p* occurs in some world that is accessible to you but not in any of the best worlds accessible to you. So, according to *MO*, "wrong" implies "can" as well.

Some may press the following objection: Why is it true that according to *MO*, if at some time *p* is wrong for you, *p* occurs in some world that is accessible to you but not in any of the best worlds accessible to you? Why does it follow from what has been said about *MO* that *p* could not occur in some world that is inaccessible to you?

Fair enough. Note, first, that if p is obligatory for you, then (simplifying) p occurs in all the best worlds accessible to you; and if p is permissible for you, then (simplifying) p occurs in some of the best worlds accessible to you. We may understand this point as follows: If MO is true, an essential constituent of the control that both obligation and right require is the ability to see to the occurrence of what is obligatory or right. Again, unless we have special reason to believe otherwise, why should this constituent of "deontic control" differ in the case of wrong? Conversely, one may argue in this way: If something *can* be morally wrong for you even though you cannot do it, why should things be different with right and obligation? As MO gives us powerful reason to accept the thesis that "ought" implies "can" and the thesis that "right," too, implies "can," then one ought not to resist the thesis that "wrong" implies "can." Second, fulfillment of an obligation or a wrong (I admit that "fulfillment of a wrong" has an odd ring, but allow it to pass) affects how the world will be; fulfilling an obligation makes the world deontically better, fulfilling a wrong makes the world deontically worse. If, by virtue of not being able to perform an action, one cannot affect for better or worse the way the world will be, it seems that action cannot be obligatory or wrong for one.

Reflection on this worldly analysis of obligation gives us reason to affirm that if one has an objective *pro tanto reason* to do something, then one can do it. If, at some time, one morally ought to do A, then (simplifying) one does A in all the best worlds *accessible* to one at this time; one does A in each one of the worlds that one can make actual. Thus, whenever one has a moral reason to do A—a reason that would be an objective *pro tanto* one to do A—by virtue of having a moral obligation to do A, there is a world *accessible* to one in which one does A, and not just some inaccessible possible world in which one A-s. There is a sense, then, in which A

is "realizable" by one if one has an objective *pro tanto* reason to do A by virtue of being morally obligated to do A. But if A is, in this sense, *realizable* by one, then one *can* do A.

The third reason to endorse the view that "wrong" implies "can" has to do with obligations to refrain from doing certain things. I start with some distinctions. One has indirect responsibility- or obligation-relevant control over something just in case one has control over it by way of having control over something else. One has direct control over something just in case one has control over it that is not indirect. Similarly, one is indirectly responsible for something just in case one is responsible for it by way of being responsible for something else; one is directly responsible for something just in case one is responsible for it but not indirectly so. And one is indirectly obligated regarding something just in case one is obligated regarding it by way of being obligated regarding something else; one is directly obligated regarding something just in case one is obligated regarding it but not indirectly so. As Zimmerman (2006, 595, 602; 2008, 90–91, 149–50) cautions, direct obligations are restricted to intentional actions that one can perform; not so with indirect obligations as Ted's case involving turning on the furnace confirms. Suppose Ted has a direct obligation to turn on the furnace. He cannot, however, turn it on without activating the relevant mechanisms within; so he ought to activate these mechanisms. This indirect obligation is one that, in his circumstances, he can perform but not intentionally.

Imagine that it is directly morally wrong for you to do something. Then you directly morally ought to refrain from doing it. Just as one can be directly responsible for something only if one can or could intentionally do it, so one can be directly obligated regarding doing something only if one can or could intentionally do it (see, for example, Zimmerman 2006, 595, 602). So if you directly morally ought to refrain from doing something, you can intentionally refrain from doing it. Such an instance of an intentional refraining would be an instance of your bringing about an intentional omission.

Intentional omission cannot be accomplished without intentionally doing something—bringing about a "positive" action, as we may say—in the place of what one omits to do (see, for example, Zimmerman 1988, 23).[5] For instance, if you intentionally refrain from turning on the light, then you bring about something—you intentionally remain seated, for example—for the purpose of the light's not going on.

Revert to a case in which you directly morally ought to refrain from doing something. Imagine that you ought not and, hence, that it is morally wrong for you, to turn on the light. Imagine, furthermore, that in your circumstances, it is a necessary prerequisite of your intentionally not turning on the light that you remain seated. Then you ought to remain seated as well. For, if you ought to do something (refrain from turning on the light in the example), and you cannot do this thing without doing something else (remaining seated in the example), because this something else is a necessary prerequisite of your doing the thing you are obligated to do, then you ought to do this something else as well.[6] Now, if you ought to remain seated, you have obligation-relevant control in remaining seated. We are supposing that an *essential* element of this control consists in your power or ability to remain seated (*Kant's Law*). Remember, if it is wrong for you to do something, then you ought not to do it. Since all wrongs are "ought nots," and "ought nots" cannot be accomplished without bringing about something that is itself obligatory, and, which is, hence, something in the bringing about of which you have obligation-relevant control, all wrongs *inherit* this very element of control.

To flesh this out, in the example, if you ought not (and, so, if it is wrong for you) to turn on the light, then you ought to remain seated. If you ought to remain seated, you can remain seated. Hence, your moral obligation that is an intentional omission—an "ought not"—can be accomplished only if you have the power to remain seated. But this "ought not" just *is* a wrong. You bring about the omission (your not turning on the light) by way—and only by way, as we have assumed—of intentionally remaining seated. There is, in the circumstances, nothing more to bringing about your intentional omission (the "ought not") than bringing about the relevant "positive" action: your intentionally remaining seated for the purpose of not turning on the light. Your control in accomplishing this "ought not" or wrong is *exhausted* by the control that you exercise in bringing about the "positive" action of your remaining seated for the purpose of not turning on the light. An essential element of this control consists in your being able to perform this positive action. This strongly suggests that "wrong" implies "can."

It may be rejoined that all this example shows is that "*S* ought not to do *A*," or "It is wrong for *S* to do *A*" imply "*S* can do what is required to avoid doing *A*," a corollary of sorts of "*S* can avoid doing *A*," and not that "*S* can do *A*." In response, I use the example to make a point about *control*. Wrong, just like obligation, requires control. If we focus on the intentional omission at issue—intentionally refraining from turning on the light—it would seem that the control required to accomplish this wrong, as I stressed, is nothing over and above the control required by the positive action of one's remaining seated for the purpose of failing to flick the light switch. The example does presuppose that you *can do* what is required to avoid switching on the light. To emphasize again, however, the *control* involved in bringing about the intentional omission—the "ought not" or "wrong"—just is the control that is involved in this "*can do*" and nothing more.

2.3.2. *Objections to "Wrong" Implies "Can"*

Let's turn to a consideration of some objections against the principle that "wrong" implies "can."

ARGUMENTS FROM FAIRNESS

Some may claim that contrary to what I have affirmed, there *is* good reason to believe that the control requirements of obligation differ from those of wrong. The asymmetry in control requirements, as these people see it, at least where the deontic notions are morally deontic notions, is associated with considerations of fairness. I start with a synopsis of this "argument from fairness."

The argument commences with reminding us that proponents of *Kant's Law* accept:

1. "*S* ought to do *A*" implies "*S* can do *A*."
2. "*S* ought not to do *A*" implies "*S* can refrain from doing *A*."

But they (generally) deny:

3. "*S* ought to do *A*" implies "*S* can refrain from doing *A*."
4. "*S* ought not to do *A*" implies "*S* can do *A*."

Invoking grounds of fairness, they engage in the following reasoning that partitions into two sub-arguments. Suppose I do *A*, and you claim that I ought not to have done *A*. This claim would seem unfair if I could not have refrained from *A*-ing. You're holding me to an obligation that I could not have met. Let's label this sub-argument "Argument A." But suppose I in fact do B, and you claim that indeed I was obligated to do B, and I ought not to have refrained from doing B. It doesn't seem that a fairness issue arises if it's the case that I couldn't have refrained from B-ing. For here, you're not holding me to an obligation that I couldn't have met. Dub this sub-argument "Argument B." From the perspective of such theorists, any control condition on deontic notions depends on plausible fairness claims. But then, while "S ought to do A" implies "S can do A," "S ought to do A" does not imply "S can refrain from doing A"; and "S ought not to do A" does not imply "S can do A," but only "S can refrain from doing A."[7]

It seems fairly evident that the conclusion of Argument B is meant to be that it's false that "ought" implies "can refrain from." One would have expected the conclusion of Argument A to be the denial of the principle that "wrong" implies "can." But it seems that this is not so. Rather, its conclusion appears to be that "ought not" (that is, "wrong") implies "can refrain from."

Regarding evaluation, I'm not sure that considerations of fairness can be successfully marshaled to support *Kant's Law* (i.e., 1 and 2). Reflect, for instance, on these remarks by David Copp who proposes that the principle that "ought" implies "can"

> rests on the intuition about the unfairness of expecting a person to do something, or of demanding or requiring that she do it, if she lacks the ability to do it. This intuition supports the idea that morality would be unfair if it implied that a person might be morally required to do something even if she lacked the ability to do it. Since it is not intelligible to suppose that morality itself might be morally unfair, it follows that any adequate moral theory would imply that if a person is morally required to do something she is able to do it. (2003, 274)

It appears that a strand of thought in this passage concerns the principle that it would be unfair to require morally someone to do something if she is unable to do it. This principle, however, is not without problems. Several moral theorists—Feldman (1986, 24–25), Zimmerman (1996, 49–50), and Haji (2002, 17–21)—believe that a person can have a moral obligation to do something even though he fails to know that he ought morally to do this thing. Failing to have knowledge that one ought to do something need not be obligation subversive according to such theorists. For instance, Mark, a strong swimmer and the only other person on the shores of the secluded lake, ought to save or try to save Matthew who has capsized, although Mark neither sees nor hears Matthew. There is a sense in which Mark cannot aid Matthew. Even so, theorists such as Feldman and Zimmerman would apparently deny that it would be unfair to require Mark to save Matthew if Mark is "unable," because of ignorance, to save Matthew. But if one would go this far, I do not see why one should also deny that it would be *unfair* to require Mark to save Matthew if Mark were psychologically unable to save Matthew, perhaps because Mark suffers from a certain phobia.

One argument in favor of "ought" implies "can" that the passage quoted above suggests is this:

> (1C1) If morality sanctioned violation of the "ought" implies "can" principle, then morality itself would be unfair. (This is because violation of this principle generates unfairness. It is unfair to require morally someone to do something if he is unable to do it.)
> (1C2) It is false that morality itself would be unfair.
> (1C3) So, it's false that morality sanctions violation of the "ought" implies "can" principle. (If the argument is sound, assume that (1C3) gives us reason to believe that the "ought" implies "can" principle is true; it is a "negative defense" of this principle.)

But the argument is not sound: (1C2) is false. Consider the principle that only the guilty ought morally to be punished. Violation of this principle would generate unfairness. Yet it is conceivable that the correct normative ethical view—one that specifies necessary and sufficient conditions for obligation—sanctions its violation. Perhaps punishing an innocent person is, alas, what one is morally required to do on some occasion because this is what one does in all the best worlds accessible to one at the time. There would then be a sense in which morality is unfair, but this is consistent with the relevant normative theory's ("morality's") being true. What is fair and what is obligatory may differ.

Maybe Copp's argument for "ought" implies "can" is even simpler amounting to this:

(2C1) If violation of some moral principle, such as *Kant's Law*, generates unfairness, then that principle is true.

(2C2) Violation of *Kant's Law* generates unfairness.

(2C3) Therefore, *Kant's Law* is true.

Thus, the principle concerning punishment—only the guilty ought to be punished—is false. But this argument would generate the result that the principle is true. Hence, this second argument is not sound either.

Perhaps there is some way to fix Copp's argument for "ought" implies "can." All the better if this is so because I think *Kant's Law* is true. However, there is a deep problem with the original argument from fairness (that has sub-arguments A and B as components). First, if considerations of fairness dictate control requirements for obligation and wrong, as the argument seems to presuppose, then, unless one has an explanation to the contrary, it would appear that such considerations should also dictate such requirements for praiseworthiness and blameworthiness and, indeed, for other normative evaluations that are conceptually or logically associated with freedom. But considerations of fairness do no such thing with, for instance, blameworthiness. So, it is not clear why one should accept the view that any control condition on deontic notions "depends on plausible fairness claims." Suppose one reasons as follows: "If one couldn't have done otherwise than what one in fact did, one isn't blameworthy for what one did. This is because it would be *unfair* to hold someone blameworthy for something that she couldn't have avoided doing." To say the least, this inference from the prior premise concerning control is highly controversial. Semi-compatibilists would reject it outright (see, for example, Fischer 2005, 343–48). They would do so *because* they don't think that freedom to do otherwise is the control that blameworthiness demands. This motivates the second more fundamental evaluative point. As semi-compatibilists regarding responsibility see it—and I agree—in this context, whether the charge of fairness is plausible *depends* on just what the control requirements of the sort of normative judgment at issue are, and not the other way around. If, for instance, freedom to do otherwise *is* the variety of freedom that blameworthiness requires, then the charge of unfairness would presumably stick in those instances in which a person could not have done otherwise. Again, I see no reason to deny that this type of view—"the priority of control over fairness"—carries over to deontic notions. Should obligation, right, and wrong require "two-way" control, then, provided one were inclined to make such claims, presumably, it would be just as plausible to claim that it is unfair to hold one to an "obligation" that one could not have refrained from performing, as it would be to claim that it is unfair to hold one to an "obligation" that one could not have met. In each case, the unfairness hinges on control requirements for obligation not being satisfied.[8]

Perhaps the justification of the principle that "ought" implies "can" has very little to do with fairness. The intuition underlying this principle is straightforward: just as responsibility requires control, so does obligation: one has a moral obligation to perform something only if one has the power to perform it—it is under one's control. And, again, unless there is strong reason to suppose differently, "wrong" has the same control requirements as "ought."

AN ARGUMENT FROM "NOT WRONG" IMPLIES "RIGHT"

Some people may question the thesis that "wrong" implies "can" on the basis of the view that "not wrong" implies "right." For example, I don't have a million dollars to give to UNICEF. Nevertheless, it may be claimed, it wouldn't be wrong for me, and so right for me, to contribute a million to UNICEF. But if it is right for me to donate a million dollars to UNICEF despite my not having a million—if "right" doesn't imply "can"—why should we accept the view that "wrong" implies "can"? It is, however, simply a mistake to suppose that "not wrong" implies "right." According to MO (and other such analyses), an act may not be right, or wrong, or obligatory if, for instance, one cannot perform it. Such an act would be "amoral." So, from the fact that an act is not wrong, it does not follow that it is right. Yet others may question the "wrong" implies "can" thesis because they believe that "not wrong" implies "not bad" or maybe even "good." But this would be another error. It is false that an amoral act or even a right act may be not bad or may not even be good. You may find yourself in an unfortunate situation in which all your options are deontically bad but one of them is least so, and because of this, obligatory for you.[9]

ARGUMENTS CONCERNING COUNTERINTUITIVE RESULTS

Some may think that the principle that "wrong" implies "can" generates highly counterintuitive results. So, it should be rejected. Let's reflect on some versions of this concern.

Consider the commandments not to commit adultery and not to covet one's neighbor's wife. Suppose one believes it is morally obligatory not to do these things, that they are morally wrong, as many do. And suppose I cannot commit adultery because I am not married. And I cannot covet my neighbor's wife because she is not in the least bit attractive to me. Most people would say that it remains morally obligatory for me not to do these things because it is morally obligatory for everyone not to do them, even if some are unable to do them.

I start with a preliminary comment: Suppose you cannot save a child who is drowning because you simply can't get to this child in time. Some people may say, or may have the intuition that, despite your not being able to reach the child, you ought to rescue the child. I confess to not seeing any relevant difference between this sort of scenario where it is *Kant's Law* that is up for assessment, and the scenarios involving adultery or coveting your neighbor's wife where it is the "wrong" implies "can" principle that is up for evaluation. It seems that should one insist that it is wrong to do the relevant things in the latter scenarios even though one cannot do them, one should (unless one has a compelling tale to tell about why the control requirements of wrong differ from those of obligation) also insist that it is obligatory for you to save the child in the initial scenario despite your not being able to save the child.

Regarding the latter scenarios it is, minimally, controversial whether, at any time, it is wrong for any person at that time to commit adultery or to covet one's neighbor's wife. With an account such as *MO*, there doesn't seem to be any barrier against its being possible that, as of some time, I covet my neighbor's wife in some world accessible to me, and there is no accessible world that is deontically as good as or better than this world in which I refrain from coveting my neighbor's wife. Furthermore, it is one thing to claim that most people would say that when I cannot do these things, it remains morally wrong for me to commit adultery or to covet my neighbor's wife, or that they have the *intuition* that these things are wrong but quite another to argue that they are wrong. Perhaps some competitor of *MO*, in conjunction with relevant facts, including facts about the substantive account of deontic value being assumed, implies, for instance, that committing adultery is always wrong for any person. But then we should assess whether such a competitor, together with its presuppositions, is superior to *MO* before we can arrive at an overall verdict about whether this objection is cogent.

Or consider this sort of case: Suppose you know that if you press a red button a bomb will go off, and as a result, a number of innocent people in a room will die. One might recommend that, barring other complications, it is wrong for you to press the button even if, unbeknown to you, you cannot press the button. My reply is forthright. If one wishes to claim that despite your not being able to press the button, it is still wrong for you to press the button, the two salient options one has are these: (1) deny that wrong, unlike obligation, requires control, or (2) concur that wrong does require control but maintain that this sort of control, whatever it is, differs from the sort that obligation requires. The first option strikes me as implausible. The second also has its shortcomings. First, I am unsure what motivates it. One might aver that the example itself is sufficiently compelling to support the proposal concerning asymmetric control requirements for obligation and wrong. This sort of response, however, won't convince anyone who believes that the variety of control "can" expresses in *Kant's Law* and in the "wrong" implies "can" principle is pretty basic to deontic appraisals. Second, if "wrong" does not imply "can" but does require some type of control, we are owed some account of in what this control consists. Third, in the absence of other reasons to accept the proposed asymmetry regarding obligation and wrong, I'm not sure why we should go along with it. I suggest that it would be better to preserve the symmetry between obligation and wrong concerning control (both imply "can"), and submit that whereas, for instance, it would be bad to press the button, and a great misfortune that the innocent die, it is not wrong to press the button if you cannot press it.

It seems that none of these arguments against "wrong" implies "can" is knockdown. Indeed, I think we have good reason to believe that each of "moral ought," "moral right," and "moral wrong" implies "can."

2.4. AN ALTERNATIVE POSSIBILITIES REQUIREMENT FOR "RIGHT," "WRONG," AND "OBLIGATION"

Reverting, now, to reasons-wise obligation, the reasons-wise "ought" implies "can" principle, just like *Kant's Law* expresses the control that "obligations" of reason require. There is, it seems, no reason to believe that the control requirements of the moral "ought" differ from those of the reasons "ought." As I previously ventured, *Kant's Law* is just a special case of the general principle that reasons-wise "ought" implies "can." And again, *precluding compelling reasons to think otherwise*, if reasons-wise "ought" requires a species of control, reasons-wise "right" and reasons-wise "wrong" require this very species of control as well: if it is reasons-wise right or reasons-wise wrong for you to do something, then you can do it.

We may now proceed to show that there is a requirement of alternative possibilities for reasons-wise right, wrong, and obligation. Recall principle *Reason Ought/Can*:

> *Reason Ought/Can*: If S has most reason to do something, A, and, thus, if S reasons-wise ought to do A, then S can do A.

Reason Ought/Can's corollary is

> *Reasons-Wise "Ought Not" Implies "Can Refrain From" (Reason Ought Not/Can Refrain From)*: If S reasons-wise ought not to do something, A, then S can refrain from doing A.

Moreover, we should, I believe, accept this principle:

> *Reasons-Wise "Ought Not" is equivalent to Reasons-Wise "Wrong" (Reason Ought Not/Wrong)*: S reasons-wise ought not to do A if and only if it is reasons-wise wrong for S to do A.

One would think to say that some action is reasons-wise wrong (that is, reasons-wise forbidden or impermissible) for you is just to say that you reasons-wise ought—you have decisive reason—not to do it or reason requires that you not do it. But then it would seem that it is reasons-wise obligatory for you not to do an act—reason *requires* that you not do it—if and only if it is reasons-wise wrong for you to do it; this is just what *Reason Ought Not/Wrong* says.

From *Reason Ought Not/Can Refrain From* and *Reason Ought Not/Wrong*, we derive:

Reasons-Wise Wrongness Requires Alternatives (Reason/Wrong Alternative): If it is reasons-wise wrong for *S* to do *A*, then *S* can refrain from doing *A*.

Reason/Wrong Alternative, in conjunction with the principle that reasons-wise "wrong" implies "can," establishes that there is a requirement of alternative possibilities for *reasons-wise* wrongness. In a nutshell, if it is wrong for one to do something, one ought not to do it (from "ought not" is equivalent to "wrong"). If one ought not to do something, one can refrain from doing it (from *Kant's Law*). Hence, if it wrong for one to do something, one can refrain from doing it. But it is also true that if it is wrong for one to do something, one can do it. So, there is an alternative possibilities requirement for "wrong."

Consider, next, reasons-wise obligation. If it is reasons-wise obligatory for one to refrain from doing something, then it is reasons-wise wrong for one to do it (from reasons-wise "ought not" amounts to reasons-wise "wrong"). Furthermore, if it is reasons-wise wrong for one to do something, then one can do it (from reasons-wise "wrong" implies "can"). Therefore, if it is reasons-wise obligatory for one to refrain from doing something, then one can do it. But it is also true that if it is reasons-wise obligatory for one to refrain from doing something, then one can refrain from doing it (from *Kant's Law*). In other words, just as there is a requirement of alternative possibilities for reasons-wise wrongness, so there is such a requirement for reasons-wise obligation.

If reasons-wise wrongness and reasons-wise obligation require alternative possibilities, I see little reason to deny that reasons-why rightness, too, requires alternatives. We may conclude that there is an alternative possibilities requirement for the truth of judgments of objective *pro tanto* reasons.

2.5. SOME OBJECTIONS

"Not so fast!" it may be chided. Against the "ought not" implies "can refrain from" principle William Mann writes:

> If the principle is to stand a chance of being plausible, it must be made compatible with the fact that for many people the present structure of their character renders them unable to avoid doing what they know they ought not to do. . . . A person whose upbringing involved considerable exposure to bigotry may find that he still sometimes makes judgments about members of other races . . . which he now knows to be bigoted. He recognizes that he ought not to make such judgments, but his habits are so strong that on some occasions—involving, say, haste and pressure—he cannot avoid making them (1983, 80)

Mann's objection to the "ought not" implies "can refrain from" principle amounts to this: It seems that both the following can be true:

M1: S knows that S ought not to do A.
M2: S cannot refrain from doing A.

But if principle "ought not" implies "can refrain from" is true, then it is not possible that M1 and M2 both be true: M1 entails that S ought not to do A, but this principle and M2 entail that it is false that S ought not to do A.

The objection, however, is not decisive. For appropriately reformulated versions of M1 and M2 enable us to retain the intuition that M1 and M2 can both be true consistent with its being the case that "ought not" implies "can refrain from." We simply need to pay close attention to the double time indexes of "ought" statements. One is the time when the obligation is incurred, the other when the obligation is to be executed. Suppose that, as of time t_1, S can avoid doing A (making bigoted judgments) at a later time t_3. Then this can be true consistent with its being true that "ought not" implies "can refrain from":

M$_1$*: S knows that, as of t_1, S ought to avoid doing A at t_3.

Now suppose due to haste or pressure:

M$_2$*: As of t_2, S cannot refrain from doing A at t_3.

Imagine that, at t_2, S's inclination to make bigoted judgments gets the better of S so that as of this time S finds that S cannot avoid making such judgments at t_3. Still, M$_1$* and M$_2$* can both be true consistent with its being that case that "ought not" implies "can refrain from."

I want to make a slightly different point, however, about Mann's case. Consider this modification of the case designed to cast doubt on "wrong" implies "can": If the principle ("wrong" implies "can") is to stand a chance of being plausible, it must be made compatible with the fact that for many people the present structure of their character renders them unable to do what they know they ought not to do. A person whose upbringing involved considerable exposure to the commandments may find that he cannot covet his neighbor's wife.

We introduce M$_3$ and M$_4$:

M$_3$: S knows that it is wrong for S to covet S's neighbor's wife.
M$_4$: S cannot covet S's neighbor's wife.

The objection this time is that M3 and M4 can both be true. If M3 and M4 are consistent, then it is false that "wrong" implies "can."

My challenge is simply the following: If this variation of Mann's case that supposedly impugns "wrong" implies "can" convinces one, I see little reason for one to resist Mann's original case against "ought not" implies "can refrain from." Presumably, however, the original case should be resisted.

Or, again, in opposition to the "ought" implies "can refrain from" principle, and the "right" implies "can" principle, one might add that if it is morally obligatory for one to feed a starving child, then one can do so. But I may be very compassionate, so much so that when I see the child in such a horrid condition I cannot help but feed it. It remains morally obligatory and hence morally right for me to feed this child. So doing otherwise does not seem to be required for having a moral obligation to do something, though being able to do it is required. And being able to do something does not seem to be required for having a moral obligation not to do it, though being able to avoid doing it is required.[10]

Nevertheless, it is one thing to have the intuition that you morally ought to feed the child even when you can't refrain; quite another to argue for it. Consider this variation of the case: Suppose, whenever you see a starving child, you can't but refrain from killing it because of your psychological profile. Now consider another permutation. Whenever you see a starving child, you can't but kill it. Do you do wrong when you kill the child you could not have refrained from killing? (Note: the concern isn't whether you bring about something that is deontically monstrous when you kill the child.) I have strong doubts that you in fact do moral wrong in this sort of case, and I have these doubts simply because moral obligation, just like moral responsibility, requires control. An analogy that comes to mind is this: some are willing to say or have the intuition that a "willing addict" exercises freedom-level control in shooting up even though her shooting up on a particular occasion causally and nondeviantly issues from an irresistible desire. I have my reservations: if the desire *is* irresistible, on the occasion in question, this addict does not act freely.[11] (Whether she is morally responsible for shooting up on that occasion is another matter.)

The claim that "ought" implies "can refrain" is intuitively plausible. Zimmerman (2008, 147) proposes that the idea that one can be obligated to do something (refrain from killing the child in the example) that one cannot avoid doing suggests, paradoxically, that morality's demands can be empty or trivial.

Looking to *other* resources to break the deadlock in the sorts of case presented above (the cases involving adultery or feeding a starving child) in which intuitions conflict is one way to proceed. What, for instance, do plausible analyses of the concept of obligation imply about whether, for example, "right" implies "can"? There are at least two different analyses and a "deontic system" that independently provide support for this principle. As I have stated, Feldman's (1986) and Zimmerman's (1996; 2008) approach both validate this principle as well as *Kant's Law*. A deontic system models the logical structure of fundamental features of common sense morality. A distinctive feature of Paul McNamara's recently developed, elegant deontic system is that it represents among other deontic notions, those of right, wrong, obligation, exceeding the moral minimum (cf. "action beyond the call of duty" or "supererogation"), and permissible suboptimality (cf. "suberogation"); as well as responsibility notions such as praiseworthiness and blameworthiness (McNamara 2008; 2011). The model validates *Kant's Law* and the moral "right" implies "can" principle as well. So we have independent confirming evidence for these principles.

Suppose being able to do something is an essential constituent of the control that obligation and right require. Then, echoing a point I previously made, I cannot see why the control requirement for wrong should differ in this respect. There is nothing special about wrong. Indeed, the morally deontic concepts of right, wrong, and obligation are interdefinable in this sense: if you take one as primitive, the other two are definable in terms of the primitive. It is curious that we often take "ought" so to speak as "primary." But this is purely arbitrary, or so it seems to me and, I presume, to some deontic logicians. We could take "wrong" as primary. Then we would say things such as "if it wrong, as of some time, for you to do something, then at that time you can do it" and "if it is wrong, as of some time, for you to refrain from doing something, then at that time you can refrain from doing it." Deontic logicians should find nothing amiss with proceeding in this way. Again, the primary point is simply that if obligation and right require control, and if an essential element of this control is the ability to do the pertinent thing, then barring persuasive reason to believe otherwise, I do not see why this control element is not also one of wrong.

One may agree that there is a symmetry of sorts between obligation and wrong having to do with control. But that symmetry, it may be pointed out, is captured by (1a) If one ought to do something, then one can do it, and (2) If one ought not to do something, then one can refrain from doing it. Both "ought" and "ought not" involve an element of control, but the control in the one case is being able to do what you ought to do; in the other case, being able to not do what you ought not to do. This captures both the similarity *and* the difference between "ought" and "ought not" (that is, "wrong"). But it does not follow from any of this that (1a*) if one ought to do something, then one can refrain from doing it, and (2*) if one ought not to do something, then one can do it.

I concur that because "ought" implies "can," one should accept the principle that "ought not" implies "can refrain from"; in short, one should accept *Kant's Law*. But I have *not* claimed that it follows from *these and solely these principles* that "ought" implies "can refrain" or that "wrong" implies "can." Rather, I gave independent reasons to sustain these latter principles. Moreover, regarding obligation, *Kant's Law* underscores the view that control is relevant to both obligatory *commissions* and obligatory *omissions*. This is the symmetry that (1a) and (2) capture. I have argued that right and wrong do not differ from obligation in this very respect: control is required for both permissible or impermissible *commissions* and for permissible or impermissible *omissions*. Clearly, (1a) and (2) do not do justice to this symmetry.

Finally, some might be concerned that I have relied far too heavily on the doing-the-best-we-can apparatus to sustain the thesis that there is an alternative possibilities requirement for our having objective *pro tanto* reasons. Aren't there other (perhaps better) accounts of the relevant normative phenomena? In reply, to appreciate the relatively limited role of the doing-the-best-we-can analysis to motivate this thesis, bear in mind that the central argument for the thesis appeals to the principles that the "ought" of objective reasons implies "can" (that is, if, from the standpoint of objective reasons, one ought to do something, then one can do it), "wrong," too, implies "can," and one ought not to do something if and only if it is wrong for one to do it. It goes without saying that the third principle is uncontroversial. The doing-the-best-we-can account validates *Kant's Law* (or the generalized reasons version of this law). As I see it, that is its primary role. But many others who would (or presumably would) *reject* the doing-the-best-we-can analysis endorse this principle. For example, many deontologists and nonconsequentialists, such as Kant and Ross, accept *Kant's Law*. (I do not, of course, mean to suggest that *Kant's Law* does not have its fair share of dissenters.[12]) The *core* argument for the third principle that "wrong" implies "can" rests on the contention that, unless we have good reasons to believe otherwise, the control requirements of "wrong" (and "right") mirror those of "obligation." This core argument has nothing essential to do with the doing-the-best-we-can analysis. I should stress, however, that I have no qualms whatsoever about invoking this analysis because, to my mind, it is sophisticated, elegant, and highly plausible.

I conclude that although these sorts of objection against "ought" implies "can refrain," "right" implies "can," and "wrong" implies "can" are suggestive, they fall far short of showing that these principles are false.

I end on this note. I said at the onset of this chapter that I do not have an account of practical reasons and that such an account is not required for the primary concerns of this work. But this might be challenged. I have presupposed that there are objective reasons, something that is controversial: the divide between the friends and foes of objective reasons is well documented. So, let me formulate my relevant position more carefully. I certainly believe that there are objective reasons. Examples, such as the following, are partly responsible for my belief:

Steve knows that he could reduce the suffering of innocent people massively merely by pushing a button that is right in front of him, which would cost him nothing beyond a millisecond of time. But he has no desire at all to push this button, and he would not reach such a desire by engaging in procedurally rational deliberation—because, even if he were presented with vivid empirical information about the suffering of these people, he would not care at all about their plight. (Hooker and Streumer 2004, 73)

The controversy over whether there are external reasons is not by any means resolved. So it would be well worthwhile to explore whether, *if* there are such reasons, our having them requires our having alternatives. Suppose there are no such reasons. Then if obligation or intrinsic value is essentially tied to our having reasons, one could conclude either that there are no true judgments of obligation or intrinsic value if these reasons are external, or that there are such true judgments, but the germane reasons are internal (or, better perhaps, these reasons are not external). Even if one opts or argues for the latter, one may well accept principles such as *Reason Ought/Can, Reason Ought Not/Can Refrain From, Reason Ought Not/Wrong,* and *Reason/Wrong Alternative.* Their attraction is not in any way diminished if it turns out that there are no practical reasons that are objective. It may, consequently, be thought that such principles are "in force" or "apply" even if all practical reasons are internal. But then one will be committed to the view that there is an alternative possibilities requirement for practical reasons that are not external, too. By virtue of such a requirement, one will also be committed to the view that there is such a requirement for, for instance, the truth of judgments of obligation and intrinsic value.

NOTES

1. A highly instructive paper on, among other things, *pro tanto* reasons is Broome 2004.
2. I take the canonical form of "ought" statements to be agent- and time-relativized in this way: as of t_1, agent S ought to do action, A, at time t_2 (where t_2 may be identical to t_1 or later than t_1). For simplicity, in the text, I will frequently suppress reference to the double temporal indices in pertinent "ought" statements.
3. See Feldman 1986, 16–25 for more on accessibility.
4. Zimmerman constructs and defends an analysis similar to Feldman's (1996, chap. 2). In his recent book (2008), he advances a different analysis but one that still validates the "wrong" implies "can" principle.

5. A more cautious view, which would suffice for purposes of this third consideration, is that *some* intentional omissions cannot be accomplished without intentionally bringing about some "positive" action.

6. It is this principle that has been implicitly presupposed in Ted's case involving the furnace. The principle requires qualification in order to avoid Good-Samaritan–type paradoxes. The following qualification seems adequate: if one cannot do *p* without doing *q* (perhaps because *q* is a logical consequence of *p*), and if one can refrain from doing *q*, then if one ought to do *p*, one ought also to do *q*. This principle is discussed, among other places, in Zimmerman 1996, sec. 2.3; and in Feldman 1990.

7. I've pretty much reproduced verbatim this version of the argument of fairness supplied by an anonymous reader for Oxford University Press.

8. I have more to say on the argument from unfairness in Haji 2006.

9. I thank Michael Zimmerman for these observations.

10. I owe this example, the previous ones involving adultery and coveting one's neighbor's wife, and the objections with which these examples are associated, to Bob Kane.

11. Some may propose that in such a case the willing addict's act of shooting up is indirectly free if, for instance, she freely decided and took appropriate measures to become an addict.

12. This is something that I address in Haji 2002.

Chapter 3

Moral Obligation, Prudential Obligation, and Alternative Possibilities

3.1. INTRODUCTION

In this chapter, I argue that there is a requirement of alternative possibilities for the truth of judgments of moral and prudential obligation. There is such a requirement because, although not *only* because, both these species of obligation are conceptually associated with our having objective *pro tanto* reasons.

3.2. MORAL OBLIGATION, REASON, AND ALTERNATIVE POSSIBILITIES

The primary argument for the view that one cannot have a moral obligation to do something unless one could have done otherwise streamlines to the following: if one morally ought to do something, one has an objective *pro tanto* reason to do it; if one has such a reason to do something, one could have done otherwise; so, if one morally ought to do something, one could have done otherwise. We may reformulate the argument in this way:

The Primary Argument

(OR) *Obligations are tied to reasons*: If an agent, *S*, has a moral obligation to do something, *A*, then *S* has an objective *pro tanto* reason to do *A*.

(RA) *Reasons are tied to alternatives*: If an agent, *S*, has an objective *pro tanto* reason to do something, *A*, then *S* could have done other than *A*.

Therefore:

If an agent, *S*, has a moral obligation to do something, *A*, then *S* could have done other than *A*.

Prior to addressing this argument, I begin with a summary of why the issue of whether there is an alternative possibilities requirement for the truth of judgments of moral obligation should command the interest even of those who are convinced by or at least receptive to the view that there is no such requirement for the truth of judgments of moral responsibility.

There are at least three reasons to be concerned with whether moral obligation requires alternatives. The first has to do with a putative connection between moral obligation and moral responsibility. Many theorists are drawn to the principles that you can't be praiseworthy for something that isn't obligatory or at least permissible, and you can't be blameworthy for something that isn't impermissible:

Praiseworthiness presupposes Obligation (PO): An agent, *S*, is morally praiseworthy for doing something, *A*, only if it is overall morally obligatory or overall morally permissible for *S* to do *A*.

Blameworthiness presupposes Wrongness (BO): An agent, *S*, is morally blameworthy for doing something, *A*, only if it is overall morally wrong for *S* to do *A*.[1]

Suppose that there is an alternative possibilities requirement for the truth of judgments of moral obligation, right, and wrong or, in short, there is such a requirement for the truth of morally deontic judgments. Then if praiseworthiness requires obligation or permissibility, and blameworthiness requires impermissibility, praiseworthiness and blameworthiness also presuppose our having alternatives. This, in turn, galvanizes a traditional worry about the incompatibility of determinism and moral responsibility. We said that *incompatibilism concerning responsibility* is the thesis that determinism is incompatible with moral responsibility. Of the many different arguments that have been advanced for this variety of incompatibilism, a venerable and relatively traditional one distils to this: If determinism is true, then we can't do otherwise.[2] If we can't do otherwise, we can't be morally responsible for any of our behavior. Therefore, if determinism is true, we can't be morally responsible for any of our behavior.

I reintroduce one principle and supplement it with a second:

The Principle of Alternative Possibilities Regarding Responsibility (PAP-R): A person is morally responsible for what she has done only if she could have done otherwise.

The Principle of Alternative Possibilities Regarding Obligation (PAP-O): It is morally obligatory for a person to do something only if she could have done otherwise.

The second premise of the traditional incompatibility argument—if one can't do otherwise, then one can't be responsible—just is a restatement of *PAP-R* (see chap. 1). *PAP-R*, in tandem with the assumption that responsibility requires control, and this control consists of the freedom to do otherwise, provides the bridge between the first premise (if determinism is true, then one can't do otherwise) and the skeptical conclusion (determinism rules out responsibility).

Frankfurt examples conceived as they originally were as counterexamples to the principle of alternative possibilities concerning responsibility (*PAP-R*), if cogent, tell against the second premise. If, however, such examples do not impugn the principle of alternative possibilities concerning obligation (*PAP-O*), and if there are strong independent reasons to favor *PAP-O*, then provided one accepts both the principle that praiseworthiness requires moral permissibility or obligation and the principle that blameworthiness requires moral impermissibility, one won't be able to escape the traditional argument merely by jettisoning its second premise.

The second reason regarding why the issue of whether moral obligation requires alternatives is significant concerns the impact of determinism on obligation. *Incompatibilism concerning obligation* is the thesis that determinism is incompatible with moral obligation. If there is a requirement of alternative possibilities for the truth of morally deontic judgments, then it would seem that determinism threatens obligation by virtue of eliminating alternatives. Specifically, one may argue as follows: If determinism is true, we can't do otherwise; if we can't do otherwise, nothing is every obligatory for any of us; hence, if determinism is true, nothing is every obligatory for any of us. This argument just mimics the traditional incompatibility argument for determinism and responsibility.

Finally, the third reason concerning the importance of whether obligation requires alternatives has to do with the arresting proposal, which a number of people defend, that although determinism undermines moral responsibility and other moral assessments that are conceptually or logically associated with praiseworthiness and blameworthiness, determinism leaves intact other normative appraisals, particularly, appraisals of moral right, wrong, and obligation (Pereboom 2001; 2002; 2007).[3] Again, if Frankfurt examples (or other considerations) do not cast doubt on the principle that something is obligatory for one only if one could have done otherwise, and there are independent reasons to accept this principle, the credentials of the arresting proposal will have to be reassessed. Determinism, as we will see, may well threaten obligation by virtue of eliminating alternatives.

Reverting to the primary argument, its first premise—if one has a moral obligation to do something, then one has an objective *pro tanto* reason to do it (OR)—captures the view that (overall) moral obligation provides us with reasons. I don't know what sort of argument may be advanced to support this principle because it seems no less basic than the principle that obligation and responsibility require control. It may simply be that obligations of any kind are conceptually linked to reasons of the given kind, moral obligations to moral reasons, for instance (see, for example, Vranas 2007, 172–73). I offer little here on the concept of obligation save that as it occurs in the first premise, "obligation" refers to *all in* obligation in contrast to *prima facie* obligation.

I have said (and will frequently say) that obligation or wrong *provides* us with reasons. Regarding wrong, for instance, one may wonder whether I am inclined toward the thesis that something's being morally wrong provides, or may provide, a reason to respond disfavorably toward it. I am, in fact, partial to another thesis: an act's being wrong just is its being such that there is an objective moral reason not to do it. Nothing substantial, however, regarding what I am concerned to show about obligation and freedom to do otherwise, hinges on which of these two theses one prefers.

The primary argument's second premise—if one has an objective *pro tanto* reason to do something, one could have done otherwise (RA)—was addressed in the previous chapter.

Why believe, however, that moral obligations are tied to objective *pro tanto* reasons and not to Davidsonian or to subjective reasons? The crux of the matter is that the view, roughly, that some things are morally wrong or obligatory for an agent irrespective of what desires or beliefs the agent has is compelling.[4] Doctor House may believe, on the evidence available to him, that giving medicine M to a sick patient will cure the patient. But if giving M will in fact kill the patient, House does wrong in giving M. He does wrong despite his subjective reason: even if he believes that he has an objective *pro tanto* reason to give M, in fact he has no such reason. Indeed, House has a decisive objective *pro tanto* reason *not* to give M. Similarly, House does wrong despite his pertinent Davidsonian reasons: He desires to cure the patient, and he believes that he can cure the patient by administering M; House's having of this desire and belief, in conjunction with other pertinent antecedents of action, causally and nondeviantly issues in his giving M. None of this, however, need tell against House's act not being wrong for House.[5]

3.3. OBJECTIONS TO THE VIEW THAT MORAL OBLIGATION REQUIRES ALTERNATIVES

I now summarize and respond to some objections to the conclusion that moral obligation requires alternative possibilities.

3.3.1. A Problem with the Derivation

We have seen that principle *Reason/Wrong Alternative*—if it is reasons-wise wrong to do something, one can refrain from doing it—together with the principle that reasons-wise "wrong" implies "can," validates the view that reasons-wise wrongness requires alternatives. To recapitulate, if it is reasons-wise wrong for one to do something, one reasons-wise ought not to do it (because "ought not" is equivalent to "wrong"); if one reasons-wise ought not to do something, one can refrain from doing it; so, if it is reasons-wise wrong for one to do something, one can refrain from doing it (this is *Reason/Wrong Alternative*). As reasons-wise "wrong" also implies "can," there is an alternative possibilities requirement for "wrong."

The first objection questions the derivation that "wrong" implies "can refrain from" from the principles "ought not" implies "can refrain from" and "ought not" is equivalent to "wrong." In a nutshell, the objection is that it's false that "ought not" implies "can refrain from" is a legitimate corollary of "ought" implies "can," and so it is nonproprietary to invoke the former to sustain "wrong" implies "can refrain from." More fully, the objection is this: Suppose, as of some time, you morally ought to do what you do in (simplifying) all the best worlds accessible to you at this time. Suppose, also, that the universe is deterministic. Then on any occasion on which you act, there is only *one* world on that occasion that is accessible to you, given pertinent incompatibilist presuppositions, and so there is only one world on each such occasion that is best for you: the only one accessible to you at that time. It would then follow that you would, whenever you act, be morally obligated to perform just one action—the one you perform; you would be morally obligated to do just what you do. This would not have any effect on the legitimacy of *Reason Ought/Can* (if one reasons-wise ought to do something, one can do it). However, the objection continues, it appears that the principle that if one reasons-wise ought not to do something, one can refrain from doing it would be undercut. For, in a deterministic universe in which an agent is morally obligated to perform some action, while reasons-wise "ought" implies "can" is still true, it is not true that the putative corollary of "ought" implies "can" is "ought not" implies "can refrain from," for it is not true that the agent in question can refrain from performing just what he performed.

The objection can be parried: If reasons-wise "ought" implies "can" is true, it is necessarily true. In this respect, its alethic modal standing would be no different from that of the principle of alternative possibilities concerning responsibility (*PAP-R*): if *PAP-R* is true, it is true across all worlds. If reasons-wise "ought" implies "can" is necessarily true, then so is the principle, if true, that reasons-wise "ought not" implies "can refrain from" (*Reason Ought Not/Can Refrain From*). There is no reason to deny that *Reason Ought Not/Can Refrain From* is noncontingent provided reasons-wise "ought" implies "can" is necessarily true. But then, of course, if *Reason Ought Not/Can Refrain From* is necessarily true, it is true in all deterministic worlds. Its alethic modal status will not "shift" merely because in such worlds an agent cannot refrain from doing what he or she in fact does. What would be true is that in such worlds, nothing could be morally wrong for an agent, assuming that "ought not" is equivalent to "wrong." (Compare: if the principle of alternative possibilities concerning responsibility—*PAP-R*—is true, it is true in all worlds including deterministic worlds. If you cannot do otherwise than what you in fact do in such worlds, this does not undermine *PAP-R*: it just shows that *PAP-R* cannot be satisfied in these worlds.)

This result, however, that nothing can be morally wrong for one if one cannot refrain from doing what one does may prompt the following concern: how then can anything be morally *obligatory*, or for that matter morally *permissible*, for anyone in such a world? The right answer to this concern, as I intimated in the previous chapter, is that nothing can in fact be morally obligatory or permissible for anyone in such a world. Rather, each thing one does in a world of this sort—a world in which one can't refrain from doing whatever one does—is what can be labeled "amoral": it is not morally obligatory, permissible, or impermissible. If we call the moral statuses of *being morally obligatory, being morally right,* and *being morally wrong* the "primary moral statuses," the simple lesson is that lack of alternatives undermines the primary moral statuses. With this in mind, one may wish to amend one's analysis of moral obligation in this way:

> *Moral Obligation Revised*: A person, *S*, ought, as of *t*, to see to the occurrence of a state of affairs, *p*, if and only if *p* occurs in some world, *w*, accessible to *S* at *t* (there is a world accessible to *S* at *t* in which *S* brings about *p*), *not-p* occurs in some world, *w**, accessible to *S* at *t* (there is a world accessible to *S* at *t* in which *S* refrains from bringing about *p*), and it is not the case that *not-p* occurs in any accessible world deontically as good as or deontically better than *w*.

In brief, and simplifying, as of some time, *S* ought to do *A* if and only if *S* can do *A*, *S* can refrain from doing *A*, and any accessible world in which *S* refrains from doing *A* is deontically inferior to some accessible world in which *S* does *A*. This revised view of moral obligation has it that moral "obligation," moral "right," and moral "wrong," each implies "can refrain." On the revised view, it is false that it is morally obligatory, or morally permissible, or morally wrong for you to take some deadly pill, or kill someone, if you cannot refrain from taking the pill, or you cannot refrain from killing the person; again, we can opt for the view that it is amoral for you to take the pill or to kill the person. Obligation requires "two-way" control. If you do not have such control with respect to doing something, then it is amoral for you. Again, compare: responsibility requires control. If you don't have responsibility-level control regarding doing something, then you can't be praiseworthy or blameworthy for doing it (although, what you do may be morally grotesque).

Responding directly to the objection under scrutiny, the way is now clear to defend reasons-wise "wrong" implies "can refrain from" partly on the basis of reasons-wise "ought not" implies "can refrain from" because the modified analysis of obligation (*Moral Obligation Revised*) does not in any way jeopardize the principles that reasons-wise "ought" implies "can" or reasons-wise "ought not" implies "can refrain from."

One may yet worry, however, that if each action one performs is amoral for one if one never has alternatives, then why should the primary argument summarized at the onset of this chapter be of any import? Why proceed to show that moral obligation requires alternatives in virtue of obligations being tied to objective *pro tanto* reasons when there is a much simpler route to this same conclusion: an analysis of moral obligation (*Moral Obligation Revised*) entails that if one cannot refrain from performing any action that one performs, then that action is amoral for one? Why indeed proceed with the more complicated route involving objective *pro tanto* reasons?

First, note that one may well be motivated to move from the original analysis of moral obligation to the revised analysis by reflecting on the fact that moral obligation is tied to objective *pro tanto reasons*, and there is an alternative possibilities requirement for the truth of judgments of reasons of this sort. Second, one may in fact construe what I have offered so far as two *divergent* routes to the conclusion that lack of alternatives precludes obligation; one invokes the link between moral obligation and objective *pro tanto* reasons, and the other, an analysis of moral obligation. Common to both routes are, among other principles, the principle that "wrong" implies "can." One may not accept the analysis of moral obligation I favor. Still, this does *not* jeopardize the principle that "wrong" implies "can." Recall, three *independent* considerations for this principle were supplied, one having to do with an analysis of something's *being morally obligatory*, and the other two, roughly, with considerations of control. A partial negative defense that deflects objections against this principle was also provided. The "wrong" implies "can" principle, in conjunction with other principles, such as reasons-wise "ought not" implies "can refrain from" and "ought not" is equivalent to "wrong," show that there is an alternative possibilities requirement for having objective *pro-tanto* reasons. This requirement, together with the thesis that obligations of a certain kind are conceptually tied to reasons of the relevant kind, sustains the conclusion that there is an alternative possibilities requirement for something's being morally obligatory. Third, independent lines of reasoning, one *via* reasons and the other *via* an analysis of moral obligation, to the same conclusion (that lack of alternatives precludes moral obligation) may, if anything, bolster our confidence in the truth of that conclusion. Fourth, the primary argument developed in this chapter, in tandem with considerations from the prior chapter, for the view that moral obligation requires alternatives proceeds by showing that there is an alternative possibilities requirement for having objective *pro tanto* reasons.

Establishing the thesis that having such reasons requires having alternatives is significant. Apart from its intrinsic interest, this thesis is of special import if we accept, as I think we should, the compelling principle that obligations of various kinds are conceptually linked to objective *pro tanto* reasons of the given kind. For, then it follows, from this thesis about our having objective *pro tanto* reasons and this principle regarding an association between having obligations and having objective *pro tanto* reasons, that our having obligations of these kinds presupposes our having alternatives. Quite apart from the issue of whether determinism effaces alternatives, and so quite apart from the debate regarding the compatibility of determinism with these kinds of obligation, it is philosophically rewarding to be able to support intuitively attractive principles, such as the principle that moral obligation presupposes our being able to do otherwise, by drawing on fundamental, widely accepted principles such as "ought" implies "can," "ought not" implies "can refrain from," and "ought not" is equivalent to "wrong."

3.3.2. The Challenge of Frankfurt Examples

Each of PAP-R (a person is morally responsible for doing something only if she could have done otherwise) and PAP-O (a person ought morally to do something only if she could have done otherwise) affirms that alternative possibilities are required for the truth of a certain species of normative judgment. The second objection appeals to Frankfurt examples to turn the tables on the second premise (OR) of the primary argument that moral obligation is conceptually tied to objective *pro tanto* reasons. The objection seeks to convince us that obligation is associated, rather, with normative *Davidsonian* reasons. If this is so, there is no reason to think that obligation requires alternatives because there is no good reason to believe that possessing Davidsonian reasons requires our being able to do otherwise or, at least, so it is averred.

To formulate and assess this objection, I start with an outline of a typical Frankfurt example. Think of such an example as unfolding in two stages. In Stage 1, an agent, Yasmin, decides to do something, *x*, and intentionally *x*-s. For instance, she decides to donate a large sum of money to an excellent charity, such as UNICEF. We are to assume that whether you are a libertarian or a compatibilist, on your account of free action and moral responsibility, Stage 1 Yasmin *is* morally responsible for deciding to x (and for x-ing).[6] In Stage 2, the scenario is developed in a way in which something, a fail-safe mechanism, ensures that Yasmin (Stage 2 Yasmin) decides to x—this thing supposedly precludes Yasmin from deciding to do other than x—*without* in any way interfering in Yasmin's deciding to x. We are meant to draw the conclusion that because Stage 1 Yasmin is morally responsible for deciding to x, and because Stage 2 Yasmin does not differ relevantly from Stage 1 Yasmin with respect to deciding to x, Stage 2 Yasmin is also morally responsible for deciding to x although she could not have refrained from deciding to x.

The following cautionary remark should be heeded. One may allow that in Stage 2, Yasmin has a general ability to refrain from x-ing. One can have this sort of ability, for example, even if one is asleep. One can have the general ability to donate to some charity or to refrain from donating to some charity even if there are no charities. What is true, however, is that in Stage 2, it is false that Yasmin has the capacity to *exercise* the general ability to refrain from donating, or that it is *open* to her or up to her to exercise this ability, or that she has a *choice* about whether to exercise this ability.[7] Partisans of *PAP-R*, it seems, should claim that it is one or more of these "stronger" abilities that responsibility requires and that the fail-safe mechanism in Frankfurt cases is supposed to impair.[8]

Individual Frankfurt examples may differ over what is offered in Stage 2 as the fail-safe mechanism. In Harry Frankfurt's original case, a "counterfactual intervener"—Black—who can manipulate the agent's mind is supposed to turn the trick (Frankfurt 1969, 835–36). Stage 2 Yasmin decides and does exactly what Black wants her to decide and do, and Black never intercedes.

Had Stage 2 Yasmin showed, for example, any involuntary sign of not deciding to donate to UNICEF, Black would have intervened and forced Yasmin to decide to donate to this charity. Owing to Yasmin's deciding to donate to the charity on her own—the insurance policy is never invoked—it seems highly reasonable that Yasmin acts freely and is, it appears, morally praiseworthy for deciding to contribute to the charity (and, subsequently, for contributing). She is praiseworthy, partisans of Frankfurt have judged, despite not having alternative possibilities regarding this decision and action. Thus, it has been thought that Frankfurt examples provide strong *prima facie* reason to believe that alternative possibilities are *not* required for moral praiseworthiness or responsibility in general.

Assume that in Stage 1 Yasmin's deciding to contribute and her contributing are overall and not just *prima facie* morally obligatory for her. If this is so, then it would *seem* that in Stage 2 Yasmin's deciding to contribute and her contributing should also be overall morally obligatory for her. After all, in Stage 2 she acts in the absence of any intervention from Black in just the way in which she did in Stage 1.

To develop the objection that moral obligation is tied not to objective *pro tanto* reasons but to normative Davidsonian ones, first, one insists that in Stage 2 Yasmin ought morally to donate to UNICEF despite not having alternatives, and this is, again, because she conducts herself no differently in this stage than she does in Stage 1 in which it is assumed that she does have such an obligation. Second, one concedes that obligations are conceptually tied to reasons. Third, one then infers that obligations are *not* conceptually associated with objective *pro tanto* reasons. The proponent of this objection is, in effect, proposing that careful reflection on Frankfurt examples reveals, or should reveal, that it is more plausible that (1a) Yasmin in Stage 2 is morally obligated to donate to UNICEF than that (1b) obligations are conceptually linked to objective *pro tanto* reasons. But if one ventures that Frankfurt examples lend more credibility to (1a) than to (1b), then, it seems, in one's estimation the reasons Frankfurt examples provide to favor the proposal that (1a) Yasmin in Stage 2 ought morally to donate, are stronger than the reasons that (1c) considerations independent of anything having to do with Frankfurt examples provide to favor the principles that reasons-wise "ought" as well as reasons-wise "ought not" imply "can," and "ought not" is equivalent to "wrong." (Or, alternatively, one believes that the reasons Frankfurt examples provide to accept (1a) are more compelling than the reasons that (1d) independent considerations provide to favor the proviso that one cannot have a reason to do something which it is impossible for one to do.) To what factors may we appeal to break this impasse? It would not do simply to dig in one's heels and insist that (1c) is more evident than (1a) or to insist on the reverse. But if we note that the sorts of reason available to Yasmin in Stage 2 of the Frankfurt example are normative Davidsonian, or so grant, then there is reason to be optimistic about the balance of critical judgment being tipped in the direction of (1c). And this reason has to do with a thesis previously registered: some things are morally wrong or morally obligatory for an agent irrespective of what desires or beliefs that agent has regarding those things.

One might rightly think that Frankfurt examples signal another sort of objection: if such examples undermine the principle of alternative possibilities regarding moral responsibility (*PAP-R*), don't they also undermine the principle of alternative possibilities regarding obligation (*PAP-O*)? I tackle this sort of objection later (sec. 3.5.3) when I discuss prudential obligation.

3.3.3. Reliance on "Ought" Implies "Can"

The third objection centers on "ought" implies "can." As should be clear, I endorse a number of such principles including versions of the principle where the "ought" is a moral "ought" or a reasons-wise "ought." But then, it may be tendered, isn't there an easy way to resist the view that having objective *pro tanto* reasons requires having alternatives? Simply reject these versions of the "ought" implies "can" principle.

It would be foolish not to recognize the controversy over whether the moral or the reasons-wise "ought" implies "can." Both proponents and opponents of these principles (I have in mind, especially, *Kant's Law*[9]) have written much on them. This is surely not the proper venue to assess this dispute. What I can say, however, is that it is not *evident* that these principles are false, and they do enjoy at least *prima facie* independent credibility. The argument I have outlined for lack of alternatives precluding having objective *pro tanto* reasons draws, at critical junctures, on these principles. One may, of course, opt to reject these principles. One may, for instance, engage in an extended debate about the plausibility of these principles and may, in the end, decide that these principles are not on target. I prefer to leave this debate open. Conceding that not everyone accepts these principles but mindful of the fact that many others do accept them, one might want to put this difference aside and ask: If these principles are true, what should we conclude about not having alternatives, on the one hand, and the truth of judgments of objective *pro tanto* reasons, on the other? In other words, it would be useful to trace some pertinent implications of normative principles that many but not all regard as highly plausible. Parties to the debate would, presumably, learn something from what one is committed to concerning the compatibility or incompatibility of not having alternatives and having objective *pro tanto* reasons if one were to accept these principles.

3.4. PRUDENTIAL OBLIGATION, REASON, AND ALTERNATIVE POSSIBILITIES

Next, I show that prudential obligation requires alternatives. We may understand prudential obligation in a fashion analogous in many respects to the fashion in which we understand moral obligation: on a worldly account of prudential obligation, actions are judged not by appeal to the values of their outcomes but by appeal to the values of the accessible worlds in which they are performed. Since we are attempting to give an account of prudential obligation, worlds are to be evaluated in terms of their value *for the agent*. To determine the value of a world for an agent, we consider how good or bad that world is for this agent. To keep things simple, assume that the worldly value for an agent is an objective measure of the extent to which the agent enjoys goods and suffers evils in the world. Each world is as good for the agent as, or better for the agent than, or worse for the agent than each other world. A world is best for an agent if and only if no other world is better for the agent than it is. The view can now be stated in this way:

> *Prudential Obligation*: A person, S, prudentially ought, as of time, *t*, to see to the occurrence of a state of affairs, *p*, if and only if *p* occurs in some world, *w*, accessible to S at *t*, and it is not the case that *not-p* occurs in any accessible world as good for S or better for S than *w*. (Feldman 1988, 309–10).

More intuitively, the best worlds for you at *t* are the best-for-you worlds accessible to you at *t*. What you prudentially ought to do is what is best for you. According to *Prudential Obligation*, as of some time, an act is prudentially obligatory for you if and only if you can do it and (simplifying) it occurs in all the best-for-you worlds accessible to you at this time. (For the reasons previously explained in connection with moral obligation, one may want to refine the analysis in this way: you prudentially ought, as of *t*, to do some action if and only if you can do it, you can refrain from doing it, and any accessible world in which you refrain from doing it is deontically inferior for you than some accessible world in which you do it.)

It is relatively straightforward to establish that lack of alternatives undermines such obligation. Again, the primary argument to secure this view parallels the primary argument that shows that lack of alternatives undermines moral obligation:

(P1) *Obligations are tied to reasons*: If one prudentially ought to do something, then one has an objective *pro tanto* reason to do it.

(P2) *Reasons are tied to alternatives*: If one has an objective *pro tanto* reason to do something, then one could have done otherwise.

Therefore:

If one prudentially ought to do something, then one could have done otherwise.[10]

Again, the rationale for (P1) is just that obligations of any kind are conceptually linked to reasons of the given kind, prudential obligation to prudential reasons.[11] If, on a certain occasion, it is objectively *pro tanto* best for you to exercise now, then you have most reason that need not be an all things considered reason to exercise now; if, on that occasion, it is worst for you to nap on the couch now, then you have decisive reason not to nap now.

The rationale for (P2) should be transparent: it rests on the argument, discussed in the previous chapter, for the view that there is an alternative possibilities requirement for having objective *pro tanto* reasons.

3.5. OBJECTIONS TO THE VIEW THAT PRUDENTIAL OBLIGATION REQUIRES ALTERNATIVES

In each of the following three subsections I take up an objection to the view that lack of alternatives precludes prudential obligation.

3.5.1. Prudence or Self-Interest?

The first challenges the view that prudential obligation is to be understood in the fashion in which I have proposed. Perhaps there is a subtle but real distinction between self-interest and prudence. According to the objection what has been offered in sec. 3.4 has to do with self-interest and not prudence. In response, if there is such a distinction, I concede it. Reinterpret my primary objective as establishing that lack of freedom to do otherwise undermines considerations of self-interest.

3.5.2. Prudential Obligation and Objective Pro Tanto Reasons

The second objection concurs that obligations of any kind are conceptually associated with reasons of the given kind, but questions whether *all* prudential obligations are linked solely to objective *pro tanto* reasons. My response to this objection is, again, conciliatory: maybe some prudential obligations are not conceptually tied to objective *pro tanto* reasons (although I have real doubts about this as I explain later); but it would be farfetched to suppose that none is.

3.5.3. A Challenge from Frankfurt Examples

The third objection is that if Frankfurt examples impugn the principle of alternative possibilities regarding moral responsibility (*PAP-R*), then such examples should also impugn the principle that persons are prudentially obligated to do something only if they can do otherwise. The principle in question can be restated in this way:

> *Prudential "Ought" Implies "Can Refrain From"* (*PAP-PR*): If an agent, S, prudentially ought to do A, then S can refrain from doing A. (Compare: If an agent is morally responsible for doing A, then the agent could have refrained from doing A.)

(Again, one argument presented for *PAP-PR* reduces to this: If one prudentially ought to do something, one has an objective *pro tanto* reason to do it. If one has such a reason to do that thing, one can refrain from doing it. So, if one prudentially ought to do something, one can refrain from doing it.)

To energize the third objection, assume this time around that in Stage 1 Yasmin's deciding to donate and her donating are prudentially obligatory for her (she couldn't live with herself if she didn't donate because she would be overcome with guilt, she wouldn't receive the large tax break, etc.) If this is so, then it would seem that in Stage 2 Yasmin's deciding to donate and her donating should also be prudentially obligatory for her. After all, in Stage 2 Yasmin acts in the absence of any intervention from Black in just the way in which she did in Stage 1. So, it may be thought, Frankfurt examples should also undercut the principle that persons have a prudential obligation to do something only if they can do otherwise *if* such examples undercut the principle that persons are morally responsible for doing something only if they could have done otherwise.

I'll formulate the objection more carefully, labeling relevant parts for easy, subsequent reference. A "Frankfurt proponent" may propose, first, that the truth of responsibility judgments, just like the truth of judgments of prudential obligation, is conceptually linked to reasons (FP-1). The responsibility analogue of the principle captured in premise P1 (if one has a prudential obligation to do something, then one has an objective *pro tanto* reason to do it) is, roughly, this: if one is morally responsible for doing something, then one has a reason to do it. So we have:

> *Responsibility Requires Reasons*: If an agent, *S*, is morally responsible for doing something, *A*, then *S* has a reason to do *A*.

Ignoring, for the moment, the ambiguity that infects "reason," *Responsibility Requires Reasons* is, some may claim, just as plausible as its prudential counterpart:

> *Prudential Obligation Requires Reasons*: If one prudentially ought to do something, then one has a reason to do it.

That moral responsibility requires reasons is widely endorsed by many libertarians and compatibilists who, despite their other differences over the precise requirements of free action or moral responsibility, by and large concur that, first, responsibility requires control, second, this control is a species of causal control, and, third, the control one has in, for instance, performing an action consists, largely, in this action's being nondeviantly caused by one's having reasons.[12]

Second, the Frankfurt proponent may claim that although responsibility judgments *are* conceptually tied to reasons, the reasons are not objective *pro tanto* reasons (FP-2). Rather, they are a species of Davidsonian reason (a normative as opposed to a merely explanatory reason), which the following simple illustration seems to confirm: Imagine nonculpably believing that you have most reason—you have objective *pro tanto* reasons—to administer medicine A to a patient because you nonculpably believe, on excellent authority, that giving A will save this patient. You believe, too, that you morally ought to administer A. However, you have decisive objective *pro tanto* reasons against giving A because doing so will kill the patient. Suppose you give A with the intention of saving the patient. Suppose, additionally, that you give A partly on the basis of the belief that you morally ought to do so. Aren't you morally praiseworthy for giving A although you have no objective *pro tanto* reasons to give A to this patient? Moreover, it appears that the sorts of reasons for which you give A are Davidsonian. Suppose, again, that you desire to save the patient. You believe that you have decisive objective *pro tanto* reasons to give A to the patient (you believe that you can save the patient by giving A); and you believe, as well, that you morally ought to give A. Assume that your desire to save the patient, together with these beliefs, nondeviantly and causally issues in your forming an intention to give A, which you then execute. Your normative Davidsonian reasons to give A include the belief that you have decisive reason to give A that is false. Still, you give A *for reasons* that you have although these reasons are not objective *pro tanto* reasons.

Third, the Frankfurt proponent may insist that the Frankfurt example involving Yasmin gives us strong reason to believe that there is no requirement of alternative possibilities for our having normative Davidsonian reasons (FP-3). Finally, the Frankfurt proponent, again, falling back on the Frankfurt example involving Yasmin, may claim that judgments of prudential obligation, no different than judgments of moral responsibility, also require normative Davidsonian reasons the truth of judgments of which do not presuppose our having access to alternatives (FP-4).

Commenting on the progression of reasoning from FP-1 to FP-4, I accept the view that the truth of responsibility judgments is conceptually tied to reasons (FP-1). Regarding FP2—that these reasons are normative Davidsonian reasons—two remarks are in order. First, theorists—perhaps "Parfittians"—convinced that all reasons are, in the end, objective won't accept FP-2.[13] One may think it is implausible that there are no reasons other than objective ones. But the proof really lies in the pudding: What does the best account of practical reason imply about the existence of reasons that are not objective? (For what it's worth, I certainly think there are normative Davidsonian reasons.) Second, there are at least preliminary considerations to support the view that prudential obligation *is* tied to objective *pro tanto* reason. You may falsely believe that it is best for you to invest in bonds rather than in stocks, and your transferring a large proportion of your savings into bonds may well be the causal upshot of normative Davidsonian reasons. Still, assuming that your pertinent prudential obligation is to sink money in stocks, this obligation is, it appears, tied to relevant objective *pro tanto* reasons of yours.

Perhaps one may reply that "best for you" is ambiguous. Attending to Davidsonian reasons nicely brings this out. On the one hand, you may evaluate the object of the desire—what you desire—of the desire component of your Davidsonian reason to invest in bonds, and you might conclude that, from *your perspective* of what is best for you, you should invest in bonds rather than in stocks. Dub this perspective the "personal perspective." On the other hand, there is some "objective" perspective, such as the doing-the-best-for-you perspective, to assess what is best for you. The suggestion is that first, prudential obligation is associated with the personal perspective, and second, there is no reason to believe that if associated with this perspective, having a prudential obligation to do something entails having an objective *pro tanto* reason to do it. Again, however, this suggestion is controversial. Surely, you can be doing what is best for you from the personal perspective without doing what is in fact best for you. You might do what you mistakenly think is best for you.

Alternatively, it might be proposed that one gauge the strength of a Davidsonian reason in, roughly, this way: assess what is desired on a scale of "objective worth," on how "objectively good" it is. On this view if the scale of objective goodness, whatever it precisely amounts to, rules that the object of one of two "competing" desires of yours is objectively better than the object of the second, the object of the first dictates what is best for you. For example, if investing in bonds—the object of one of your desires—is objectively better than investing in stocks—the object of a competing desire—then, on this alternative, it is best for you to invest in bonds. And, similarly again, the proposal is that from the perspective of objective worth, there is no reason to believe that prudential obligation is conceptually linked to objective *pro tanto* reasons. However, even assuming that there is scale of objective worth, it would seem that what is objectively best need not be what is *best for you*. Maybe your investing in bonds is objectively best, in the relevant sense, but without strong supporting reason, why think that investing in bonds is, in virtue of being objectively best, prudentially best for you? In sum, I believe there are good initial considerations to support the view that prudential obligation is conceptually associated with objective *pro tanto* reasons.

Addressing FP-3—the proposal that there is no requirement of alternative possibilities for Davidsonian (normative or otherwise) reasons—this proposal is not as forthright as one might initially believe. The Frankfurt example involving Yasmin seems to show that responsibility judgments require reasons that are "internal" insofar as these reasons are essentially "agent-dependent": they are *constituted* by the desires or beliefs of the agent. In this way, they are not agent-independent "external" reasons. One may think that if the pertinent reasons are internal in this sense, then Frankfurt examples lend strong credibility to the view that the truth of judgments of such "internal" Davidsonian reasons is divorced from any requirement of alternative possibilities. But this is much too quick. It is so because there is nothing to preclude a proponent of even "internal" reasons from partnering such an account of reasons with an alternative-possibilities requirement for reasons; indeed, there is a fair bit to be said in favor of such an alliance.

Echoing what I proposed toward the end of chapter 2, suppose you are an "internalist" or an "externalist" about reasons, and you accept as a constraint on practical reasons the *independently plausible* principles: reasons-wise "ought" implies "can" (*Reason Ought/Can*), reasons-wise "ought not" implies "can refrain from" (*Reason Ought Not/Can Refrain From*), and reasons-wise "ought not" is equivalent to "wrong" (*Reason Ought Not/Wrong*). (You may accept as a further constraint on reasons, whether "internal" agent-dependent ones or "external" agent-independent ones, the proviso that you cannot have a reason to do something if it is impossible for you to do it.[14]) Then you will be committed to the view that there is a requirement of alternative possibilities for the truth of judgments of practical reason because principles *Reason Ought/Can, Reason Ought Not/Can Refrain From*, etc, imply that your having such reasons commits you to having alternatives. Consequently, you will be able to hold on to the view that there is no requirement of alternative possibilities for the truth of "internal" Davidsonian reasons only by paying a theoretical cost many will deem too high: regardless of whether you are an "internalist" or "externalist" about reasons, you have to renounce principles *Reason Ought/Can, Reason Ought Not/ Can Refrain From,* and *Reason Ought Not/Wrong.*[15] I return to this issue in section 6.6.

Regarding FP-4—prudential obligation requires our having alternatives—my reply turns on the view that responsibility judgments and judgments of prudential obligation have different objects of evaluation; the first assesses persons, the second actions. In other works, I have proposed that appraisals of moral responsibility are, first and foremost, appraisals of the *person*—they are agent-focused (see, for e.g., Haji 2002, 146–47). With responsibility judgments, when, for example, we hold an agent morally to blame, we are primarily *faulting the agent* and not what she has done. Such judgments disclose the moral worth of an agent with respect to some episode in her life—a person "expresses what she morally stands for" when she is morally responsible for some deed. When blameworthy, one typically expresses "ill will" toward another—the willingness to do wrong involving the other—and it is the expression of such ill will that, partly, sanctions the judgment that one's moral worth with respect to the relevant action has been diminished. I say "typically," because, for instance, in cases of culpable negligence, agents often do not express ill will. On the view I defend, an expression of such ill will is manifested when one nonculpably believes that some act is morally wrong, and despite this belief, performs the act; in short, when blameworthy, one acts in light of the nonculpable belief that one is doing moral wrong.[16] Similarly, when one is praiseworthy, one typically expresses good will toward another, and it is the expression of such good will that partly validates the judgment that one's moral worth vis-à-vis the relevant deed has been augmented. When praiseworthy, one acts on the basis of the nonculpable belief that one is doing what is morally obligatory or morally permissible.

Regarding responsibility appraisals, an agent can manifest ill will or good will by an action she performs—she can disclose what she morally stands for on the particular occasion—even when she lacks, as she would in a Frankfurt situation, alternative possibilities. This is because such expression does not presuppose the availability of alternative options. Since an agent, in a Frankfurt scenario, discerns her situation and subsequently acts in just the way in which she would discern her situation and then act as if there were no counterfactual intervener or some other fail-safe gismo in the wings, in such cases agent-focused appraisals of responsibility should not be affected merely because the agent lacks alternatives. Or, coming at this point from another direction, if an act from your perspective is morally wrong—if you take yourself to be doing intentional moral wrong—then even if you lack alternatives and, thus, your act is not in fact wrong, you can still express ill will in your conduct; and, similarly, if you take yourself to be doing something that is morally obligatory, even without alternatives, you can still express good will in your conduct.[17]

In contrast, appraisals of prudential obligation are pronouncedly *non*-agent-focused; they are *act-focused*. They are *not* connected, in any necessary fashion, with how the agent perceives the situation or with the agent's germane motivations or beliefs. Whether an agent's act has the sanction or condemnation of prudence—whether it has the property of *being prudentially permissible, being prudentially impermissible,* or *being prudentially obligatory*—then, is *not* essentially associated with, for example, whether the agent performs that action in the belief that it has the support or censure of prudence, or more generally, with the agent's perception of what she prudentially ought or ought not to do. Act-focused appraisals of prudence, unlike those of responsibility, turn primarily on whether it is indeed best for the agent to perform or refrain from performing the pertinent act. If responsibility appraisals are different in kind from appraisals of prudence, there is no reason to assume that the conditions requiring satisfaction for one to be apt must be the very ones requiring satisfaction for the other to be apt. For instance, freedom to do otherwise may well be necessary for the latter sorts of appraisal but not for the former sorts. In light of this, there is little preliminary reason to believe that a counterexample against a proposed condition for the appropriateness of one sort of normative appraisal, for instance, Frankfurt examples as proposed counterexamples to the principle of alternative possibilities regarding responsibility, will also be a counterexample to an analogous condition for the other. Hence, although some may take Frankfurt examples to cast doubt on the principle of alternative possibilities regarding responsibility, it is not clear that they cast doubt on the prudential "ought" implies "can refrain from" principle (PAP-PR).

We may conclude that there is a requirement of alternative possibilities for both moral and prudential obligation because of the essential association between each of these sorts of obligation and objective *pro tanto* reasons.

NOTES

1. See, for instance, Smith 1991, 279; Widerker 1991, 223; Fields 1994, 408–9; Copp 1997; 2003, 286–87; Fischer 2006, 218, Arpaly 2006, 91, n. 3. I've argued against these principles. See, for example, Haji 2002.
2. On the Consequence Argument that attempts to show that determinism effaces alternatives, see, for example, Wiggins 1973; Ginet 1990; 2003; van Inwagen 1983.

3. On a similar theme, see, for example, Waller 1990; Double 1991; 2004; Honderich 1993; and Trakakis 2008.

4. I realize that this claim would be rejected by those people—Bernard Williams (1981), for example, and more recently Mark Schroeder (2007)—who think that *pro tanto* reasons in some way depend on desires.

5. Some may, of course, say that if a doctor gives a medicine to a patient that the doctor sincerely and responsibly believes will cure the patient, what the doctor does is not wrong even if it turns out that the medicine unexpectedly kills the patient. Intuitions about these sorts of cases can conflict. I'm inclined to claim that the doctor does objective wrong but is not blameworthy; and that the doctor fulfils his subjective obligation: she does what she believes she has an objective obligation to do.

6. A more cautious manner of arguing would be to assume only that it is not demonstrated that the agent is not morally responsible (see, for example, Fischer, 1999; and Haji and McKenna, 2004; 2006). But for present purposes, we can work with the stronger assumption.

7. But see Vihvelin 2008b. Fischer's response (2008a) to Vihvelin is highly interesting as is Vihvelin's paper.

8. See, for instance, Clarke 2008; Berofsky 2011; and Fischer 2011 for more on this point.

9. In defense of the moral "ought" implies "can" principle, see, for instance Zimmmerman 1996, chap. 3; Streumer 2007b, Vranas 2007; Haji 2002; 2009a.

10. Further discussion on reason, prudential obligation, and alternative possibilities can be found in Haji 2010.

11. See, for example, Vranas 2007, 172–73.

12. Non-causalists such as Ginet (1990); Goetz (1998); McCann (1998); and Widerker (2009) do not accept any such causal conception of control.

13. See Parfit 1997; 2001; forthcoming. If one takes all reasons to be (objective) *pro tanto* reasons, then one, perhaps, shouldn't accept *Responsibility Requires Reasons*.

14. On such a condition, see, for instance, Streumer 2007a; 2010. Crisp (2006, 43) rejects this condition.

15. It is interesting to note the following: Bernard Williams has proposed that an agent has an "internal" reason to do something—*a*—only if she would arrive at a motivation (or desire—here, I use the terms interchangeably) to *a* were she to deliberate rationally from her current "motivational set," where this set has been corrected to exclude false beliefs and include all relevant true beliefs (Williams 1981, 102–3; 1995a, 36; See, also Smith 1994, 156; Parfit 1997, 100). But Williams also seems to endorse a "reason implies can" principle: if you have an (internal) reason to *a*, you must be capable of *a*-ing (Williams 1995b, 189–90).

16. The analysis of blameworthiness I have defended is, roughly, this: *S* is blameworthy for doing *A* if and only if *S* does *A* freely, *S* does *A* on the basis of the nonculpable belief that *S* is doing moral wrong in *A*-ing, and *A* causally and nondeviantly issues from pertinent springs of actions (such as desires or beliefs) that with respect to which *S* is autonomous. See Haji 1998; 2002; 2009a.

17. I concede that there is a potential problem with this line of reasoning if a Davidsonian account of reasons is paired with principles *Reason Ought/Can*, *Reason Ought Not/Can Refrain From*, and *Reason Ought Not/Wrong*, or, more generally, with the proviso that you cannot have a reason to do something if it is impossible for you to do that thing. For more on this problem with Frankfurt examples, see Haji 2011.

Chapter 4

Axiological Appraisals and Alternative Possibilities

4.1. INTRODUCTION

G. E. Moore (1903) called the value that something has for its own sake "intrinsic value," presumably because he took such value to supervene solely on the intrinsic properties of its bearers. Some people reject this supervenience thesis but still use the term "intrinsic value" to refer to the kind of nonderivative value at issue (e.g., Kagan 1998), while others opt instead for such labels as "final value" (e.g., Rabinowicz and Rønnow-Rasmussen 1999). Although I subscribe to the supervenience thesis, almost nothing of substance in this chapter turns on this thesis. Thus, I use the term "intrinsic value" to refer to the sort of value that interests me.

My primary concerns in this chapter pivot on the freedom presuppositions of the truth of judgments of or involving intrinsic value. Specifically, I address the following issue: Is there reason to think that the truth of judgments of intrinsic value presupposes our having alternatives owing to a necessary connection between intrinsic value and objective *pro tanto* reasons? I defend an affirmative answer. Toward the end of the chapter, I say something on the tie between (1) pleasure and reasons and (2) virtue appraisals and reasons.

4.2. INTRINSIC VALUE AND REASONS

As a point of departure consider this attractive thesis:

> (*IValue-1*): Necessarily, x is intrinsically good if and only if any-
> one who were to contemplate x would have a (practical) reason
> to favor x for its own sake.[1]

Here, "intrinsically good" refers, again, to the sort of Moorean impersonal, nonderivative value that presumably precludes partiality;
and "favor" is an umbrella term covering any sort of pro-attitude
toward x.[2] There are analogous principles concerning intrinsic badness, intrinsic neutrality, and intrinsic betterness:

> (*1Value-2*): Necessarily, x is intrinsically bad if and only if anyone
> who were to contemplate x would have a reason to disfavor x for
> its own sake.
>
> (*IValue-3*): Necessarily, x is intrinsically neutral if and only if any-
> one who were to contemplate x would have a reason to be indif-
> ferent toward x for its own sake.
>
> (*1Value-4*): Necessarily, x is intrinsically better than y if and only
> if anyone who were to contemplate both x and y would have a
> reason to prefer x for its own sake to y for its own sake.

IValue-1 should be differentiated from the stronger so-called
buck-passing account of value which it resembles:

> *Buck Passing*: x is intrinsically good = df. anyone who were to
> contemplate x would have a reason to favor x for its own sake.

According to the buck-passing account, it is not x's being good that
gives a person who contemplates x reason to favor it or, as some

would prefer to say, it is not *x*'s being good that renders it fitting of a favorable response; rather, it is those properties in virtue of which *x* is good that do so (see, e.g., Ewing 1939; 1948; Scanlon 1998). Although many have endorsed this view, others have rejected it, insisting that the reason why it is fitting to favor what is good is the fact that it *is* good (e.g., Blanshard 1961, 284. Zimmerman 2007, 346–51; 2011,452). As these people see it, goodness has a priority over fittingness of or reasons to favor that is inconsistent with the buck-passer's fundamental contention that goodness may be ana-lyzed in terms of fittingness of or reasons to favor. Unlike the buck-passing account, *IValue-1* is perfectly compatible with the pri-ority of goodness over fittingness. It is to *IValue-1* (or at least to *IValue-1*–like principles) that attention is confined.

If intrinsic value is associated with practical reasons in the way in which *IValue-1* affirms, what sorts of reason are at issue? Are the rea-sons subjective, Davidsonian, or objective? "A reason" in *IValue-1* cannot plausibly refer to a subjective reason. Reflect on the part of the biconditional that says that if anyone who contemplates *x* has reason to favor *x* for its own sake, then *x* is intrinsically good. Sup-pose you have subjective reason to favor something—*Alf's taking displeasure (to some specified degree), at noon, in the fact that his son has been injured*: you believe, upon contemplating it, that you have an objective *pro tanto* reason to favor this state for its own sake. (Here, "state" may refer either to Kim-like concrete states, that is, states as finely individuated concrete occurrences (Kim 1976), or to states of affairs; the distinction is of no moment for present con-cerns.) But suppose this belief is false. Then contrary to what this part of *IValue-1* implies, there is no reason to think that this state is intrinsically good.

It is also true that "a reason" in *IValue-1* cannot plausibly refer to a Davidsonian reason. Suppose that the object of one of your intrinsic desires is the state *Ralph's taking displeasure (to some specified degree), at noon, in the fact that he misses the big game tonight*; and suppose this desire, together with a suitable belief, constitutes a Davidsonian reason of yours for seeing to the occurrence of this state when you contemplate it. This fact, in conjunction with the part of *IValue-1*: if anyone who contemplates x has reason to favor x for its own sake, then x is intrinsically good, when "a reason" in this condition denotes a Davidsonian reason, implies, falsely, that *Ralph's taking displeasure (to some specified degree), at noon, in the fact that he misses the big game tonight* is intrinsically good. There is an equally pressing problem in the other direction of the biconditional: if x is intrinsically good, then anyone who contemplates x has reason to favor x for its own sake. For it may well be that although *Ralph's taking pleasure (to some specified degree)at noon, in the fact that his beer is frosty cold* is intrinsically good, someone else may not have any Davidsonian reason to favor this state of affairs for its own sake upon contemplating it.

I propose, then, that "a reason" in *IValue-1* refers to an objective *pro tanto* reason. If *IValue-1* is true, there is such a reason for anyone who contemplates x to favor x for its own sake if x is intrinsically good. And I concur with relevant partisans that there is such a reason *because x* is intrinsically good; x is worthy of being favored for its own sake. More fully, I am partial to what I take to be Michael Zimmerman's proposal (2011, 453–54) that it would be better to understand *IValue-1* in this way:

(*IValue-1**): Necessarily, x is intrinsically good if and only if (1) x is object worthy, that is, x is worthy of being favored for its own sake; and

(2) anyone who contemplates x has a reason of the right kind to favor x for its own sake, where this sort of reason is constituted by x's being worthy of being favored for its own sake or x's deserving to be favored for its own sake.

A concern with clause (1) is that it might well be the case that object worthiness is tied to intrinsic goodness in a way which threatens *IValue-1**, to wit, something is object worthy only if it is intrinsically good. Be that as it may, it is *IValue-1** that I assume attempts to capture an important truth about intrinsic value. The kernel of truth of significance for the objectives of this work is, roughly, that the fact that something is intrinsically good is a reason to desire, or pursue, or favor (however precisely "favoring" is to be construed) it.

4.3. A REQUIREMENT OF ALTERNATIVE POSSIBILITIES FOR INTRINSIC VALUE

We have seen that there is an alternative possibilities requirement for having objective *pro tanto* reasons. As this is so, we may now argue for the view that intrinsic value also presupposes our having alternatives.

Assume that an objective *pro tanto* reason to *favor* something is not relevantly different from such a reason to *do* something in that, with a reason of this sort for either sort of thing, it is not possible to have a reason to favor something or to do something if one cannot favor or do that thing. Without justification to believe otherwise, it is implausible to suppose that this asymmetry obtains: whereas one cannot have an objective *pro tanto* reason to do something unless one can do it, one can have such a reason to favor something despite one's not being able to favor it. So, assume that the principles reasons-wise "ought" implies "can," reasons-wise "ought not" implies "can refrain from," and reasons-wise "ought not" is equivalent to "wrong" "apply" even when it is favoring that is of concern. Then it will be true that if you have a reason to favor *x*, you can refrain from favoring *x*. We may now invoke this argument to show that the truth of judgments of intrinsic value requires our having alternatives: If something is intrinsically good, one has an objective *pro tanto* reason to favor it; if one has such a reason to favor something, one could have refrained from favoring it; so, if something is intrinsically good, one had relevant alternatives. The argument can be presented a bit more carefully in this fashion:

> (AX-1) If something, *x*, is intrinsically good, then one would have an objective *pro tanto* reason to favor *x* were one to contemplate *x*.
> (AX-2) If one would have an objective *pro tanto* reason to favor *x* were one to contemplate *x*, then one could refrain from favoring *x* (because there is an alternative possibilities requirement for having objective *pro tanto* reasons).
> Therefore:
> If *x* is intrinsically good, then one could refrain from favoring *x*.

I now outline and respond to one objection to this line of reasoning. The objection consists in denying the reasons-"can" thesis I assert, where, again, "can," as I have cautioned, expresses a form of personal possibility stronger than mere logical possibility.

Commenting on a version of (*IValue-1*),

> (*IValue-1Z*): Necessarily, *x* is intrinsically good if and only if one's contemplation of *x* morally requires that one favor *x* for its own sake,

Zimmerman explains that one can be morally required, in the relevant sense of "morally required," to do something or to favor something despite one's not being able, in the personal sense of "able," to do it or to favor it. What is required is, roughly, what is most appropriate or most fitting. To flesh out the latter, Zimmerman introduces an example:

> Suppose that you have gratuitously insulted Bert and that you must now make amends. Perhaps it will be most appropriate if you apologize to Bert in person. Or perhaps it will be equally appropriate if you send Bert flowers with a card expressing your remorse. It may be less appropriate, but nonetheless suitable, if you leave a brief message of apology on Bert's answering machine. However, you will be overdoing it if you buy Bert a new TV, and it may even be positively inappropriate if you buy Bert a new car. (2001, 92)

Zimmerman then proposes that the sort of appropriateness or requirement at issue is more closely related to what is sometimes called the "ought-to-be" or to what is ideal as opposed to the "ought-to-do" or the "ought" of obligation (2001, 93). He claims that whereas the "ought" of obligation implies "can," the ideal "ought" does not:

> I don't think that "require" or "appropriate," as they are to be understood in the present context . . . imply "can." For example, it would remain true that it would be most appropriate for you to send Bert flowers by way of an apology, even if there were no flowers available. (That is, it's not just that this would be the, or a, most appropriate thing for you to do *if you could*; it would be the most appropriate thing *period*.) Similarly, it would be inappropriate for you to buy Bert a new car, even if you lacked the means to do so (2001, 94).

I reproduce one more passage from a later work of Zimmerman that is revealing:

Imagine that John becomes aware of something that is intrinsi-cally good . . . for example, he sees a news report of some mother in a foreign land crying tears of joy when her child is rescued from a burning building—but he does not respond positively towards it. He is unmoved. You accuse him of being hard-hearted. He replies: "What has that child's being saved got to do with me? *I* have no reason to be glad about it." Surely this reply is defective. But how? It is true that John has no prudential reason to be glad at the news; *he* is no better off for it. Likewise he has no legal or aesthetic reason to be glad at it. I submit that he has a moral rea-son to be glad at it; his failure so to respond is indicative of a moral deficiency, an ethical insensitivity, in him. . . . To forestall one possible misunderstanding: in saying that John has a moral reason to be glad at the news, I am not saying that he is morally obligated (even prima facie) so to respond. One can be morally obligated to do something only if one is in control of doing it, and John might not be in control of such a response. But even if he cannot control his response, it makes sense to say that his being glad at the news would be a morally *fitting* way to respond to it—that the news *calls for* or *requires* such a response from him. To say, then, that John has a moral reason to be glad at the news is to say that there is a moral requirement that he so respond, even if this requirement is not tantamount to an obligation. (2007, 329–30, notes omitted.)

If the "ought" of requirement does not presuppose one's having control, this would lend support to the view that this sort of "ought" does not imply "can." Or coming at this same concern another way, if one is not in control of the apt response, and there is a moral requirement to respond in this way, then, seemingly, it is easier to maintain that the "ought" of requirement does not entail "can." So, I address this issue of control first. According to (*IValue-1*) or (*IValue-1Z*), or more generally, the fitting-attitude account, something is intrinsically good just in case it would be fitting to favor it if one were to contemplate it as such; the account requires that one have epistemic familiarity with the object of contemplation. As Krister Bykvist remarks, such epistemic familiarity will minimally involve a grasp of all the intrinsic features of the thing considered (2009, 4). For ease of discussion, I assume the fitting attitude, whatever it precisely is, is some attitude that is directed onto objects. I neither pretend to know what this attitude is, nor deny that there are trenchant problems with identifying the pertinent attitude (Bykvist 2009). I simply set these legitimate concerns aside. In addition, to make headway, I assume that the attitude is one of desiring, in a sense of having a disposition to bringing about the relevant object (although I doubt that this is indeed so). The focal question now is: Does the agent have control in responding to the pertinent object in this way? We note that we can acquire desires on the basis of practical reasoning. Presumably, when we do acquire desires in this way, we have indirect control in acquiring them by virtue of our having direct control with respect to our reasoning. What about control, however, regarding grasping propositions or grasping the intrinsic features of objects? With the former, typically we grasp certain propositions but not others. It appears it is up to us, in some hard to specify way of *being up to us*, that we grasp a proposition when we do. Grasping a proposition is not just something that happens to us. If it were, it would be difficult to explain why we grasp the propositions that we do but not others: it would be chancy which propositions we grasped if grasping itself were not in our control. But this is not so.

With respect to grasping the intrinsic features of objects we contemplate as such, it seems that grasping such features is more like acquiring desires on the basis of practical reasoning, than, for instance, acquiring desires because of the way we feel. But we have already registered that the former involves control. So, presumably, the latter should as well. Moreover, grasping the intrinsic features of an object, when we do grasp these features, is akin to grasping a proposition, insofar as it is not chancy. However, if we failed to have control in grasping the intrinsic features of something, then it seems that grasping such features when we did *would* be chancy. This gives us additional reason to believe that when we grasp the intrinsic features of an object, we have control in grasping such features. And this, in turn, imparts further support to the view that in responding as we do to something that is intrinsically good, we may well be in at least indirect control of such a response; this is because we presumably have direct control in grasping its intrinsic properties.

Addressing, next, Zimmerman's rationale to associate or liken requirement with the ideal "ought" rather than with the "ought" of obligation, although this rationale is interesting, it is not beyond dispute.[3] Suppose that in virtue of its relevant aesthetic features a painting merits a certain sort of aesthetic response; it would be most appropriate to respond to it in the pertinent way upon contemplating its intrinsic features. Suppose, however, that you have no aesthetic sense and so cannot respond to the painting in the most appropriate way called for by its contemplation. Is it evidently the case that it would be most appropriate for *you* to respond in the specified way? The issue is, of course, not whether it would remain true that it would be most appropriate for you to respond in the specified way *if you could*. The question, How can it be *required* of you to respond in the particular fashion when you cannot so respond, and How can this be so even if the painting or its contemplation calls for such a response? is not inappropriate. Or imagine an elegant computer program that enables you quickly and easily to edit a manuscript. Some might venture that this program calls for a certain response. But suppose you know nothing whatsoever about such programs; you could not discriminate between elegant and ungainly ones. Again, it does not strike me as out of the ordinary to affirm that, although, owing to its mathematical elegance, the program (generally) calls for a certain response, there is no (moral) requirement for *you* to respond in the appropriate way. Similarly, one might wonder how it can be required that you do something, such as send flowers to Bert, when you cannot send flowers. One need not, I think, deny that it *ought to be* that you respond to the painting or program in the specified way, or that it ought to be that you send flowers to Bert by way of an apology, while consistently maintaining that it is *not* most appropriate for you to respond or to send flowers because you cannot do these things.

I have suggested that it is not clear, in cases such as Bert's, that it remains most appropriate for one to do something when one cannot do it. But why think that Zimmerman needs to show that this is *clearly* rather than, say, plausibly the case? One might further demand that because my thesis—it is controversial that it remains most appropriate for one to do something which one cannot do—is *counterintuitive*, I should shoulder the burden of proof, and therefore the onus is on me to construct the clear counterexample.

I have conceded that Zimmerman's position is plausible. What I have on offer is a contrary position, which, admittedly, I do not find counterintuitive and which I think is plausible.[4] Is there anything more that can be said to bolster my alternative? Bykvist advances this example:

> Take, for instance,
> there being happy egrets but no past, present or future agents
> (i.e., beings who intentionally bring something about).

This is a good state of affairs that it is not fitting to intentionally bring about, for the simple reason that it is logically impossible to intentionally bring it about that there is no present, past or future agent who brings anything about. I am here relying on the uncontroversial principle that what it is fitting to favour must be logically possible to favour. (2009, 35, notes omitted.)

Exploiting some elements in this passage, consider: (1) It is not appropriate, and so not most appropriate, for you intentionally to bring about something that it is not logically possible for you to bring about. Similarly, (2) it is not appropriate for you intentionally to bring it about that a temporally nonrelational fact about the past, such as, yesterday, Stefaan took pleasure to degree +5 in puffing on his Havana, not be a fact about the past. But if we grant (1) and (2), I see no reason to deny (3) it is not appropriate for you intentionally to bring about something you cannot bring about unless you acquire beliefs that you cannot, in your circumstances, acquire, or (4) it is not appropriate for you intentionally to send flowers to Bert when you cannot send flowers. Insofar as bringing about impossible states of affairs, or "fully past" contingent states of affairs, the bringing about of which would require altering the past, or bringing about "future" contingent states of affairs which you cannot, in some personal sense of "cannot," bring about, such as sending flowers to Bert when there are no flowers to send, you are in the same predicament: in your circumstances, you *cannot* bring about the relevant state of affairs. You are just as disabled—you do not have the power (or opportunity) to bring about the germane state of affairs—irrespective of whether the state of affairs occurs in no possible world or whether the non-actual state of affairs occurs in some possible world that is either "close" or "distant" to the actual world. In brief, if a certain logical modality—*its being impossible*—of a certain state of affairs, or its having the feature of *being fully past*, counts against there being a *requirement* to bring about this state of affairs, why should the fact that you cannot bring about a future contingent state of affairs, such as your sending flowers to Bert, also not speak against there being a requirement to bring about such a state of affairs?

Zimmerman also proposes that just as there is a connection between the "ought" of obligation and reason, so there is a connection between requirement and reason:

> If you have a prima facie moral obligation to do something, you have one type of moral reason to do it. You have a reason of this type, for instance, if you have a prima facie obligation to apologize to Bert in person. (Some may prefer to say that your having such an obligation implies only that *there is* such a reason, and that *you have* such a reason only if you're aware of your obligation.) If this prima facie obligation is matched or overridden by some conflicting prima facie obligation, then your reason to apologize to Bert in person is not a conclusive reason of this type; otherwise, it is. There arises a second type of moral reason, though, simply in virtue of one's being morally required to do something. For, as noted . . ., requirement isn't restricted, as obligation is, to what you can do. If what would be most fitting is something that you cannot achieve (such as sending Bert flowers when none are available), then there is a moral reason of the second type, even though not of the first type, to do the thing in question. (To say that "you have" this reason might in this case seem rather awkward.) (2001, 95–96)

Again, I have my doubts about whether one can *have* reasons of the second type that Zimmerman's describes in this passage when one cannot bring about the relevant state of affairs. Suppose, contrary to what I have proposed, that you can be required to do something, send flowers to Bert, for instance, that you cannot do. There might, at best, be a reason for you to send flowers, although I am highly suspicious about this claim. But I think, contrary to Zimmerman, that it is implausible to believe that you have—you possess—a reason to do what it is not within your power to do. You cannot, for instance, (1) have a reason to bring it about that some square is round; nor can you (2) have a reason to bring it about that some fact that is fully about the past or fully "settled" is not a fact about the past. But then, I see no reason to deny that you cannot (3) have a reason to send flowers to Bert when there are no flowers to send.

To recapitulate, on one position—the *Value-Requirement* position—intrinsic value, via its association with requirement or fittingness, is tied to reasons. This position implies that if something is intrinsically good, then there is a moral requirement to favor it, and in virtue of there being such a requirement, one has a reason to favor it. But our having this species of reason to do something—a "requirement reason"—does *not* presuppose our having alternatives, let alone presupposing our being able to do that thing. On a second, competing position—the *Value-Objective Reason* position—intrinsic value is tied to objective *pro tanto* reasons, which are reasons of the sort to do something that we cannot have without having both the ability to do it and the ability to refrain from doing it. I find both views plausible, but I'm inclined to lean toward the latter. Here is one more, admittedly far from decisive, consideration in favor of the second position. Contrary to what I suggested earlier, grant that it can be appropriate or fitting to do something even if one is unable to do it, a key plank the *Value-Requirement* position exploits to sustain the view that intrinsic value is associated with reasons to do something whose possession does not require our having the ability to do it. Well, if it is, for instance, appropriate for Berta to send tulips, then, presumably, it can be fitting for her to send them (on the *Value Requirement* view) despite her not having a motivating desire to send them. (Recall, a motivating desire is an attitudinal state or its neural realizer that is, constitutes, or includes motivation.) On the *Value-Requirement* view, this can be fitting because even if Berta lacks any motivation to send tulips, there can still be a moral requirement for her to send them. In virtue of its being appropriate to send tulips, suppose, furthermore, that Berta has what I've called a "requirement reason" to send them. But this reason is, apparently, an objective reason, and it is *pro tanto*: it is a reason that is screened off from any motivating desire of Berta (and so it is objective), and it can be overridden by other reasons (and so it is *pro tanto*). But this just is the very sort of reason one would have in virtue of having a moral obligation to send tulips. *These* obligation-associated reasons, again, are objective *pro tanto*. So, one could propose the following. Should one have a reason to do something in virtue of having a requirement or its being fitting to do it, that reason is an objective *pro tanto* reason. Since we cannot have such reasons to do something without being able to do it, a requirement to do something when one cannot do it does not give rise to reasons.

Of course, some might simply find this line of thought question-begging. They might insist that what we should conclude, rather, is that requirement or fittingness *always* gives rise to objective *pro tanto* reasons, but an objective *pro tanto* reason to do something does *not* presuppose that we can do it. Here, I can only say that on careful reflection, overall I find the second of these options more plausible.

In sum, I am fairly skeptical of the view that the reasons, if any, one has in virtue of having a requirement to do something, do not presuppose that we are able to do that thing. Should one insist otherwise, then my inclination would be to distinguish *IValue-1* from *IValue-1Z*; I would be partial to the view that these are *distinct* theses.

4.4. THE MORALLY DEONTIC'S DEPENDENCE ON THE AXIOLOGICAL

I have defended the view that moral obligation requires alternatives. The defense of this view pivoted on the premise that there is a necessary connection between moral obligation and objective *pro tanto* reasons. I now offer an alternative justification for this view, one that relies on the morally deontic's dependence on the axiological.

A long-standing thesis in moral philosophy is that the morally deontic property of *being morally obligatory* supervenes on the axiological property of intrinsic goodness: roughly, on each occasion of choice, one ought to see to what is intrinsically best. With this view in mind, consider an account of moral obligation I favor:

> (*Obligation*): A person, S, morally ought, as of t, to see to the occurrence of a state of affairs, p, if and only if p occurs in some world, w, accessible to S at t, and it's not the case that *not-p* occurs in any accessible world intrinsically as good as or intrinsically better than w (Feldman 1986, 37).[5]

In short, you ought to do what you do in all the intrinsically best worlds accessible to you. I readily grant that *Obligation* is controversial, but it does have widespread support as well. In any event, I assume, without argument, that *Obligation*, or at least something like *Obligation*, when it is construed to imply that moral obligation supervenes on the intrinsic value of worlds, is in the right ballpark. Owing to the supervenience of the morally deontic on the axiological, it would be distinctly odd, perhaps even incoherent, if there were an alternative-possibilities requirement for the truth of the relevant sorts of judgment of intrinsic value but no such requirement for the truth of the morally deontic judgments of moral right, wrong, and obligation. Happily, this is not so. In this section, I argue that the truth of pertinent judgments concerning the intrinsic value of worlds presupposes our having access to alternatives. Consequently, assuming supervenience of the morally deontic on the value of worlds, the truth of right, wrong, and obligation judgments also presupposes our having access to alternatives.

Suppose some world were overall intrinsically good. Presumably, however, contemplation of it could give one both reason to favor it and to disfavor it. An application of *IValue-1* and *IValue-2* to this case generates the unacceptable result that this world is both intrinsically good and intrinsically bad. This sort of concern might, perhaps, be better appreciated in connection with a simple "conjunctive" state. Again, being indifferent to whether "state" refers either to a state of affairs or to a concrete state, consider the conjunctive state:

(S1): Jack's taking pleasure to degree +2, at noon, in the cold beer's going down his hatch, and Jill's taking displeasure to degree +3, at noon, in the beer's being warm.

Again, it seems that contemplation of S1 may well give one reason to favor and reason to disfavor it. This fact, in conjunction with *IValue-1* and *IValue-2*, yields the untenable result that S1 is both intrinsically good and intrinsically bad.

Invoking the concept of basic intrinsic value enables us to circumvent this problem (as well as, it has been proposed, to provide a solution to others, such as the computation of intrinsic value).[6] I explain briefly by introducing a simple version of hedonism.

A hedonist, could not, on pain of contradiction, both affirm that the only things that are intrinsically good are episodes of pleasure, and that some worlds, or lives, or total consequences of actions are intrinsically good, too. Rather, at the core of one sort of hedonism is the view that the sole atoms or bearers of intrinsic value are episodes of pleasure and displeasure, and that the intrinsic value of a complex object is entirely dependent on the intrinsic values of its atoms. It is incumbent on each version of hedonism (indeed, on any axiology) to identify its atoms—its basic intrinsic value states or "basics." More precisely, the *basic intrinsic value states* of each axiology are the items the axiology takes to be the most fundamental bearers of intrinsic value. Each of these items has its intrinsic value in a nonderivative way. The intrinsic value of a complex thing, such as a life or a world, is the sum (I assume, or some aggregative function) of the values of its basic intrinsic value states. According to "Simple Intrinsic Attitudinal Hedonism"—"*Simple Hedonism*"—the atoms of intrinsic value are episodes of intrinsic attitudinal pleasure and intrinsic attitudinal displeasure all relevantly like the following (positive numbers indicate degree of intrinsic pleasure, negative numbers degree of intrinsic displeasure):

> Positive Atom A: At noon on Tuesday, October 16, 2001, Jack takes intrinsic attitudinal pleasure to degree +8 in the fact that Jack's beer is frosty cold (see, for e.g., Feldman 2004, 176).
> Negative Atom B: At 9:00 p.m. on Friday, October 16, 2001, Jill takes intrinsic attitudinal displeasure to degree -10 in the fact that Jill's beer is warm.

The theory may now be formulated in this way:

Simple Hedonism

1. Every episode of intrinsic attitudinal pleasure is intrinsically good; every episode of intrinsic displeasure is intrinsically bad.

2. The intrinsic value of an episode of intrinsic attitudinal pleasure is equal to the amount of pleasure contained in that episode; the intrinsic value of an episode of intrinsic displeasure is equal to -(the amount of displeasure contained in that episode).

3. The intrinsic value of a complex object, such as a world, is entirely determined by the intrinsic values of the episodes of intrinsic attitudinal pleasure and displeasure contained in that object, in such a way that one complex object is intrinsically better than another if and only if the net amount of intrinsic attitudinal pleasure in the one is greater than the net amount of intrinsic attitudinal pleasure in the other (see Feldman 2004, 66).

Reverting to our initial problem concerning worldly intrinsic value, generated by the plausible assumption that contemplation of a world may give us reason both to favor and disfavor it, the problem can be handled by restricting the variable x in *IValue-1—IValue-4* to range over basic intrinsic value states. *IValue-1*, for instance, should be understood as claiming that:

(*IValue-1-Basic*): Necessarily, x is basically intrinsically good if and only if anyone who were to contemplate x would have a reason to favor x for its own sake.[7]

Worlds, of course, are not basic intrinsic value states.

Imagine a world that contains, on balance, more intrinsic attitudinal pleasure than intrinsic displeasure. Appealing to our illustrative hedonistic axiology, this world is overall, intrinsically good. If no basics were true at this world—or, as I'll say, if the world contained no atoms of value—then it would be bereft of intrinsic value. We may, hence, conclude that, necessarily, if a world is intrinsically good, it contains an atom, which is such that anyone who contemplates this atom has an objective *pro tanto* reason to favor it for its own sake. Thus, if it is false that one has such reasons to favor, or to disfavor, or to be indifferent to the atoms a world contains upon contemplating these atoms, then that world is not intrinsically good, intrinsically bad, or intrinsically neutral. We have argued that one's having an objective *pro tanto* reason requires one's having alternatives. Thus, we may further conclude that if a world is intrinsically good, it contains an atom, which is such that anyone who contemplates this atom can refrain from favoring it for its own sake. In other words, there is an alternative possibilities requirement for the truth of judgments of worldy intrinsic value. If moral obligation, in turn, supervenes on worldly intrinsic value in the fashion in which *Obligation* specifies (roughly, what we morally ought to do is what is intrinsically best), it follows that there is an alternative possibilities requirement for the truth of morally deontic judgments as well.

4.5. PLEASURE AND REASONS

Suppose *S* is pleased about something; *S* takes intrinsic attitudinal pleasure in it. Are there grounds to believe that, necessarily, if *S* takes pleasure in something, then *S* has a reason to take pleasure in it (allowing for the possibility that *S* does not take pleasure in it *for* this reason)?

Attitudinal pleasures are propositional attitudes; they are always directed onto objects. In this respect, such pleasures are just like beliefs, fears, and hopes. If you hope for something, or you fear something, or you believe something, presumably you have a reason to hope, fear, or believe. Maybe this gives us some reason to think that when a person takes attitudinal pleasure in some fact, this person has a reason to be pleased about this fact.

I want to pursue another thought about why it is plausible to think that there is an interesting connection between intrinsic attitudinal pleasures, or intrinsic attitudinal displeasures, and reasons. If S is pleased about p, the fact that S is pleased about p is intrinsically good, and *this* fact is a reason for S to look favorably upon this fact. To elaborate, assuming the variety of attitudinal hedonism introduced earlier—*Simple Hedonism*—we said that a bearer of positive intrinsic value is a state of affairs of this sort:

> Positive Atom A: At noon on Tuesday, October 16, 2001, Jack takes intrinsic attitudinal pleasure to degree +8 in the fact that Jack's beer is frosty cold.

State of affairs A is intrinsically good; it has positive intrinsic value. The fact that something is intrinsically good is an objective *pro tanto* reason, roughly, to want, or pursue, or enjoy, or, more generally, to favor it. Again, I use "favor" as a placeholder for any sort of germane pro-attitude toward a positive atom. Necessarily, if someone takes pleasure in something at a time, a basic relevantly like A obtains at that time. Moreover, such an atom is intrinsically good. So if someone takes intrinsic attitudinal pleasure in some object at a time, there is a fact, which is such that this person has an objective *pro tanto* reason to favor it for its own sake. It seems, then, that this is true:

> *Pleasure/Reason*: Necessarily, if, at t, S takes intrinsic attitudinal pleasure to degree n in some state of affairs, p, then, at t, this positive

atom, A, obtains: *S is pleased at t to degree n about p,* and at *t S* has an objective *pro tanto* reason to favor *A* for its own sake.

Briefly, necessarily, if at *t*, *S* is pleased about *p*, then the fact that *S* is pleased about *p* is a reason for *S*, at *t*, to favor this fact.

Perhaps one might worry that if someone is unaware that a state of affairs obtains, one cannot favor it. So although at *t S* may be pleased about *p*, at *t S* may be unaware that *S* is pleased about *p*, and so unaware at *t* that the state of affairs, *S's being pleased about p,* obtains. On the connection between attitudinal pleasure and knowledge, Feldman writes:

> Someone might think that if you are pleased about something, then you must know that you are pleased about it. This seems not true. At least, it is not true as a matter of conceptual necessity. I think it is possible for there to be a person who is confused or self-deceived about his own mental states. Consider the case of Stan, the overly competitive indoor rower. He finds that one of his rivals has just been diagnosed with a serious illness. Perhaps Stan is pleased about this, but is too ashamed of himself to acknowledge that he is pleased about it; perhaps he finds it difficult to admit to himself that he is the kind of person who could be pleased about a rival's illness. In such a case, Stan is pleased about something but seems not to know that he is pleased about it. (2010, 116)

Partly on the basis of what Feldman says in this passage, one might object that it is false that whenever someone takes attitudinal pleasure in something at a time, at that time one has an objective *pro tanto* reason to favor the fact that one takes attitudinal pleasure in that thing. Rather, what's true is something weaker: whenever someone takes attitudinal pleasure in something at a time, at that time one *would* have an objective *pro tanto* reason to favor the fact that one takes attitudinal pleasure in that thing if one *were* aware of this fact.

It's interesting that in earlier work, however, Feldman proposes that one can be pleased about something without being *fully aware* of the fact that he is pleased about it. Feldman adds the following:

> I am almost inclined to say that at least this much must be true: if you are taking pleasure in something, then if someone were to ask you, you would immediately recognize that you are taking pleasure in it. But, of course, the subjunctive conditional is too crude. You might be taking pleasure in something [in your wood-work project, for instance], but if someone were to ask, you would be so annoyed by the intrusion that you would lose your temper, put down your chisel and mallet, and storm out of the room. You might never recall that you had been enjoying yourself. . . . In this respect, pleasure is like belief. After the fact, if someone were to ask you if you earlier believed a certain tool to be a chisel, you might say that you had done so. You could say this truly, even if you had not consciously thought, "this is a chisel," while you were working on the tenons. (2004, 58–59)

In any event, it seems that the following line of reasoning is still cogent. Call the state of affairs, *S is pleased about p*, "*A*."

1. If at *t S* is pleased about *p*, then at *t S* would have an objective *pro tanto* reason to favor *A* if *S* at *t* were to contemplate *A*.
2. If at *t S* would have an objective *pro tanto* reason to favor *A* if *S* at *t* were to contemplate *A*, then at *t S* could favor *A* and *S* could refrain from favoring *A*. (Again, this is because having objective *pro tanto* reasons to favor something entails having alternatives.)

3. Therefore, if at *t*, *S* is pleased about *p*, then at *t* *S* could favor *A* and *S* could refrain from favoring *A*.

Otherwise put, if at some time, one is pleased about something, then, one could both favor and refrain from favoring the fact that, at that time, one is pleased about that thing. Corresponding things that I've said about the connection between positive atoms and reasons are also true regarding negative atoms and reasons. A bearer of negative intrinsic value *Simple Hedonism* recognizes is an atom of this sort:

Negative Atom B: At 9:00 p.m. on Friday, October 16, 2001, Jill takes intrinsic attitudinal displeasure to degree -10 in the fact that Jill's beer is warm.

The fact that something is intrinsically bad is an objective *pro tanto* reason to have some con-attitude toward it—to disfavor it for its own sake. If someone takes intrinsic attitudinal displeasure in some state of affairs at a time, there is a fact—*this person's being displeased about this state of affairs*—which is an objective *pro tanto* reason for this person to disfavor this fact for its own sake. So this is true, too:

Displeasure/Reason: Necessarily, if, at *t*, *S* takes intrinsic attitudinal displeasure to degree *n* in some state of affairs, *p*, then, at *t*, this negative atom, *B*, obtains: *S is displeased at t to degree n about p,* and at *t* *S* has an objective *pro tanto* reason to disfavor *B* for its own sake.

As with atoms of attitudinal pleasure, one might want to be more circumspect and claim that if at some time, one is displeased about something, one *could* both favor and refrain from favoring the fact that, at that time, one is displeased about that thing.

I have argued that if some state of affairs is a positive atom of intrinsic value, then one can favor it and one can refrain from favoring it. Maybe it would be better to be more precise: if some state of affairs is a positive atom of intrinsic value, one could favor it and one could refrain from favoring it. Similarly, if some state of affairs is a negative atom of intrinsic value, one could disfavor it and one could refrain from disfavoring it. Also, if some state of affairs is a neutral atom, one could be or could refrain from being indifferent toward it. We may, thus, draw these conclusions: First, if, at *t*, *S* takes intrinsic attitudinal pleasure to degree *n* in some state of affairs, *p*, then, at *t*, *S* could both favor and refrain from favoring *p*. Second, similarly, if, at *t*, *S* takes intrinsic attitudinal displeasure to degree *n* in some state of affairs, *p*, then, at *t*, *S* could both disfavor and refrain from disfavoring *p*. Third, to capture neutrality, we may say that if at *t*, *S* is pleasure- or displeasure-wise indifferent to degree *n* in some state of affairs, *p*, then, at *t*, *S* could both be indifferent and refrain from being indifferent toward *p*. In other words, there is an alternative possibilities requirement for being pleased or displeased about something.

4.6. VIRTUE AND REASONS

I end this chapter with some brief observations on virtue ethics and reasons. The overall thrust of my comments is that certain approaches to virtue ethics cannot be divorced from alternative possibilities because of the essential connection between elements of these approaches and our having objective *pro tanto* reasons.

In a chapter in *From Morality and Virtue*, Michael Slote (1992) proposes that close analogues of deontic notions, such as moral

wrongness and moral obligation, can be developed on a purely aretaic basis, and that virtue ethics can be expressed in terms of precepts
recommending concern for oneself and others in the imperative
mood. He first argues that aretaic notions like "good" or "bad,"
and "admirable" or "deplorable" can have a force of requirement or
prohibition—*a practical or action-guiding force*—similar to that of
standard deontic notions like "obligatory" or "wrong" (1992, 159–
63). He then offers virtue-ethical analogues of rightness, wrongness,
and obligatoriness:

> [A]retaic ethics can easily express its own equivalent of rightness
> by speaking of what is "not deplorable (or criticizable)." . . . The
> virtue-ethical analogue of (moral) wrongness is deplorability or
> (some appropriate degree of) criticizability, and to the extent
> rightness is conceived simply as the contradictory or negation of
> wrongness, that is, as permissibility or acceptability, it would ap-
> pear that non-deplorability or non-criticizability is the virtue-
> theoretic equivalent of (moral) rightness. . . . To the extent that
> claims of moral wrongness are thought to justify "ought" claims
> and imperatives, we are entitled to claim that someone ought not
> to do something and to use a grammatical imperative to tell her
> not to do that thing, once the claim that it is wrong has been
> justified; likewise, within the aretaic realm, the claim that some-
> thing is deplorable can at the very least justify imperatives and
> "ought" claims that stand to more familiar, deontic imperatives
> and "ought" claims as deplorability stands to wrongness. Where
> a given act would be deplorable, we can say "don't do it" or claim
> that one ought not to do it, and such utterances will be deriva-
> tively or analogically deontic, if we insist that aretaic notions are
> fundamentally non-deontic. Such an insistence may possibly be
> warranted even in the face of the earlier-given arguments for the

equivalent force of (morally) aretaic and (morally) deontic claims, respectively, of badness/deplorability and of wrongness. But in fact I am not sure how one can uphold the aretaic/deontic distinction while granting the equivalence in force of aretaic and deontic judgments, and so, although there is more, much more, that needs to be said on this issue, I think we should at this point at least mention the possibility—relative to what has been argued above—that there may be no significant fundamental distinction between aretaic and deontic notions. (1992, 164, note omitted)

It would seem that if the virtue-ethical analogue of wrongness is deplorability or criticizability, then doing something deplorable or criticizable is a reason for one not to do it. What sort of reason? If there is "no fundamental distinction between aretaic and deontic notions," we may plausibly take these reasons to be objective *pro tanto* because, for instance, the fact that something is wrong for one (or one's recognizing that this is so) is such a reason for one not to do it.

Perhaps this connection between virtues (or vices) and objective reasons can be more fully appreciated by reflecting on Gary Watson's template of a virtue ethics. Watson suggests that an Aristotelian ethics of virtue will have the following basic structure:

(1) *The claim of explanatory primacy* Right and proper conduct is conduct that is contrary to no virtue (does not exemplify a vice). Good conduct is conduct that displays a virtue. Wrong or improper conduct is conduct that is contrary to some virtue (or exemplifies a vice).

(2) *The theory of virtue* Virtues are (a subset of the) human excellences, that is, those traits that enable one to live a characteristically human life, or to live in accordance with one's nature as a human being. (1993, 455)

Elaborating, Watson explains that we may depict the appraisal of conduct on an Aristotelian ethics of virtue with the following schema:

1. Living a characteristically human life (functioning well as a human being) requires possessing and exemplifying certain traits, *T*.
2. *T* are therefore human excellences and render their possessors to that extent good human beings.
3. Acting in way *W* is in accordance with *T* (or exemplifies or is contrary to *T*).
4. Therefore, *W* is right (good or wrong). (1993, 459)

Suppose acting in way *W* exemplifies an excellence or various excellences. Then it would appear that, necessarily, the fact (or one's recognizing the fact) that acting in this way exemplifies an excellence is an objective *pro tanto* reason for one to act in this way. One may have no Davidsonian reason to act in this way; one may not have the relevant desire, for instance, to act in way *W*. Still, because acting in way *W exemplifies an excellence,* independently of whether one has a desire to act in way *W*, the fact that acting in way *W* exemplifies an excellence is an objective *pro tanto* reason to act in this way.

Here's an alternative strategy to develop a sort of Aristotelian ethics of virtue. On this approach, the primary normative status of an act (whether it is morally right, wrong, or obligatory) is a function of the net amount of virtue its agent manifests in performing this act. Assume that we have a list of all the virtues and the vices. Assume, moreover, that for any possible action, there is a number that represents its "virtue value": take the total amount of virtue its agent would manifest if this agent performed it and subtract from it the total amount of vice its agent would manifest if this agent performed it. This sort of virtue ethical theory (VET) would then say: an act is right if and only if no alternative has higher virtue value than it has.

Needless to say, this sort of virtue ethical theory is committed to our having alternatives. If an act is (VET)-right for one, one has an objective *pro tanto* reason to perform it, and so one has relevant alternatives.

Given the association I have outlined between the virtues (or vices) and objective *pro tanto* reasons, or the association between obligation as it is identified by some permutation of a virtue ethical theory, such as VET, and such reasons, it appears that prominent approaches to virtue ethics are committed to our having alternatives.

In sum, I have argued in this chapter that various axiological appraisals and virtue appraisals on at least some key approaches to understanding an ethics of virtue, are partnered with our having alternatives. Again, this is because there is a necessary connection between the truth of such appraisals and our having objective *pro tanto* reasons.

NOTES

1. This view is suggested by Brentano 1969, 18; Broad 1930, 283; Ross 1939, 275–76, Ewing 1948, 152, Chisholm 1986, 52; Lemos 1994, 12, 15; Scanlon 1998, 96; Zimmerman 2001, sec. 3.6; 2007, 346; 2011.
2. Pinning down the relevant favoring attitudes promises to unearth a host of difficulties for *IV-1* as Bykvist (2009) discusses in his engaging paper.
3. On requirement not being restricted to what one can do, see also Ewing 1948, 150, 171; and Olson 2009, 375.
4. Maybe there is a real distinction between something's calling for a response, and one's being required to respond to it in some way.

5. See also Zimmerman 1996, chap. 2. Recently, Zimmerman (2008) has renounced this view in favor of an alternative: roughly, on the alternative, you ought to perform the option that is prospectively best, where an option is prospectively best if it is supported by relevant evidence.

6. On basic intrinsic value and the computation of intrinsic value, see e.g., Harman 1967; Feldman 2000; 2004; Zimmerman 2001.

7. Zimmerman (2011, 475–76) recommends this very formulation to develop an interesting response to a thorny problem concerning intrinsic value and partiality. See Bykvist 2009 for comments on this proposed solution.

Chapter 5

Moral Sentiments and Alternative Possibilities

5.1. INTRODUCTION

Interpersonal relationships we deeply value implicate various moral sentiments. Peter Strawson (1962/1982), for example, proposes that some of the sentiments constitutive of, or integral to, these relationships are indignation, moral resentment, guilt, forgiveness, gratitude, and mature love. In this chapter, I expose a necessary connection between our having some of these moral sentiments and our having objective *pro tanto* reasons. As there is an alternative possibilities requirement for having such reasons, without alternatives, the appropriateness—or more broadly, the rationality—of our having these sentiments is called into question.

5.2. FORGIVENESS AND REASONS

What is the connection, if any, between attitudes or emotions such as forgiveness, guilt, gratitude, and indignation, on the one hand, and reasons, on the other?[1] I begin with forgiveness.

Forgiveness is associated with reasons in a number of ways. For instance, forgiving someone gives us reasons to do things.

Your forgiving may give you reason to strengthen the relationship with the person you have forgiven. Or your forgiving may give you occasion to reflect on what you may have done that might have triggered the other party to hurt you. But forgiveness is also tied to reasons in another way on which I wish to focus: *we forgive for reasons.* There may be many different reasons why we forgive when we do. You may forgive because you think it is morally obligatory for you to do so. Or you may forgive because you believe that doing so would please someone else, and you want to please this other person. Or, you may forgive because *you are willing to cease to regard the wrong done to you as a reason to weaken or dissolve the relationship.* This last reason—reason "FR"—is of special interest. It differs from the others in a pivotal respect. A contrast will highlight this difference. Suppose you forgive because you believe that doing so will please someone else, and you desire to please this person. Failing to have this Davidsonian reason to forgive when you forgive does not cast doubt on this sentiment's or attitude's being an instance of forgiving. It seems, however, that you cannot *fail* to have reason FR when you forgive. If you fail to have this reason, then the state you are allegedly in when you allegedly forgive is not a state of forgiveness. So, necessarily, when one forgives, one has reason FR. Part of the explanation for this difference is that *being willing to cease to regard some wrong as a reason to weaken or terminate a relationship* is essential to forgiveness. Another has to do with the fact that reason FR *is* a reason to forgive.[2]

When one forgives, we should be careful to distinguish between *having* reason FR as a reason for forgiving and forgiving *for* this reason. My claim has to do with the former and not the latter, and an analogy will help to explain the distinction. Reconsider:

Obligations are tied to reasons (*OR*): If an agent has a moral obligation to do something, *A*, then the agent has an objective *pro tanto* reason to do *A*.

By their very nature *pro tanto* reasons are reasons that other reasons can outweigh; in this respect they differ from all-things-considered reasons, which cannot be outweighed. Suppose you morally ought to visit your friend in hospital. Then you have an objective *pro tanto* reason to visit: *your being obligated to visit.* You may, of course, have other reasons to visit. For example, you may believe that if you fail to visit, you will feel guilty, and you want to avoid feeling guilty; or if you do not visit you will incur the disfavor of the sick's person's spouse, something distasteful to you. Suppose that it is some such Davidsonian reason for which you visit. It does not follow that you do not have the relevant objective *pro tanto* reason, the reason that it is obligatory for you to visit. Similarly, you may forgive because you think that it is morally obligatory for you to do so. Or alternatively, you may forgive because you believe that doing so will please someone else, and you desire to please this person. In these cases, nothing precludes you from having reason FR (being willing to cease to regard the wrong done as a reason to weaken or dissolve some relationship) to forgive; it is simply that you do not, in these cases, forgive *for* FR.

The principle that expresses the connection of interest between forgiveness and reasons can preliminarily be stated in this way:

Forgiveness-pre: Necessarily, if *S* forgives *T* for something, then *S* has a *pro tanto* reason (reason FR) to forgive *T*.

To refine this principle, we ask whether reason FR (ceasing to regard the wrong done as a reason to weaken or end the relationship) is a Davidsonian or an objective reason. As hinted at previously, on the face of it FR appears to be an objective reason. Why might one conjecture otherwise? We said that a motivating desire is an attitudinal state of mind (or the neural realizer of this state) that is, that constitutes, or that includes motivation. One might think that you cannot be willing to cease to regard something as such and such, or you cannot cease to regard something as such and such, without having a pertinent motivating desire. But this is false. One's being willing to regard something—a brusque remark, for instance—as being out of character does not imply that one has a motivating desire concerning being willing to regard the remark as out of character. As another example, you may be willing to regard some person you know to be culpable as innocent—as a person who did not commit the vicious crime—without having any motivating desire to regard this person as innocent. Alternatively, one might argue that to regard something as such and such is to engage in mental activity. Perhaps, when you regard something as such and such, you perform a mental action or you engage in mental activity that is somewhat similar to performing a mental action in that this mental activity may well have causal antecedents such as beliefs and desires. But then, it may be claimed, regarding something as such and such *is* indirectly linked to some motivating desire. Suppose we agree that being willing to regard something as such and such, or regarding something as such and such, qualifies as a mental action, and, furthermore, we concur that as a mental action, there is some motivating desire that this action has in its etiology. It would, however, not follow that reason FR itself is a motivating desire. Nor would it follow that FR has a motivating desire as a *proper* constituent (see chap. 2). I can think of no other reasons to disqualify reason FR from being an objective reason. Principle *Forgiveness-pre* may now be regimented in this way:

Forgiveness: Necessarily, if S forgives T for something, then S has an objective *pro tanto* reason—being willing to cease to regard the wrong done to S as a reason to weaken or dissolve the relationship—to forgive T.

5.3. INDIGNATION AND REASONS

Next, consider indignation or anger. We express anger for sundry reasons but restrict attention to one of these reasons. Aristotle proposed that anger, when justified or legitimate, *essentially* involves the correct judgment that one has been wronged and not just that something bad has befallen one (1941, bk. 2, 1378a 30–32). "Essentially" here implies that without the presence of such a judgment, the psychological state in question is not anger. Your having been wronged gives you a reason to be angry. In justified cases of anger, the psychological state that is anger would not qualify as a state of being in anger if you did not have this reason. Once again, this reason has nothing essential to do with pertinent desires. It appears to be an objective reason. So, the following principle seems eminently reasonable:

Indignation: Necessarily, if S feels (justified) indignation, then S has an objective *pro tanto* reason—S's having been wronged— for feeling indignation.

5.4. GUILT, SORROW, AND REASONS

Reflect, now, on guilt. Confine attention to cases in which the agent experiences legitimate guilt. These are cases in which the agent experiences guilt upon doing moral wrong or doing what he takes to be moral wrong, for example, as opposed to feeling "guilt," even when the agent believes correctly that he has done no wrong. Guilt, just like forgiveness, is associated with reasons. For our purposes, just as we asked "Why forgive?" so we may ask "Why feel guilt?" One key answer—reason "GR"—is that *one takes oneself to have intentionally done wrong*. Reason GR is analogous to reason FR (*being willing to cease to regard the wrong done to one as a reason to weaken or dissolve some relationship*) in crucial respects: It appears, similarly, that you cannot fail to *have* reason GR when you feel guilt. If you fail to have this reason, then the state you are allegedly in when you allegedly feel guilt is not a state of legitimate guilt. This is largely because your taking yourself to have intentionally done wrong is essential to guilt (recall, we are restricting ourselves to cases in which you feel bona fide or legitimate guilt). As before, bear in mind here the distinction between having reason GR when one feels guilt and feeling guilt for reason GR. The pertinent principle of interest has to do with the former and not the latter. It is concerned with the sort of reason, whether Davidsonian or objective, that reason GR is. Consonant with what I previously proposed, this reason is an objective one: GR is not a motivating desire of its agent, it does not have a motivating desire as a proper constituent, and it is not, even in part, a fact, truth, proposition, or the like about any actual motivating desire of its agent. The pertinent principle can be summarized in this fashion:

> *Guilt*: Necessarily, if S feels (legitimate) guilt for doing something, then S has an objective *pro tanto* reason—taking S's self to have intentionally done wrong—for feeling guilt.

Hard incompatibilism is the position that in the absence of any action (mental or otherwise) being agent caused, moral responsibility is incompatible with any action being either deterministically caused or indeterministically caused (Pereboom 2001, 127–28). In his insightful and provocative discussion on guilt and remorse, Derk Pereboom explains that hard incompatibilism seems to endanger remorse and guilt, insofar as they presuppose blameworthiness. It may be proposed that if some individual were deprived of remorse and guilt, she would be incapable of mending any relationships with people whom she has intentionally wronged; and having intentionally done wrong, she would lack any motivation to restore her own moral integrity and thus to develop morally. However, Pereboom recommends that even if one believed in hard incompatibilism, one may feel profound *sorrow* and *regret* on being the instrument of wrongdoing despite believing that one was not in any way blameworthy. Sorrow and regret, Pereboom proposes, can play the pertinent roles that remorse and guilt typically do in interpersonal relationships. For example, sorrow and regret may generate a repentant attitude and thus induce the agent not to perform her immoral action again; they may motivate the agent to make amends by seeking to alleviate the suffering caused to others; and they may help to heal the relationship by impelling the agent to express misgiving about her untoward behavior (Pereboom 2001, 205–6).[3] So, although gratitude and guilt "would likely be theoretically irrational for a hard incompatibilist," these attitudes "have analogs that could play the same role they typically have" (2001, 206).

Imagine an instance in which one feels sorrow upon intentionally doing wrong. If one feels sorrow, presumably one does so for a reason. What sort of reason would this be, Davidsonian or objective? If one feels sorrow because one takes oneself to have intentionally done wrong, then the reason for which one feels sorrow (reason GR) is an objective one. Indeed, the phenomenology of feeling sorrow strongly suggests that it would be out of the ordinary to feel sorrow for some Davidsonian reason. Typically, when one feels sorrow, it is not as though one has an antecedent desire, for instance, to make amends and a belief that by feeling sorrow one can motivate oneself to do so. Nor is it the case normally that one has an antecedent desire not to perform yet again the sort of impermissible action one did and a belief that by feeling sorrow, one would generate a repentant attitude that is instrumental to one's not performing in the future the sort of wrong one did. This simply does not ring true to the facts. In brief, when one feels sorrow, typically one does not have some antecedent desire, which on its own or together with some apt belief, is the Davidsonian reason for which one feels sorrow. Rather, it appears consonant with the facts that one feels sorrow for some objective reason, and one's feeling sorrow subsequently may generate desires, which conjoined with suitable beliefs perhaps, may give one Davidsonian reasons to do various things.

5.5. GRATITUDE, JOY, THANKFULNESS, AND REASONS

Regarding gratitude, Pereboom writes:

Gratitude might well require the supposition that the person to whom one is grateful is morally responsible for an other-regarding act, and therefore hard incompatibilism might well undermine gratitude. However, certain aspects of this attitude would be left untouched, aspects that can play the role gratitude commonly has in interpersonal relationships. First, gratitude includes an element of thankfulness toward those who have benefited us. Sometimes, being thankful involves the belief that the object of one's attitude is praiseworthy for some action. But one can also be thankful to a pet or a small child for some favor, even if one does not believe that he is morally responsible. Perhaps one can even be thankful for the sun or the rain even if one does not believe that these elements are backed by morally responsible agency. In general, if one believed hard incompatibilism, one's thankfulness might lack features that it would have if one did not, but nevertheless, this aspect of gratitude can survive. . . . Gratitude involves an aspect of joy upon being benefited by another. But no feature of the hard incompatibilist position conflicts with one's being joyful and expressing joy when people are especially considerate, generous, or courageous in one's behalf. Such expressions of joy can produce the sense of mutual well-being and respect frequently brought about by gratitude. Moreover, when one expresses joy for what another person has done, one can do so with the intention of developing a human relationship. (2001, 201–2)

If one is thankful for something, then there is a reason for being thankful for this thing. Indeed, this principle, it appears, is true:

Thankfulness: Necessarily, if S is thankful for something, Y, then there is a reason for S to be thankful for Y.

Similarly,

Joy: Necessarily, if S takes joy in Y, then there is a reason for S to take joy in Y.

Are the reasons for which one takes joy or is thankful when one is grateful Davidsonian or objective? Again, typically, when one expresses gratitude, one does not have an antecedent desire, for example to thank one's benefactor, which when conjoined with appropriate beliefs, causally gives rise to one's giving thanks.

Rather, the explanation seems to run in the other direction along these lines: the benefactor's kindness or considerateness, for example, is the reason for one to express thanks. This reason, customarily, is an objective one.

One may rejoin that mentally healthy adult human beings normally have a disposition to give thanks to others who have been kind to them; frequently, people have a standing or dispositional desire to give thanks upon being beneficiaries of some good or kindness. The standing desire simply requires "activation" by appropriate conditions to produce action; the activated desire, in consort with apt beliefs, may then be the Davidsonian reasons for which one expresses thanks or joy. But all of this is consistent with the fact that the benefactor's having been kind or considerate is an objective reason: reflection on or one's awareness of this reason causally contributes to the activation of the dispositional desire to give thanks or to express joy.

In summary, there is a range of emotions or sentiments we experience when we are involved in interpersonal relationships. In virtue of entering into various relationships with others, we feel or express emotions or adopt attitudes such as forgiveness, guilt, sorrow, gratitude, thankfulness, joy, and indignation. For each of these things, there are reasons why we feel the emotion or adopt the attitude. Regarding forgiveness, guilt, and indignation, I argued that, necessarily, if one forgives, feels guilt, or expresses indignation, then one has an objective *pro tanto* reason for forgiving, feeling guilt, or expressing anger (although one may not forgive, feel guilty, or express anger *for* this objective reason). With respect to sorrow, gratitude, thankfulness, and joy, my conclusion is more tempered. I suggested that, typically, when we feel sorrow, we feel sorrow for objective reasons and, typically, when we are thankful or feel joy, we are thankful or feel joy for such reasons as well.

5.6. THE MORAL SENTIMENTS AND ALTERNATIVE POSSIBILITIES

Let's revisit principles *Forgiveness*, *Guilt*, and *Indignation*:

> *Forgiveness*: Necessarily, if S forgives T for something, then S has an objective *pro tanto* reason—being willing to cease to regard the wrong done to S as a reason to weaken or dissolve the relationship—to forgive T.
>
> *Guilt*: Necessarily, if S feels (legitimate) guilt for doing something, then S has an objective *pro tanto* reason—taking S's self to have intentionally done wrong—for feeling guilt.
>
> *Indignation*: Necessarily, if S feels (justified) indignation, then S has an objective *pro tanto* reason—S's having been wronged—for feeling indignation.

I argued (chap. 2) that there is an alternative possibilities requirement for having objective *pro tanto* reasons. This fact, together with this trio of principles, entails that legitimate instances of forgiveness, guilt, and indignation all presuppose our having alternatives.

I proposed that there are other emotions or attitudes, such as thankfulness, sorrow, regret, and joy, intimately associated with interpersonal relationships. In addition, that, typically, when one feels these emotions or adopts these attitudes, one does so for objective reasons. Insofar as we express these emotions on occasions for objective *pro tanto* reasons, we have pertinent alternatives.

There is another path to the conclusion that a cluster of the moral sentiments presupposes our having alternatives. Some sentiments or attitudes are essentially associated with moral rightness, wrongness, or obligatoriness. Forgiveness and indignation, for instance, are sentiments of this sort; each is essentially tied to moral wrongness. Since there is an alternative possibilities requirement for the truth of the morally deontic judgments, it follows that there is such a requirement for our having these sentiments as well.

We may conclude that various sentiments or attitudes, such as thankfulness, sorrow, regret, and joy, which are intimately associated with interpersonal relationships, are imperiled in the absence of our having pertinent alternatives.

NOTES

1. I do not discuss love in what follows as Cuypers and I have done so elsewhere (see Haji and Cuypers 2008).
2. Compare what I say here with Angela Smith's (2005; 2008) pertinent views. She claims that various emotions essentially express certain judgments; these judgments are partly constitutive of these emotions. For instance, she proposes that to feel contempt toward some person "involves the judgment that she has some feature or has behaved in some way which makes her unworthy of one's respect" (2005, 250.)
3. Critical discussion of this view is found in Haji and Cuypers 2008.

Chapter 6

Determinism's Impact on Normative Judgments

6.1. INTRODUCTION

What impact, if any, would determinism have on the truth of judgments of obligation, intrinsic value concerning basic intrinsic value states, moral responsibility, and an important cluster of moral sentiments? Assuming, first, the perspective of the incompatibilist and then that of the compatibilist will facilitate the discussion.

6.2. INCOMPATIBILISM, STRONG ALTERNATIVES, AND NORMATIVE ASSESSMENTS

We remind ourselves of the distinction between strong and weak alternatives. S has a strong alternative at time, t, to doing action, A, in world w if the combination of w's past and w's laws of nature is consistent with S's not A-ing at t. There are good reasons to believe that determinism expunges strong alternatives; in what follows, I assume that this is so.

Weak alternatives are alternatives one can have consistent with determinism's obtaining. Traditional compatibilists offered a conditional analysis of such alternatives or "can." On one such conditional view, an agent could have done other than what she in fact did if and only if it is true that had she wanted, or tried, or intended, or chosen to do something else instead, she would have done this other thing (Hobart 1934; Ayer 1954; Smart 1961; Berofsky 2003).[1] It has been well documented that this conditional analysis of ability has various shortcomings. In one of J. L. Austin's cases (1961) a skilled golfer misses a short putt of the sort he has successfully made several times before. It seems that Austin's golfer could, on the occasion he misses, have made the putt despite having failed to succeed when he attempted to do so. There are concerns in the other direction as well: It may well be true that had she wanted or tried to take a dip in the ocean, Jane, who suffers from aquaphobia, would have succeeded. But it is false that in her situation, Jane could have entered the waters.

Some have tried to improve on this conditional analysis. Kadri Vihvelin offers this revised analysis:

> S has the ability at time t to do X iff, for some intrinsic property or set of properties B that S has at t, for some time t' after t, if S chose (decided, intended, or tried) at t to do X, and S were to retain B until t', S's choosing (deciding, intending, or trying) to do X and S's having of B would jointly be an S-complete cause of S's doing X. (2004, 438)

An S-complete cause is a "cause complete in so far as havings of properties intrinsic to . . . [S] are concerned, though perhaps omitting some events extrinsic to . . . [S]" (Lewis, 1997, 156).

This refined analysis, however, seems to succumb to one of the same sorts of concern that Austin raised against the traditional conditional analysis: Austin's golfer is able to sink the putt, but Vihvelin's analysis implies that he lacks that ability (see, e.g., Berofsky 2011; Speak 2011, 123–24).

Michael Smith (2003) has offered yet another analysis of weak "can" or ability to act otherwise construed in terms of a capacity to have believed or desired differently.[2]

My intention here is not to argue for or against any one of these or other proposed analyses of weak "can." I use these illustrations to highlight the distinction between such weak, compatibilist analyses and the strong incompatibilist analysis. I proceed on the supposition that incompatibilists conceive of the alternatives, if any, required for the truth of judgments of prudential obligation, moral obligation, moral responsibility, intrinsic value regarding basic intrinsic value states, and aretaic appraisals, too, on some approaches to virtue ethics, as strong. This is merely a simplifying supposition; needless to say, some incompatibilists may well reject it.

I have argued that the truth of judgments of each of this sort requires our having alternatives. From the incompatibilist perspective, determinism precludes the truth of such judgments on the presumption that determinism effaces strong alternatives. Thus, assuming this perspective, the costs of living without free will may already be judged to be substantial.

6.2.1. Incompatibilism, Strong Alternatives, and Intrinsic Value

Some may think that I have been too quick with intrinsic value. I entertain two preliminary objections to the conclusion that determinism imperils intrinsic value, assuming the pertinent alternatives are strong, and then a somewhat more involved objection.

Each of the preliminary objections concerns the characterization of intrinsic value I invoked:

(*IValue-1*): Necessarily, *x* is intrinsically good if and only if anyone who were to contemplate *x* would have a reason to favor *x* for its own sake.

I don't regard *IValue-1* as giving an analysis of *something's being intrinsically good*.[3] But then one might claim that if *IValue-1* does not give an analysis, it merely picks out intrinsic goodness. Furthermore, if it simply picks out intrinsic goodness, then the fact, if it is one, that agents lack the ability to favor *x* or to refrain from favoring *x* (whatever the case may be) owing to determinism would be entirely consistent with *x's* being intrinsically good. In brief, from the fact, if it is one, that determinism precludes agents from responding appropriately to certain states that are supposedly intrinsically good, it does not follow that those states are not intrinsically good provided *IValue-1* does not give a "reductive" analysis of intrinsic goodness.

First, I'm not so sure about this claim concerning a "reductive analysis." For, what is required to motivate the concern about the incompatibility of determinism and intrinsic value is the view that, necessarily, something can't be intrinsically good if it doesn't provide us with objective *pro tanto* reasons. Presumably, a "reductive analysis," if there is one, would have to respect this claim. Second, whether one accepts this objection turns on whether intrinsic goodness is, as some have characterized it, a "response-dependent property." Roughly, to say that some property is response-dependent is to say that its instantiation in an object consists in the disposition of that object to give rise to certain kinds of response, in certain sorts of agents, in certain sorts of circumstances (see, e.g., Cuneo 2001). It seems that the objection presupposes that intrinsic goodness is *not* such a property: on this view something can be intrinsically good even if its contemplation, roughly, does not elicit appropriate responses. But this is controversial. People such as Moore (1903) and Ross (1939) favored a nonresponse-dependent characterization of intrinsic value; but many others (see chap. 4, n.1) favor a response-dependent characterization. Which of these characterizations is correct is something that needs to be fought out elsewhere. I am, though, quite willing to be concessive here: if a nonresponse-dependent characterization has the upper hand, then perhaps the concerns about determinism's imperiling intrinsic value that I have raised may fall by the way.

The second preliminary objection introduces the option of being an internalist about intrinsic value: such an internalist holds that if x is intrinsically good, then a rational agent contemplating x, or judging x to be intrinsically good, necessarily will have some kind of pro-attitude—such as favoring—with regard to x. A comparison may help: it may be proposed that if one recognizes or judges that one ought morally to do something, y, then one's recognizing this fact or this reason for doing y necessarily motivates one to do y; having the reason, or judging that y is intrinsically good, has "built in" motivation. It is further claimed that if this sort of judgment internalism about intrinsic value is plausible, it dispenses with the "can," and so, once again, escapes worries concerning determinism's impact, if any, on whether one can (or can refrain from) favoring various things. In response, two comments are in order. First, even the internalist view in consideration may not be able to dispense with "can." The concern here is similar to a concern with judgment internalism with respect to moral "oughts": Imagine that at the very moment when some rational agent judges that some state, x-1, is intrinsically good, a powerful demon "inactivates" neural processes essential to this agent's eliciting the apt response. Then it is false that this agent's contemplating x-1, necessarily, will have the suitable pro-attitude with regard to x. To evade this sort of counterexample, it would seem that the judgment internalist would have to amend the condition along these lines that incorporates ability: if x is intrinsically good, a rational agent contemplating x necessarily will have some kind of pro-attitude with regard to x if this agent can, at the apt time, have this sort of pro-attitude toward x. Second, once again I am willing to be concessive. Maybe some sort of plausible judgment internalism regarding intrinsic value can be developed. Then whether the conclusion that determinism imperils intrinsic value is acceptable will depend partly but vitally on whether this species of internalism about intrinsic value is superior to rivals such as *IValue-1*.

Turning, now, to the more involved concern, some may object that even if there is a values-reasons connection, it is not clear that it must take the form of *IValue-1-Basic*.

> *IValue-1-Basic*: Necessarily, x is basically intrinsically good if and only if anyone who were to contemplate x would have a reason to favor x for its own sake.

It might be claimed, instead, that this "conditional" rival is more plausible:

> *IValue-Conditional-1*: Necessarily, x is basically intrinsically good if and only if anyone who were to contemplate x would have a reason to favor x for its own sake *if one can favor x*.

It may be helpful to reformulate *IValue-Conditional-1* in this way:

> *IValue-Conditional-2*: Necessarily, x is basically intrinsically good if and only for any agent, y, if y can favor x, then if y were to contemplate x, y would have a reason to favor x for its own sake.

This conditional values-reasons thesis, it may be proposed, does not support the view that determinism undermines values. But this is not quite right. After all, determinism would not preclude people from favoring or disfavoring basics upon contemplating them if these basics were intrinsically good or intrinsically bad, whatever the case might be. However, if one has an objective *pro tanto* reason to favor *x*, then one can favor *x* *and* one can refrain from favoring *x*. Suppose one contemplates a basic, *x*, and one favors it. If determinism is true, and "can" is used in its strong sense, one cannot refrain from favoring *x*. But then despite one's being able to favor *x*, one cannot have an objective *pro tanto* reason to favor *x* because there is an alternative possibilities requirement for having such reasons.

A more promising conditional thesis is, roughly, that something, *x*, is intrinsically good if and only if any person who contemplates *x* has a reason to favor *x* for its own sake if the person both can favor and refrain from favoring *x*. More precisely:

> *IValue-Conditional-3*: Necessarily, *x* is basically intrinsically good if and only if for any agent *y*, if *y* can favor *x* and *y* can refrain from favoring *x*, then if *y* were to contemplate *x*, *y* would have a reason to favor *x* for its own sake.

But this conditional thesis has little going for it. Data of Star Trek fame, it may be assumed, is "attitudinally dead." He can't favor or disfavor anything. Suppose *x-1* is a basic, and Data were to contemplate *x-1*. Then since the right hand side of *IValue-Conditional-3* is true (because its antecedent is false), it follows that *x-1* is intrinsically good. Now consider:

> *IValue-Conditional-4*: Necessarily, *x* is basically intrinsically bad if and only if for any agent, *y*, if *y* can disfavor *x* and *y* can refrain

from disfavoring x, and y were to contemplate x, then y would have a reason to disfavor x for its own sake.

Suppose that Data were, again, to contemplate x-1. The right hand side of *IValue-Conditional-4* is true (because its antecedent is false). It follows that x-1 is intrinsically bad. But a basic cannot be both intrinsically good and intrinsically bad. So we ought to reject both *IValue-Conditional-3* and *IValue-Conditional-4*.

One might propose instead:

IValue-Conditional 5a: Necessarily, x is basically intrinsically good if and only if for any agent, y, if it were the case that y can favor x and y can refrain from favoring x, then it would be the case that if y were to contemplate x, y would have a reason to favor x for its own sake;

and

IValue-Conditional-5b: Necessarily, x is basically intrinsically bad if and only if for any agent, y, if it were the case that y can disfavor x and y can refrain from disfavoring x, then it would be the case that if y were to contemplate x, y would have a reason to disfavor x for its own sake.

In support of this way of formulating the "fitting attitude" account, one might draw attention to these formulations of the unconditional view:

(1a): x is intrinsically good if and only if for any agent, y, if y contemplates x, then y has a reason to favor x for its own sake;

and

(1b): x is intrinsically good if and only if for any agent, y, if y were to contemplate x, then y would have a reason to favor x for its own sake.

It may be proposed that if the conditional in the right hand side of (1a) is the material conditional, we would have the absurd result that any basic that is not contemplated is good. So (1b) is to be preferred to (1a). Similar considerations, it may be further claimed, support the move from *IValue-Conditional-3* to *IValue-Conditional-5a*.

But there are problems with *IValue-Conditional-5a*, too. All counterfactuals with a necessarily false antecedent are vacuously true. Suppose Data is such that essentially, he cannot favor anything; there is no world in which he can favor anything. Then the right side of *IValue-Conditional-5a* is a counterfactual with a necessarily false antecedent. Suppose Data contemplates basic *x-1*. *IValue-Conditional-5a* in conjunction with this fact implies that this basic is intrinsically good. *IValue-Conditional-5b* in conjunction with this fact implies that this basic is intrinsically bad. It cannot be, however, that basic *x-1* is both intrinsically good and intrinsically bad. So *IValue-Conditional-5a* and *IValue-Conditional-5b* ought to be rejected.

There is a second problem. Presumably the favoring attitude, whatever it precisely amounts to, is analogous to attitudes such as taking pleasure in something, or being displeased about something, or being indignant about some matter in that these attitudes are "naturalistic"; they have neurophysiological underpinnings. (Should the favoring attitude not be an attitude of this sort, so much the worse for this attitude and for the fitting attitude account of intrinsic value.) These neurophysiological roots can be tempered with. Imagine a case in which new wave psychosurgeons alter relevant parts of Zoe's brain in such a way that when she contemplates a "positive" basic, such as *a mother's taking pleasure in her child's being saved* (*pbasic*), when left to her own devices, she disfavors this basic rather than favoring it as she would were she not subject to "inversion surgery." She is so altered that when she grasps the intrinsic features of the state she is contemplating, she regards these features as giving her reason to disfavor the state. It is not that the surgery renders her unable to favor *pbasic*. Rather, she would favor this basic only if there is a partial eclipse of the moon. Under these conditions, I doubt whether it would be fitting for Zoe to favor *pbasic* if she were to contemplate it: just as it is not fitting to favor something that it is logically impossible to favor, so, it seems, it is not fitting to favor something one can favor but only under highly restrictive conditions that won't obtain during the agent's life time. Analogously, I have my doubts whether Zoe would have reason to favor *pbasic* were she to contemplate it. Unlike Zoe, mentally healthy Zahara has a reason to favor *pbasic* for its own sake when she contemplates this basic intrinsic value state. Contrary to conditional view *IValue-Conditional-5a*, *pbasic* would not be intrinsically good. For, whereas Zoe would not have a reason to favor *pbasic*, Zahara would have a reason to favor this state.

In view of this difficulty, one might propose yet another modification of conditional view *IValue-Conditional-5a* along these lines:

> *IValue-Conditional-6*: Necessarily, *x* is basically intrinsically good if and only if for any agent, *y*, if it were the case that *y* can favor *x* and *y* can refrain from favoring *x*, and *y* is not subject to inversion surgery, then it would be the case that if *y* were to contemplate *x*, *y* would have a reason to favor *x* for its own sake.

IValue-Conditional-6 is unacceptable as well. We can imagine that a mutation results in Zoe's offspring, Zach, having "inverted" favoring attitudes just as his mother does. Fill in the details of the case in such a way that an entire community of "inverts" eventually comes to flourish. Again, upon contemplating positive basics, such as *pbasic*, each of these inverts regards the intrinsic features of these basics as giving them reason to disfavor these states. Like Zoe, they *can* favor such basics but only under conditions that won't obtain during their life spans. "Non-Inverts" upon contemplating *pbasic* will have reason to favor it; inverts upon contemplating this basic will not have reason to favor it. *IValue-Conditional-6* thus fails.

Whether the properties, intrinsic or otherwise, of a thing give an agent reason to favor it, if these properties do at all, when that agent contemplates it crucially depends upon the sort of agent doing the contemplating. If the agent is essentially attitudinally "dead," then the intrinsic features of a basic such as *pbasic* will fail to give this agent reason to favor it; if the agent is an invert like Zoe, its intrinsic features will give her reason to disfavor it; if the agent is an agent like Zahara, it intrinsic features will give her reason to favor it. Although I may be wrong about this diagnosis, I think one thing Data-like examples and the inversion examples highlight is that it is a mistake to suppose that a state's having intrinsic value is conditional upon those who contemplate it having various properties such as *being attitudinally dead*, or *being inverted* or *being non-inverted*; intrinsic value does not supervene upon relational properties.

Against the conditional accounts so far canvassed, one might object that it has been assumed that the sense of "can" in these accounts is the "all-in" (incompatibilist) sense rather than some compatibilist sense, which implies merely having "one-way" control as opposed to having "two-way" control. This assumption, though, is unwarranted. Why isn't "one-way" control sufficient? There are two interpretations of this objection. The first is not on target; the second is, but it is one that I have anticipated. Addressing the first interpretation, reconsider:

IValue-Conditional-3: Necessarily, *x* is basically intrinsically good if and only for any agent *y*, if *y* can favor *x* and *y* can refrain from favoring *x*, then if *y* were to contemplate *x*, *y* would have a reason to favor *x* for its own sake.

I argued that *IValue-Conditional-3*, together with its sibling concerning intrinsic badness (*IValue-Conditional-4*) generates the unacceptable result that some basic can be both intrinsically good and intrinsically bad. The argument did not rely on the claim that "can" in the phrases "can favor *x*" and "can refrain from favoring *x*" that occur in these principles is the all-in "can." The concern of incoherence arises no matter whether "can" is understood in the all-in sense or some "compatibilist" sense.

On the second much more plausible interpretation of this objection, the problem is that even if it is, for instance, *IValue-1*, that is in question, there is no *prima facie* reason to exclude occurrences of "can" in *IValue-I* from referring to some compatibilist account of "can." But then, of course, determinism won't threaten intrinsic value. I think this is just right, but this interpretation raises a concern I expound on more fully in sec. 6.6. In brief, a "compatibilist" rendering of *IValue-1* will still be wedded to our having alternatives, albeit alternatives compatible with determinism.

To tie some ends together, either unconditional theses *IValue-1-Basic—IValue-4-Basic* capture the fitting attitude account of intrinsic value, or the conditional variants of these unconditional theses capture this account. If the latter is true, so much the worse for the fitting attitude account; I believe that the conditional variants should be rejected. If the former is true, then determinism precludes intrinsic value if the alternatives in question are strong.

We may as well record the following. Regarding the impact of determinism on the intrinsic value of worlds, again, determinism undermines such value if, as I have argued, there is an alternative possibilities requirement for having objective *pro tanto* reasons, these alternatives are strong, and no world can be intrinsically good (or intrinsically bad or intrinsically neutral) unless anyone who contemplates the atoms, if any, that the world contains has objective *pro tanto* reasons to favor (or to disfavor, or to be indifferent to) these atoms when one contemplates them. We, thus, have an alternative route to the conclusion that determinism precludes moral obligation: owing to the supervenience of the morally deontic on worldly value, determinism imperils moral obligation.

6.2.2. Incompatibilism, Strong Alternatives, Welfare, and Happiness

I have argued that there is an alternative possibilities requirement for being intrinsically pleased or intrinsically displeased about something. I have assumed that from the standpoint of the incompatibilist, the alternatives are strong. On certain views of personal well-being (or welfare) and happiness, the fact that there is an alternative possibilities requirement for intrinsic attitudinal pleasure and intrinsic displeasure, together with the view that the alternatives are strong, leads to the disturbing conclusion that incompatibilism imperils personal welfare and happiness.

According to simple intrinsic attitudinal hedonism—*Simple Hedonism*—one's life is going well for one to the extent that it contains a net balance of intrinsic attitudinal pleasure. To elucidate, a theory of welfare should start with certain "atoms" of welfare. On *Simple Hedonism* the positive atoms of well-being are states of affairs in which some person is intrinsically attitudinally pleased to some degree about something at a time; the negative atoms are states of affairs in which some person is intrinsically attitudinally displeased to some degree about something at a moment. A person's welfare level at a time is, roughly, the sum or some aggregation of the welfare-values of the atoms of welfare involving that person and occurring at that time. A person's welfare level across some interval is determined by summing, or combining in some relevant way, information about the person's welfare levels at times during the interval. Similar things are true about a theory of happiness: the theory specifies its atoms of happiness, advances an account of the happiness level of a person at a time, and provides an account of the person's happiness through an interval. On some views of happiness, the happiness atoms mirror those of the welfare atoms *Simple Hedonism* recognizes (see, for e.g., Feldman 2010).

I argued that if someone takes intrinsic attitudinal pleasure in some state of affairs at a time, then at this time, this person has an objective *pro tanto* reason to favor the fact that he is then taking intrinsic attitudinal pleasure in something. As there is an alternative possibilities requirement for having objective *pro tanto* reasons, it follows that if some person takes intrinsic attitudinal pleasure in some state of affairs at a time, then at this time, this person can refrain from favoring the fact that he is then taking intrinsic attitudinal pleasure in something. Provided such alternatives are strong, and assuming a hedonistic theory such as *Simple Hedonism*, the incompatibilist is committed to claiming that the welfare atoms and the happiness atoms are compromised: no such atoms are true at a world in which apt agents have no alternatives. This is a pretty hefty cost of living without free will.

Some may object that what I have shown in the previous, relevant section (sec. 4.5) is only that whenever someone takes attitudinal pleasure in something at a time, at that time one *would* have an objective *pro tanto* reason to favor the fact that one takes attitudinal pleasure in that thing if one *were* aware of this fact. But I also argued for these conclusions: First, if, at *t*, one takes intrinsic attitudinal pleasure to degree *n* in some state of affairs, then, at *t*, one could both favor and refrain from favoring that state of affairs; if, at *t*, one takes intrinsic attitudinal displeasure to degree *n* in some state of affairs, then, at *t*, one could both disfavor and refrain from disfavoring that state of affairs; and if at *t*, one is pleasure- or displeasure-wise indifferent to degree *n* in some state of affairs, then, at *t*, one could both be indifferent toward and refrain from being indifferent toward that state of affairs. If we conceive of the relevant alternatives as strong, then once again the incompatibilist must concede that welfare atoms (and perhaps happiness atoms), with a theory such as *Simple Hedonism*, are imperiled at a world in which agents have no such alternatives.

6.2.3. Incompatibilism, Strong Alternatives, and Moral Responsibility

What of judgments of moral responsibility? Here, I limit my remarks to the following. First, if you are a traditional incompatibilist who thinks that moral responsibility requires strong alternatives, then determinism precludes responsibility. Second, you may be a "source incompatibilist" who believes that to be morally responsible for a choice or action, you must be the "ultimate originator" of this choice or action or of at least some of your choices or actions. But as determinism precludes your being such an originator, determinism precludes moral responsibility. Source incompatibilists may concur with various compatibilists that the principle of alternative possibilities concerning responsibility (*PAP-R*) is false (see, for example, Pereboom 2002; Widerker 2011), but still look upon determinism as a threat to responsibility because they see determinism as undercutting ultimate origination. Source incompatibilists as well as traditional compatibilists, however, may well endorse the principles that praiseworthiness requires obligation or permissibility and blameworthiness requires wrongness:

> *Praiseworthiness presupposes Obligation (PO)*: An agent, *S*, is morally praiseworthy for doing something, *A*, only if it is overall morally obligatory or overall morally permissible for *S* to do *A*.
> *Blameworthiness presupposes Wrongness (BO)*: An agent, *S*, is morally blameworthy for doing something, *A*, only if it is overall morally wrong for *S* to do *A*.

Should they accept these principles, source incompatibilists who also believe that there is a requirement of strong alternatives for the truth of morally deontic judgments have an additional reason to conclude that determinism precludes moral responsibility.

6.2.4. Incompatibilism, Strong Alternatives, and the Moral Sentiments

As for the moral sentiments or attitudes, I argued previously that well-founded or "legitimate" forgiveness, guilt, and indignation all presuppose our having alternatives. If, for instance, one forgives another for something, then one has an objective *pro tanto* reason to forgive this person. Although, when one forgives, one may not forgive *for* this reason (see principle *Forgiveness*). Similar things are true with guilt and indignation, as the discussion concerning principles *Guilt* and *Indignation* confirmed. From the incompatibilist perspective we have assumed, determinism, thus, threatens the rationality of having these sentiments or attitudes. In addition, I proposed that with emotions such as thankfulness, sorrow, regret, and joy, typically, when one feels these emotions or adopts these attitudes, one has an objective *pro tanto* reason to feel these emotions or to adopt these attitudes. Again, the incompatibilist perspective in question implies that determinism compromises the rationality of such emotions or attitudes. To the extent that these emotions or attitudes are bound up with interpersonal relations, incompatibilists who opt for the view that the pertinent alternatives are strong must concede that, to this extent, the rationality of such relationships is imperiled as well.

6.3. LIBERTARIANISM, LUCK, AND NORMATIVE APPRAISALS

Prior to leaving incompatibilism, I want to digress somewhat and say a few things about the implications of a certain brand of libertarianism—*action-centered modest libertarianism*—for the truth of various sorts of normative appraisal. I argue that this type of libertarianism precludes moral responsibility, moral obligation, prudential obligation, and various axiological appraisals, and it raises problems for certain moral sentiments as well, owing to concerns of luck.

Modest libertarian accounts, like their most promising compatibilist competitors on free action, require that to choose or act freely, an agent must have the capacity to engage in practical reasoning and to guide her behavior in light of the reasons she has.[4] In addition, emulating their compatibilist rivals, such accounts are modest in that they make no appeal to Kantian noumenal selves, Cartesian minds, or the like, and they avoid agent causation altogether. Moreover, like their compatibilist challengers, they dictate that the choices or overt actions for which an agent is morally responsible be the outcomes of causal processes. Distinguishing between deterministic and indeterministic causation will be helpful in rounding out this brief sketch of modest libertarianism. One event deterministically causes a second if and only if the first causes the second, and with the laws of nature and the past as they are, there is no chance that the first occurs without causing the second. An event indeterministically causes another if and only if the former causes the latter, and it is consistent with the laws of nature and the past that the former event occurs and not have caused the latter. Now we may add that modest libertarians require that a free decision be made for reasons, and its being made for reasons consists, partially, in its being indeterministically caused in an appropriate and nondeviant way by the agent's having those reasons.

Libertarian views allow that an indirectly free action—an action whose freedom derives from the freedom of other actions to which this action is suitably related—may be determined by its immediate causal precursors. A directly free action is not indirectly free. Modest libertarian theories differ from compatibilist ones in that they imply that even the immediate causal antecedents of a directly free action do not determine that action: given these antecedents, and the natural laws, there is some chance that that action not occur.[5] On *action-centered* modest libertarian accounts, the event that is directly free and indeterministically caused is the making of a decision (Clarke 2000, 23).

Accounts of acting for a reason generally require that the connection between the agent's having the reason and her action comprise, partly, the exercise of a certain degree of control by the agent. To generate a working version of modest libertarianism start with our best compatibilist view of freedom, and then add to this "host" the requirement that free decisions themselves are indeterministically caused. The resulting event causal action-centered libertarianism specifies that an agent's control—"*proximal*" or "*active*" control—in making a decision consists in apt agent-involving events causing nondeviantly that decision. More fully, such control concerns the direct causal production of agent-involving events, such as the agent's having certain values, desires, and beliefs, his making a certain evaluative judgment, his forming a certain intention or arriving at a certain decision, his executing an intention, and his performing a nonmental action. The degree of active control the agent exercises depends on which agent-involving events actually cause the decision and on their etiologies. On such a libertarian view, the factors that constitute an agent's active control in making a free decision are the *very ones* shared by this view and its compatibilist host: roughly, deliberative processes with appropriate causal histories causing nondeviantly the decision.

If modest libertarianism does not vary from its best compatibilist rival with respect to active control (as may initially be presumed), one may well wonder why some have thought that this sort of libertarianism undermines free action, responsibility, or freedom-relevant *control*, especially on the assumption (the reader is invited to entertain) that its best compatibilist competitor does not share these faults. Speaking to this concern regarding control, I cite from a previous work:

> Suppose Peg is mulling over whether to keep a promise to visit Al. She judges that, all things considered, she ought to keep the promise, though reasons of self-interest tempt her to refrain. She decides to keep the promise, and her having certain reasons to do so, including her making the all-things-considered judgment that she ought, on this occasion, to keep the promise, nondeterministically causes her to make this decision. On an action-centered libertarian view, since Peg's decision to keep the promise is nondeterministically caused, there was a chance that

her deliberative process would terminate in a decision not to keep the promise. Had Peg made this other decision, it would have been nondeterministically caused by her having reasons of self-interest. *Everything* prior to the decision that Peg actually makes, including every feature of Peg, might have been just the same, and yet she could have made the alternative decision instead. To underscore this point, consider the nearest possible world with the same past as the past in Peg's world. This world will have a past in which Peg's prior deliberations have resulted in the best judgment that the promise ought to be honored but Peg (or if we want, one of Peg's counterparts, Peg*) decides not to keep the promise. In so deciding, Peg* acquires an intention not to keep the promise. The acquisition of this intention—the making of the decision to refrain from keeping the promise—is seemingly not explained by anything. At least, Peg*'s prior deliberations do not explain why she makes this decision. This is because these deliberations exactly mirror those of Peg's but Peg's deliberations nondeterministically give rise to the opposed decision to keep the promise. (Haji 2005, 323–24).

More needs to be said on why Peg*'s making the decision to refrain from keeping the promise has no causal explanation, especially in light of the modest libertarian's proposal that Peg*'s reason states in her non-actual world may be duly invoked to explain her making of this decision. If there is no reason to doubt that Peg*'s pertinent reason states indeterministically cause her decision, then, it appears, it would be no less plausible to suppose that Peg* exercises active control in making her decision than it would be to suppose that Peg exercises this sort of control in making the decision that she does. Furthermore, it may be thought that exercising such control in making the decision that each does would go a long way (if not the complete way) toward satisfying the requirement of acting for a reason that there be a connection between the agent's having the reason and her action that is constituted, partly, by the exercise of a certain degree of freedom-level control by the agent.[6]

Focusing on control, *if* it is supposed that Peg (or Peg*) lacks freedom-level control in making the decision that she does, just what sort of control, if any, does she lack? Not active, as we are initially supposing (we will return to this supposition later), but what I have previously referred to as "antecedent proximal control" (Haji 2002, 110–11). With fixed pasts, the difference in outcome in Peg's and Peg*'s cases appears to be merely a function of the indeterminacy in actional pathways leading to choice. I have claimed, however, that it would seem that no agent could exert active or any other sort of control over such indeterminacy to "ensure" a particular outcome. Amplifying somewhat, if t_1 is the time at which Peg makes whatever decision she makes at t_1 if she is still alive at t_1 (it is not indeterministic, for instance, whether Peg will suffer a fatal stroke at t_1), unlike her otherwise similar deterministic counterpart Peggy, Peg does not have the ability or power to ensure that at t_1 she decides in accordance with her decisive best judgment about what to do. She may judge that it is best for her to keep the promise, may muster all the powers of self-control that would ordinarily suffice for her deciding in accordance with this best judgment, but still fail to so decide. In Peg's case, her prior actional antecedents seem not to contribute sufficiently to control.

For more on antecedent proximal control, the "ensuring power," and the connection between these things, on the one hand, and acting for a reason and moral responsibility, on the other, assume that an agent is self-controlled insofar as she is not akratic. In a deterministic world, suppose that on the basis of her reasons this agent forms the all-things-considered best judgment that she ought, at *t0*, to decide to *A* at *t1*. Then barring unusual circumstances, such as unexpected death, and in the absence of any information that may influence her verdict about what is all things considered best for her, she can ensure at *t0* or at some time prior to *t1* that, at *t1*, she decides in accordance with her best judgment. *Her being able to ensure that she so decides simply amounts to her being able to so decide provided nothing goes awry in the causal trajectory of her decision.*

Why should this power or ability be thought to be relevant to free action and moral responsibility? After all, we do act akratically, and strict akratic action is *free*, intentional action that is contrary to a consciously held best or better judgment. Moreover, we *can* be morally responsible for our akratic choices or actions. To understand the significance of the ensuring power to freedom and responsibility, assume that deterministic Peggy is perfectly self-controlled. An agent is perfectly self-controlled if (1) this agent does not succumb to akratic or other irrational influences;[7] and, (2), barring unusual circumstances, such as sudden death or the occurrence of events over which she lacks any control and which would prevent her from deciding in accordance with her best (or better) judgment, and in the absence of new information, further deliberation, etc., she decides, at least in deterministic worlds, in accordance with such a judgment. I introduce a term of art: we can say that the etiology or causal trajectory, or a segment of such a trajectory, of an action, mental or otherwise, is *smooth* provided it is free of responsibility-undermining factors, such as, for instance, the influence of manipulation of the sort that vitiates responsibility. Some may claim that deterministic causation is itself responsibility-subversive. To avoid begging questions against either compatibilists or incompatibilists, assume that neither deterministic causation per se nor indeterministic causation per se qualify as responsibility undermining. Both compatibilists and incompatibilists can provisionally agree on what factors, other than the variety of causation at issue, are at least intuitively and plausibly responsibility-undermining. This assumption is not unwarranted on the constraint that modest libertarianism differs from its compatibilist rival *only* in that the former insists that directly free actions are not deterministically caused.

Imagine that perfectly self-controlled Peggy judges that of her two salient options, A and B, it is best for her to A rather than to B. Assuming that the causal pathway to her decision to A is smooth, she enjoys a certain power in her deterministic world. This is the power to "ensure" that she decides in accordance with her best judgment, and, again, the ensuring power amounts to this: If she exercises this power and the causal trajectory to her decision to A that "commences," roughly, with her deliberations about whether or not to A or to B is smooth, she will decide to A in accordance with her best judgment. Provided this segment of the trajectory is smooth, if as a self-controlled agent, Peggy fails to decide in accordance with her best judgment and decides to B rather than to A, it would appear that this decision is not free, and, hence, she would not be morally responsible for so deciding. It is not free because, assuming that free action requires control, and this control consists partially but crucially in there being an appropriate causal connection between Peggy's reason states and her making the decision that she does, there appears to be no such connection. For if she is perfectly self-controlled and she decides to B, something somewhere along the causal pathway to her decision has gone very wrong: no new considerations come to her mind prior to or after her having judged that it is best for her to A, she is uninfluenced by akratic considerations, she is not the victim of surreptitious manipulation, she has contributed all she can, consistently with what modest libertarianism allows agents to contribute, to her deciding in accordance with her best judgment to A, and so on. Her failure to so decide is freedom- and, hence, responsibility-subversive. Some may conjecture that there has been a breakdown of agency in a situation of this sort.[8] This may be so; if it is, it reinforces the judgment that Peggy is not morally responsible for deciding to B if she decides to B.

What, however, of agents like us who, unlike Peggy, are not perfectly self-controlled? Suppose that Percy, who sometimes succumbs to akratic influences, judges that of her two options, C and D, it is best for her to D. Suppose the causal pathway or its segment that "commences," roughly, with her deliberations about whether or not to C or D, to her subsequent decision to D is smooth: she musters sufficient self-control in deciding to D, she is not the victim of secretive manipulation, she is not deliberating under the influence of mind-altering drugs, etc. Like Peggy, in her deterministic world Percy possesses the power to make sure that she decides in accordance with her best judgment. Provided nothing goes amiss in the segment of the causal pathway to her D-ing, this power can be exercised to achieve Percy's proximal goal: deciding to D. If on this occasion, had Percy decided to C in the absence of akratic influences or new information that sways her reasoning, unsolicited manipulation, and the like, again, she would presumably *not* be morally responsible for deciding to C.

We may summarize the general, relevant point about antecedent proximal control in this way: Perfectly self-controlled agents and agents who, though not perfectly self-controlled but who exhibit self-control on various occasions of choice, can exercise the power to ensure that they decide in accordance with their best (or better) judgments in deterministic worlds. Should they fail to so decide, then in the absence of germane explanatory factors for this failure, they would not be morally responsible for the pertinent decisions they make. These factors should illuminate what it is about the etiology of the decisions in question that render their agents not responsible for these decisions.

Revert to our original Peg/Peg* indeterministic case. Assume, first, that Peg is perfectly self-controlled. Judging that it is best for her to A, she decides in accordance with her best judgment. The segment of the causal pathway from her deliberations about whether or not to A to her decision to A is smooth. The modest libertarian claims that, given exactly the same past up to or just prior to Peg's decision to A, and the same laws, if this decision is free, Peg was able to decide otherwise. So, consider the scenario in which holding fixed the relevant past and the laws, one of Peg's counterpart, Peg* (really, Peg) decides to B. If this decision is *not* free, then the libertarian has lost the battle because Peg* would not, in this scenario, be morally responsible for deciding to B. Assume, then, that Peg*'s decision to B is a *free*, intentional mental action. Reflect on what may be three broad possibilities concerning Peg*'s deciding to B.

First, Peg*'s reasons to B causally generate her *continent* decision to B. This option, however, is inconsistent with the assumption that the past is fixed. Recall, Peg judged that it is best for her to A, so Peg* must have judged similarly. If Peg* decides to B, then her so deciding is akratic: her deciding to B is a free, mental action that is contrary to what we may assume is a consciously held best judgment of Peg*'s.

Second, Peg*'s decision to B is akratic. One concern with this option is that it violates the assumption that Peg is perfectly self-controlled. Modest libertarianism seems to have the incredible consequence that perfectly self-controlled agents are not possible. If perfectly self-controlled Peg*'s A-ing in the actual world is to be free in accordance with modest libertarian requirements, in relevant non-actual worlds in which she, say, B-s, she akratically B-s (or seemingly so), a weakness to which perfectly self-controlled agents do not succumb. Even if this concern is set aside, there is a problem understanding the etiology of Peg*'s deciding to B. Why so? In customary accounts of akratic action, when an agent performs a strict akratic action, there is a misalignment between the motivational strength of the desire from which her act causally derives (the motivationally strongest desire) and her best judgment (see, e.g., Watson 1975/1986, 86–87; Mele 1995, chap. 2). If we accept these typical accounts, Peg*'s best judgment that she ought to keep the promise should stand opposed to her stronger desire to break the promise. With Peg*'s libertarian supposedly free decision, however, we see no such misalignment because Peg* *shares* the relevant past with Peg. Given her past, Peg*'s desire to keep the promise does not differ in motivational strength from this desire of Peg's. Regarding Peg, however, we may assume that her desire to keep the promise has *greater* motivational clout than her competing desire and, moreover, there is no misalignment between this stronger desire and her judgment that it is better for her to keep the promise. So we have a pretty obvious problem: How are we to explain Peg*'s *akratic* decision?

Elsewhere (Haji 2005), I considered this option: Robert Kane proposes that a libertarian might claim that the misalignment in question does not occur *prior* to choice but at the moment of choice. The desire to break the promise, it may be suggested, does not become the strongest desire of Peg* until she makes it so at the moment of choice. On this view, it is false that akratic misalignment preexists the pertinent choice. Rather, the akratic agents themselves create such misalignment when they choose (Kane 1999a, 114, n. 17). What, precisely, however, does the akrates do to shift the balance of motivational strength in favor of the desire that is allegedly out of kilter with her best judgment? Various explanations of the balance have been proposed, ones that make use of such things as selective focusing, failing to remind oneself how one will feel later knowing that one has acted contrary to one's better judgment, and conversely, thinking of how good one will feel afterward in light of being aware that one has successfully resisted temptation, and failing to make an effective attempt at self-control.[9] In the view that akratic misalignment occurs at the moment of choice, Peg*'s situation may be depicted in this way: Let t be the time at which Peg* makes the decision that she does. *Unlike* Peg, at t, Peg* selectively focuses, fails to make a concerted attempt at self-control, and so forth. At t, these "activities" (as we may say) of Peg*, in turn, bolster the motivational strength of her desire to break the promise, which, at t, causally gives rise to her decision to break the promise, despite her consciously held better judgment at t that she ought to keep the promise.

I limit comment to two concerns with this picture.[10] First, the actual world, where, at t, Peg decides to keep the promise, and possible world, W, in which she decides at t to break the promise, do not differ in *any* respects until t. It is, consequently, a mystery why, at t, Peg* engages in the activities that we have outlined when Peg, at this time, fails to engage in these activities. The *radical* shift, at t, in Peg*'s psychology paints an untenable picture of free agency. Engaging in these activities, or failing to do so, seems itself to be a matter of luck. Second, either these activities are free or they are not. If the latter, there is strong reason to doubt that the decision that Peg* makes is free because this decision stems from activities (that allegedly occur at the time when the decision is itself made) that are themselves not free.[11] If some of these activities, such as selective focusing, are not actions, if free, they will be indirectly free. If they are actions—an intentional omission would qualify as an action— then, again, if free, they would presumably be indirectly free. If the latter—if, that is, these activities *are* free—and if it is false that free events are uncaused, as the event causal libertarian assumes—these activities, if events, must themselves be indeterministically caused.

Again, since the actual world and world *W* are indiscernible right up until *t*, it is unclear what the causal antecedents of these activities could be. More cautiously, if these activities have causal precursors, and Peg* engages in these activities, then again it seems to be entirely a matter of luck that Peg fails to engage in these activities.

Regarding this second option, finally, it is implausible that a modest libertarian be committed to the view that in Peg/Peg*-like cases in which Peg acts continently, Peg could have freely done otherwise only if she had *akratically* done otherwise.

Perhaps some will object that the alleged difficulty in explaining Peg*'s supposedly akratic decision stems from elements of the particular conception of akratic action I have exploited. It may be proposed that we can explain why Peg*'s decision was akratic by simply appealing to the fact that she strongly desired to *B*, contrary to her judgment that it would be best to *A*. We can assume that the motivational strength of Peg's desire to *B* was stronger than the motivational strength of her *judgment* that it was best to *A*. When Peg decides to *A* she exercises self-control. Unlike Peg, failing to exercise such control, Peg* decides to *B*, and this decision is akratic. To assume that this explanation is inadequate is to assume a contentious, Hobbesian account of practical reasoning, in which deliberation is just a function of the force of the attitudes in play. But there is no reason to think the libertarian must accept this view of practical reason.

Presumably, the "non-Hobbesian" has an account of what it is for an agent, such as Peg, to exercise self-control. I assume, consistently with modest libertarian demands, that this account will appeal to relevant causal factors in the etiology of action. Imagine, then, that there is an explanation, partly in terms of Peg's desires, beliefs, best judgment, and so forth of her exercising self-control in her deciding to *A*. Once again, we find ourselves in a quandary: If

Peg has contributed all she can in exercising self-control in deciding to A, then on the stipulation that the laws and the past are fixed, and, consequently, all events right up or just prior to Peg's continently deciding to A in her world are mirrored in Peg*'s world, in virtue of what is it true that Peg* failed to exercise self-control as a result of the failure of which she decided to B? The fundamental concern regarding action explanation has not disappeared. Since she failed to exercise self-control, something in the causal history of Peg*'s deciding to B must be different from what we find in the causal history of Peg's contently deciding to A.

Nor will it do to suppose that Peg*, unlike Peg, acts perversely. "Perverse" agents differ from akratics in that they endorse and are fully "behind" their actions that run counter to their all-things considered judgments. With the past and the laws fixed, what does Peg do that Peg* does not (or the other way around) in virtue of which it is true that whereas Peg continently decides to A, Peg* "perversely" decides to B? Furthermore, if there is some difference in the etiologies of their decisions, is it a difference that a modest libertarian can accommodate, again, on the stipulation that the past and the laws are fixed?

So far, we have examined the unpromising options that Peg* continently decides to B and she akratically or "perversely" decides to B. On the third option, if Peg* decides to B in opposition to her consciously held best (or better) judgment, she has suffered a breakdown in agency. If so, she is not morally responsible for deciding to B.

In sum, the event causal libertarian says that, consistent with the past and the laws being what they are, at t Peg can either freely decide to keep the promise, or at t she can decide to break the promise, and whatever decision she makes at t, there is an action explanation of that decision. Roughly, apt reasons, it is claimed, indeterministically cause the decision that the agent makes. It seems that this view is not quite on target, as Peg*'s scenario illustrates. As remarked, active control is a function of one's actions being *appropriately* caused by agent-involving springs of action. It appears that an agent who decides akratically exercises less active control in deciding as she does than an otherwise similar agent who decides continently. So it would be too quick to claim, without further explanation, that indeterministic Peg*, who decides akratically, exercises the same degree of active control in making the decision that she does as deterministic Peggy would in making a type- or near type-identical decision when Peggy is perfectly self-controlled.

Still, one might wonder about what precisely is the connection between lack of an action explanation of Peg*'s akratic action and responsibility-level control. Modest libertarians endorse the view that acting for a reason requires that the connection between the agent's having the reason and her action constitute, partly, the exercise of a certain degree of control by the agent. I take action explanations to be causal. Kane, an event-causal libertarian, explains that an agent's decision is free only if that agent exercised plural voluntary control in making that decision. Plural voluntary control presupposes that the agent had genuine alternatives; consistent with the past and the laws remaining fixed, the agent (like Peg*) could have made an alternative decision. Assuming that the agent had these genuine options, she had plural voluntary control over these options only if she was able to bring about whichever of the options she willed (or desired) when she willed to do so, for the reasons she willed to do so, on purpose, rather than accidentally or by mistake, without being coerced or compelled in doing so or in willing to do so, or otherwise controlled in doing or in willing to do so by other agents or mechanisms (Kane 2005, 138; 2011, 384–85, 389).[12] If Peg*, then, has plural voluntary control over her akratic decision, her reason states must suitably and indeterministically cause that decision. But if there is no apt causal explanation of her decision, akratic, perverse, or what have you, in terms of her prior reasons, then we have reason to doubt that she exercises such control in making this decision.

To collect results, in Peg/Peg*-like cases, we begin with the assumption that in accordance with her best judgment Peg continently A-s at a certain time, t, in the actual world. In relevant non-actual worlds with the same past and the laws as the actual world, Peg (Peg*, if we want) B-s at this time. (We may take Peg's A-ing and Peg*'s B-ing to be Peg's deciding to A and Peg*'s deciding to B respectively.) In such cases, Peg* lacks the power to ensure that she decides in accordance with her best or better judgment even though, having formed this judgment, she does not persist in deliberation, no new information or considerations come to her mind prior to her deciding to B, etc., and there are no reasons to believe that the segment of the causal etiology of her deciding to B from the time she forms the best judgment that she ought to A to her decision to B is *not* smooth. Abbreviating, Peg* lacks antecedent proximal control in deciding as she does despite the assumption that the relevant segment of the causal etiology of her deciding to B is smooth. If, having formed the best judgment that she ought to A, Peg* does not deliberate any further, no new considerations or information come to her mind prior to her deciding to B, etc., and she lacks antecedent proximal control despite smoothness of the relevant segment of the causal etiology of her deciding as she does, then it does not seem that her reason states appropriately cause her decision to B. Each of the pertinent options—Peg* decides to B continently, she decides to B akratically (or perversely), or she suffers a breakdown of agency—are untenable (given that the past and the laws are fixed). If Peg*'s prior reason states do not appropriately cause her decision to B, however, then she lacks responsibility- or freedom-level control in deciding as she does. Recall, this control is largely causal. Provided an agent's active control in making a decision consists in apt agent-involving events causing nondeviantly that decision, we have grounds to challenge the claim that Peg* exercises active control in deciding as she does. Therefore, Peg* lacks the sort of causal control in deciding as she does that modest libertarianism requires of one to perform free actions.

It may be worth recording the following. Since modest libertarianism differs from what I have called its "compatibilist host" or its "best compatibilist rival" only in that the causation of directly free actions by reason states is indeterministic, one may wonder what advantage modest libertarianism is supposed to enjoy regarding moral responsibility over its best compatibilist rival. One might propose that having real alternatives enhances the control one has in performing actions for which one is morally responsible. This, however, is implausible. The mere fact, if it is one, that one's decisions are indeterministically caused cannot contribute to one's exercising a greater degree of control *in* making such decisions than one would exercise were one's decisions deterministically caused. There is nothing about indeterministic causation per se that is "control enhancing." Alternatively, one might propose that the indeterministic causation of one's directly free actions ensures that one has freedom of control from the past, such freedom being essential to one's directly free actions being "up to one" (see, e.g., Kane 2011, 397–98). There are strong doubts, however, with this proposal as well. If an agent has contributed *all* she can to the causal antecedents that (supposedly) generate a decision and, as the modest libertarian insists, given the past and the laws, it is still open whether a decision occurs or whether it does not, and, furthermore, the agent contributes no more to whatever decision occurs, then whether a certain decision occurs seems not to be up to the agent.

My preliminary conclusion (which I continue to endorse) is that modest libertarianism falls prey to luck: it precludes responsibility for what are meant to be directly free actions. (Should one think that agent causalists can circumvent the problem of luck, one should consult the appendix to this chapter.)

Turning, now, to luck and reasons, responsibility requires control that is incompatible with luck, but what about obligations of objective *pro tanto* reasons? Do such obligations require control as well, and if so, what sort of control over and above the ability to do otherwise? Suppose, from the perspective of objective *pro tanto* reasons, Peg ought to give medicine A to a patient—she reasons-wise ought to give A. Imagine that Peg does indeed give A, and her reason states indeterministically cause the event that is her giving A. We may suppose that her appreciation of the objective *pro tanto* reason to give A causally gives rise to an apt desire, and this desire in conjunction with suitable beliefs are in the etiology of Peg's indeterministically giving A. If she indeterministically gives A, there is a world with the same past as the actual one right up to the time or just prior to the time when she gives A in the actual world, and the same laws, in which she refrains from giving A. In this world, either Peg does not give A or any other medicine to the patient, or she gives some medicine other than A. Assume, furthermore, that partly on the basis of the objective reason she has for giving A, she forms the best judgment that she should give A, and actional members of the segment of the causal trajectory culminating in her giving A, including apt desires and beliefs, and her best judgment smoothly give rise to her giving A: no new information comes to mind prior to her giving A, she does not succumb to akratic influences, she does not suffer from a breakdown of agency, etc. Then, for the reasons adumbrated earlier in addressing responsibility and luck, it looks as though Peg's refraining from giving A in the non-actual world and, for that matter, her giving A in the actual world, is a matter of luck.

With this preparatory background, it is hard to see how Peg's refraining from giving A in the non-actual world in which she refrains is an intentional action that derives from Peg's reasons, objective or otherwise, not to give A. Elucidating, in the non-actual world, it appears that Peg does not act on the basis of reasons. It would seem that she does not do so because acting on the basis of reasons requires that her action be appropriately caused by suitable reason states, something that is *not* so in the non-actual world as, again, reflection on the previous discussion involving responsibility and luck should confirm. I admit that this is not a decisive consideration for the view that obligations of reason require a certain variety of control. But it is a consideration that seems to shore up the intuition that just as responsibility requires control, so do obligations of (objective) reasons.

As for the sort of control, I have argued that if one reasons-wise ought to do something, give medicine A for instance, then one can do that thing and one can refrain from doing it: there is an alternative possibilities requirement for reasons-wise "right," "wrong," and "obligation." But if one is to execute one's reasons-wise obligation to do something, such as giving A, one must have control both in giving A and in refraining from giving A. It is implausible to hold that although reasons-wise "ought" requires our having alternatives, it only requires control with respect to one of the alternatives but not the other (or others); for example, regarding Peg, reasons-wise "ought" only requires that Peg have control in giving A, but not in refraining from giving A (or vice versa).

It should now be relatively straightforward to see that just as luck of the variety discussed in connection with moral responsibility precludes responsibility, such luck precludes the truth of judgments of objective *pro tanto* reasons as well, or at least it is highly credible to think so. Why? Simply because the scenario in which Peg gives medicine A to the patient suggests that when she indeterministically gives A, she lacks the sort of control in giving A (or in refraining from giving A in the non-actual world or worlds in which she does not give A) that obligations of reason require.

In sum, if Peg has an objective reason to give A, then she can give A and she can refrain from giving A. Moreover, whichever of these options she elects, she has control in doing what she does if she has an objective reason to give A. This control is largely causal: apt reason states nondeviantly cause her relevant action. Whether an agent can have this sort of control if her action is indeterministically caused, as modest libertarianism requires, is suspect. I believe similar concerns arise with modest libertarianism and subjective reasons, but I won't pursue this here.

The stage is now set to derive some interesting results concerning luck, moral and prudential obligation, certain judgments of intrinsic value, and various moral sentiments. Beginning with obligation, the thought is simply that if one has a moral (or prudential) obligation to do something, then one reasons-wise ought or it is reasons-wise permissible for one to do it. Furthermore, if one reasons-wise ought or it is reasons-wise permissible for one to do something, one's doing it cannot be a matter of luck. However, if one were indeterministically to do something—if one's action itself were indeterministically caused—then one's doing it *would* be a matter of luck.[13] So it seems that indeterministic causation of the sort modest action-centered libertarianism presupposes thus precludes moral and prudential obligation. The argument, restricted to moral obligation, can more perspicuously be formulated in this way:

(1A) If S has a moral obligation to do A, then S reasons-wise ought to do A or it is reasons-wise permissible for S to do A.

(2A) If S reasons-wise ought to do A or it is reasons-wise permissible for S to do A, then S has control both in doing A and in refraining from doing A.

(3A) If S has control both in doing A and in refraining from doing A, then S's doing A cannot be indeterministically caused in the way modest (action-centered) libertarianism implies supposedly directly free actions are caused.

Therefore:

If S has a moral obligation to do A, then S's doing A cannot be indeterministically caused in the way modest (action-centered) libertarianism implies supposedly directly free actions are caused. In other words, modest libertarianism precludes moral obligation.

This same sort of argument can be tailored to show that modest libertarianism precludes the truth of various judgments of intrinsic value. Briefly, the argument is that if something is intrinsically good, then one has an objective *pro tanto* reason to favor it. If one has such a reason to favor something, then it is reasons-wise obligatory or permissible for one to favor it. If one reasons-wise ought or it is reasons-wise permissible for one to favor something, then one has control both in favoring that thing and in refraining from favoring it. However, it seems that modest libertarianism precludes having this sort of control. So, modest libertarianism precludes the truth of germane axiological judgments.

Next, what about the moral sentiments? I focus on forgiveness to tease out a general moral. If you forgive somebody for something, you have an objective *pro tanto* reason to forgive this person for this thing. Recall, the relevant principle concerning forgiveness and objective reasons is:

Forgiveness: Necessarily, if *S* forgives *T* for something, then *S* has an objective *pro tanto* reason—being willing to cease to regard the wrong done to *S* as a reason to weaken or dissolve the relationship—to forgive *T*.

Presumably, again, if one has such a reason to forgive when one forgives, this reason is either reasons-wise obligatory or reasons-wise permissible for one. If this reason is reasons-wise obligatory or permissible for one, one has control both in doing and in refraining from doing what this reason recommends one do. This requirement of two-way control precludes doing what the reason recommends one do from being indeterministically caused in the manner modest libertarianism specifies. Thus, because of the logical link between various moral sentiments and objective *pro tanto* reasons that are either reasons-wise permissible, impermissible, or obligatory, modest libertarianism generates worries of luck with such sentiments.

In summary, owing to concerns of luck, modest libertarianism imperils the truth of judgments of objective *pro tanto* reason. By virtue of doing so, it appears that modest libertarianism imperils the truth of judgments of moral obligation, prudential obligation, and pertinent judgments of intrinsic value, and it threatens some of the moral sentiments as well.

Leaving incompatibilism, we transition next to see what impact, if any, the requirement of alternative possibilities for the truth of judgments of objective *pro-tanto* reasons has on compatibilist approaches.

6.4. COMPATIBILISM, WEAK ALTERNATIVES, AND NORMATIVE JUDGMENTS

Traditional compatibilists and their modern successors agree with traditional incompatibilists that moral responsibility requires alternatives but they conceive of these alternatives as weak. So in their view, determinism will not preclude responsibility owing to determinism's precluding the species of alternative that moral responsibility requires. Similarly, such compatibilists won't be perturbed by the fact that the truth of judgments of prudential obligation, moral obligation, perhaps some aretaic assessments, and relevant axiological evaluations presupposes our having alternatives because, again, in their estimation, the alternatives are weak and so not imperiled by determinism. Such compatibilists, however, assume the heavy burden of formulating and defending an account of *something's being a weak alternative*. Furthermore, one could not, it seems, reasonably expect traditional incompatibilists to be moved by the pleas of these compatibilists that the relevant alternatives are weak.

It merits emphasis that traditional compatibilists (and some of their contemporary followers) who endorse a conditional analysis of "can," and who believe that this sort of conditional view lies at the core of the control moral responsibility requires, need to face up to Frankfurt examples. These examples, whatever their other shortcomings, appear to pose a serious challenge to such accounts of control (Haji 2002, 66–69, Fischer 2008b, 210–12). For example, in prior-sign Frankfurt examples, the counterfactual intervener might simply take an apt desire or choice, if the conditional account in question implies that one can do otherwise had one wanted or chosen to, as the cue for intervention. In the Frankfurt example involving Yasmin, for instance, contrary to the wishes of counterfactual intervener Black, had Yasmin expressed the desire not to donate to UNICEF, Black would have intervened and forced her to donate. Such an example would seem to refute the view that responsibility requires the sort of conditional variety of freedom at issue.

6.5. ON THE VIABILITY OF SEMI-COMPATIBILISM

My primary interests, however, reside in a different sort of compatibilism, semi-compatibilism because many believe, with good reason, that this is the most promising variety of compatibilism on offer. Starting with semi-compatibilism regarding moral responsibility, a compatibilist drawn to this sort of semi-compatibilism renounces appeal to alternative possibilities altogether to account for responsibility.

Semi-compatibilism with respect to responsibility, if viable, is an attractive option for a number of reasons. Among the most significant of these is that, given the two types—weak and strong—of alternative, it is not surprising that in debates on free will and moral responsibility, different parties have frequently found themselves at an impasse over whether determinism does indeed undermine moral responsibility by ruling out alternatives. These parties have arrived at this impasse because, often but not always, concurring that responsibility requires alternatives, they have disagreed on whether the alternatives are weak or strong.[14] An alluring feature of semi-compatibilism is that it promises to break, or better perhaps, circumvent this impasse altogether by insisting that moral responsibility does not require alternatives of *any* sort, strong or weak.

We recorded that semi-compatibilists do not deny that responsibility presupposes our having freedom or control; rather, they deny that this control requires our having access to alternatives. We said, in addition, that semi-compatibilists have drawn significantly on Frankfurt examples to energize their variety of compatibilism.

It is worth discussing whether semi-compatibilism with respect to responsibility is indeed viable. To make the task of tackling this difficult issue manageable, provisionally assume that Frankfurt examples impugn the principle of alternative possibilities concerning responsibility. We will return to this assumption shortly. My modest aim is to motivate the view that the rational credentials of semi-compatibilism regarding responsibility turn on whether several *other* normative principles are true or false. In what is to follow in the remainder of this section, first, I introduce some but certainly not all of these principles. Then I map out three positions regarding the viability of semi-compatibilism with respect to responsibility, the tenability of each depending upon whether a subset of these principles is true.

It will be convenient to bring together some of the principles invoked in previous chapters.

The Principle of Alternative Possibilities Concerning Responsibility (PAP-R): Persons are morally responsible for what they have done only if they could have done otherwise.

Praiseworthiness presupposes Obligation (PO): An agent, S, is morally praiseworthy for doing something, A, only if it is overall morally obligatory or overall morally permissible for S to do A.

Blameworthiness presupposes Wrongness (BO): An agent, S, is morally blameworthy for doing something, A, only if it is overall morally wrong for S to do A.

The Moral "Ought" Implies "Can" or Kant's Law: If it is morally obligatory for an agent, S, to do something, A, then S can do A; and if it is morally obligatory for S to refrain from doing A, then S can refrain from doing A.

Obligations are tied to reasons (OR): If an agent has a moral obligation to do something, A, then the agent has an objective *pro tanto* reason to do A.

The Reasons Cluster:

Reasons-Wise "Ought" Implies "Can" (Reason Ought/Can): If an agent, *S*, has most reason to do something, *A*, and, thus, if *S* reasons-wise ought to do *A*, then *S* can do *A*. (There are parallel principles concerning reasons-wise "right" and reasons-wise "wrong.")

Reasons-Wise "Ought Not" Implies "Can Refrain From" (Reason Ought Not/Can Refrain From): If an agent, *S*, reasons-wise ought not to do something, *A*, then *S* can refrain from doing *A*.

Reasons-Wise "Ought Not" is equivalent to Reasons-Wise "Wrong" (Reason Ought Not/Wrong): An agent, *S*, reasons-wise ought not to do *A* if and only if it is reasons-wise wrong for *S* to do *A*.

Reasons-Wise Wrongness Requires Alternatives (Reason/Wrong Alternative): If it is reasons-wise wrong for an agent, *S*, to do *A*, then *S* can refrain from doing *A*. (Again, there are parallel principles concerning reasons-wise "right" and reasons-wise "obligation.")

To facilitate mapping out various positions concerning the viability of semi-compatibilism, assume that the principle if one is morally obligated to do something, then one has an objective *pro tanto* reason to do it (*OR*), is true. It's hard to see how one can deny this principle. Here are three relevant options:

Position 1: Accept PO (praiseworthiness requires obligation or permissibility), BO (blameworthiness requires wrongness), and the principles in the Reasons Cluster.

This position implies that semi-compatibilism is not viable. More circumspectly, if *PO*, *BO*, and the principles in the *Reasons Cluster* are true, then semi-compatibilism with respect to moral responsibility is in jeopardy. To explain: if moral praiseworthiness is tied to moral obligation or moral right (*PO*), moral blameworthiness is tied to moral wrong (*BO*), these deontic evaluations are associated with objective *pro tanto* reasons (in the manner explained in section 2.2.), and there is an alternative possibilities requirement for having such reasons, then both moral praiseworthiness and moral blameworthiness presuppose our having alternatives. So, if one accepts *PO*, *BO*, and the *Reasons Cluster*, then one should accept the principle of alternative possibilities regarding responsibility as well. (Or, more cautiously, if one accepts *PO*, *BO*, and the *Reasons Cluster*, then one should also accept the principle that persons are praiseworthy or blameworthy for what they have done only if they could have done otherwise.) One should, consequently, be suspicious about Frankfurt examples.[15]

> *Position 2: Accept PO (praiseworthiness requires obligation or permissibility) and BO (blameworthiness requires wrongness); discard reasons-wise "ought" implies "can."*

Just as some have rejected the moral "ought" implies "can" principle, so these persons may reject the reasons-wise "ought" implies "can" principle. On this position, semi-compatibilism would be viable but at a cost some would deem too high.[16]

It may be worth noting the following. What we may call the "*Obligation Cluster*" is a set of principles with these members:

> *Moral "Ought" Implies "Can" or Kant's Law*: If it is morally obligatory for an agent, *S*, to do something, *A*, then *S* can do *A*; and if it is morally obligatory for *S* to refrain from doing something, *A*, then *S* can refrain from doing *A*. (There are parallel principles concerning moral "right" and moral "wrong.")
>
> *Moral "Ought" Implies "Can Refrain From" (Moral Ought/Can Refrain From)*: If it is morally obligatory for an agent, *S*, to do

something, *A*, then *S* can refrain from doing *A*; and if it is morally obligatory for *S* to refrain from doing *A*, then *S* can do *A*. (There are similar principles concerning moral "right" and moral "wrong.")

Moral "Ought not" is equivalent to moral "Wrong" (Moral Ought Not/Wrong): Agent, *S*, morally ought not to do *A* if and only if it is morally wrong (i.e., morally impermissible) for *S* to do *A*.

An argument structurally parallel to the one for the conclusion that reasons-wise "ought" implies reasons-wise "can refrain from," in which occurrences of "reasons-wise 'ought'," "reasons-wise 'right'," and "reasons-wise 'wrong'" are replaced by "moral 'ought'," "moral 'right'," and "moral 'wrong'" establishes the moral "ought" implies "can refrain from" principle (*Moral Ought/Can Refrain From*) and the analogous principles concerning "right" and "wrong."

Here, very briefly, is the pertinent sequence of reasoning. Commencing with moral wrong, it is straightforward to confirm that "wrong" implies "can refrain from." For: if it's morally wrong for one to do something, one morally ought not to do it; if one morally ought not to do something, one can refrain from doing it (from *Kant's Law*); therefore, if it's morally wrong for one to do something, one can refrain from doing it. This conclusion, together with the moral "wrong" implies "can" principle, confirms that there is an alternative possibilities requirement for moral "wrong."

Regarding obligation, if one morally ought to refrain from doing something, it's morally wrong for one to do it (from "ought not" is equivalent to "wrong"); if it's morally wrong for one to do something, one can do it (from "wrong" implies "can"); therefore, if one morally ought to refrain from doing something, one can do it. This conclusion, in turn, in conjunction with the principle that if one ought to refrain from doing something, one can refrain from doing it, establishes that there is an alternative possibilities requirement for obligation.

Finally, there is no similar way to derive the proposition that rightness, likewise, requires alternative possibilities. For even if it is agreed that "right" implies "can," there is no principle like the principle that moral "ought not" is equivalent to "wrong" that will allow us to infer that "right" implies "can refrain." Nevertheless, it is very plausible that "right" does imply "can refrain." For, first, as I have previously underscored, unless we have sound reason to believe otherwise, the control requirements of right should not differ from those of obligation and wrong. Second, if we deny that "right" implies "can refrain," inasmuch as obligatoriness and wrongness do require alternative possibilities, we are in danger of being encumbered with the dubious view that it is morally right for one to do whatever acts, heinous or otherwise, that one cannot avoid doing.

Should one accept the principle that praiseworthiness requires obligation or permissibility, blameworthiness requires wrongness, and the *Obligation Cluster*, then again one should not accept semi-compatibilism. If one finds compelling the analysis of moral obligation in terms of worldly value that I adumbrated earlier (sec. 4.4 in chap. 4), one would have strong grounds to accept the *Obligation Cluster*.

Position 3: Reject PO (praiseworthiness requires obligation or permissibility) and BO (blameworthiness requires wrongness); accept the Reasons Cluster, or the Obligation Cluster, or both these clusters).

On this option, semi-compatibilism is still in the running. This is the option I favor (and for which I have argued elsewhere, e.g., Haji 2002), but some may find the price of renouncing the principles that praiseworthiness requires obligation or that permissibility and blameworthiness requires wrongness exceedingly high. In my view, moral praiseworthiness and moral blameworthiness are conceptually tied to nonculpable belief in what is overall morally obligatory, overall morally right, overall morally wrong, or deontic value in the fashion to be explained in the next section, and not to what is in fact overall obligatory, right, or wrong.

Worthy of mention is the following. McNamara (2008; 2011), as I summarized before, has defended a deontic system that represents the deontic notions, among others, of right, wrong, obligation, exceeding the moral minimum, and permissible suboptimality; as well as responsibility notions such as praiseworthiness and blameworthiness. Not only does the model validate *Kant's Law* and the moral "right" implies "can" principle, it validates as well the *falsity* of the praiseworthiness requires obligation or permissibility principle (*PO*) and the blameworthiness requires wrongness principle (*BO*).

6.6. REVISITING FRANKFURT EXAMPLES

Are Frankfurt examples indeed cogent? I start with two initial points, and then examine one argument against the effectiveness of such examples and a reply to this argument.

As for the initial points, first, in the example with which we have worked, on the basis of certain reasons Yasmin decides to donate to UNICEF in Stage 1. Assume (although I think this assumption is open to serious doubt) that these reasons are objective *pro tanto* reasons. If it is such reasons that causally issue in her deciding to donate, then owing to there being a requirement of alternative possibilities for having such reasons, in Stage 1 she could have decided to refrain from donating. To be clear, if Yasmin decides to donate for an objective *pro tanto* reason, then she could have refrained from deciding to donate because there is an alternative possibilities requirement for deciding or forming intentions on the basis of such reasons. In Stage 2, however, provided all relevant alternatives are expunged, Yasmin's deciding to donate could not have causally issued from her having objective *pro tanto* reasons. Some theorists who are inclined toward the view that all reasons are, in the end, objective should not accept one alleged moral of Frankfurt examples, to wit, the principle of alternative possibilities regarding responsibility is false. Other theorists who accept the view that having objective *pro tanto* reasons requires having access to alternatives might argue that another lesson to be learned from Frankfurt examples, in addition to the proposed lesson that responsibility does not require alternatives, is that although responsibility presupposes our having reasons—if one is morally responsible for doing something, then one has a reason for doing it—responsibility does not presuppose our having objective *pro tanto* reasons; perhaps responsibility only presupposes possession of normative Davidsonian reasons. These considerations highlight the fact that Frankfurt examples are not neutral regarding the sorts of reason responsibility requires.

Still, one may press this issue that I previously touched upon (in section 3.5.3, in chap. 3): *is* there a symmetry concerning an alternative possibilities requirement with respect to Davidsonian and objective reasons? Specifically, do both sorts of reason presuppose that if one has a reason of either sort to do something, then one could have done otherwise? Symmetry would, of course, threaten the view that Frankfurt cases undermine the principle of alternative possibilities concerning responsibility. However, there are, I think, reasonable grounds to deny this symmetry in a fashion congenial to the Frankfurt proponent: even if responsibility requires normative Davidsonian reasons, there is no requirement of alternative possibilities for having such reasons. For one thing, lack of alternatives does not preclude one from having desires and beliefs, the fundamental constituents of typical Davidsonian reasons. For another thing, suppose you have an objective reason to give medicine A to a patient owing to your having a moral obligation to give A to this patient. The objective reasons-wise "ought" implies "can" (and the objective reasons-wise "ought not" implies "can refrain from"); I don't see any reason to deny this. As we saw, crucially these principles, in combination with others, lead to the conclusion that there is an alternative possibilities requirement for reasons-wise right, wrong, and obligation when the reasons are objective. Suppose, now, you believe falsely that on a certain occasion you morally ought to give A to save the patient. This belief, together with a desire of yours to do what you morally ought to do to save the patient on this occasion, is a normative Davidsonian reason you have to save the patient. But one's believing that one ought to give A—a subjective reason—unlike its being true that one ought to give A, does *not* entail that one can give A. At least I doubt that this is so. Since, "ought" implies "can" doesn't "apply," as we may say, with such subjective reasons, these being constituents of pertinent Davidsonian reasons, one might plausibly deny that there is an alternative possibilities requirement for having normative Davidsonian reasons. In brief, one can't persuasively argue from the premise that pertinent subjective reasons that are constituents of Davidsonian reasons, such as the reason that one believes that one morally ought to give A, imply "can," in consort with other principles, such as "ought not" is equivalent to "wrong," entail that there is an alternative possibilities requirement for such subjective reasons, and, hence, by generalization, for Davidsonian reasons. The argument falls at its first premise.

Second, imagine that Yasmin is putatively morally praiseworthy for doing what it is that she supposedly cannot, in her situation, avoid doing: deciding to donate to UNICEF. If *PO*, however, is true—if moral praiseworthiness requires moral obligation or moral permissibility—and there is an alternative possibilities requirement for the truth of morally deontic judgments, then it would seem that Frankfurt-examples are not as decisive as one might initially have thought them to be. Assessing Frankfurt examples independently of assessing *PO* and *BO* may be injudicious if one is interested in whether moral praiseworthiness and moral blameworthiness require alternatives.

This brings us to one instructive dispute in the extensive and interesting debate on whether or not Frankfurt examples are persuasive. Introduce a slight change in the Frankfurt example involving Yasmin: Suppose Yasmin decides to spend the money on some trifles although she is aware that she morally should have donated to UNICEF, and she is supposedly morally blameworthy for making this decision. So modified, the Frankfurt example seeks to show that Yasmin is morally to blame despite not being able to do otherwise. Now, however, consider this argument that David Copp and David Widerker independently develop against Frankfurt examples:

> (1) If one is blameworthy for doing something, then one ought not to do it (from the blameworthiness requires wrongness principle, *BO*).
>
> (2) If one ought not to do something (such as deciding to spend money on trifles), then one can refrain from doing it (from *Kant's Law*).
>
> (3) Therefore, if one is blameworthy for doing something, then one can refrain from doing it (Widerker 1991; Copp 1997; 2003).

Since, as we are taking for granted, Yasmin cannot refrain from deciding to spend on trifles (and she cannot, subsequently, refrain from spending), (3)—the last line of the above argument that blameworthiness for something requires the ability to refrain from dong that thing—in conjunction with these facts imply that Yasmin, in her "Frankfurt situation," is not blameworthy for deciding to spend; nor is she blameworthy for spending. So it is concluded that Frankfurt examples do not impugn the principle of alternative possibilities regarding moral blameworthiness.

Fischer advances considerations against *Kant's Law*, thus undermining premise (2) of the Copp/Widerker argument, to defend Frankfurt. To adumbrate Fischer's reply (see Fischer 1999; 2003), suppose that some agent, *S*, is blameworthy for an intentional omission:

(1F) *S* is blameworthy for failing to do *A* (or for not-*A*-ing).

Appealing to the blameworthiness requires wrongness principle:

(*Bo*): *S* is morally blameworthy for not doing *A* only if *S* morally ought to do *A*,

it may be inferred that *S*'s failing to do what *S* did is wrong:

(2F) *S*'s not-*A*-ing is wrong; that is, *S* ought not to fail to do *A*.

In addition, if *Kant's Law* is true, in particular if "ought not" implies "can refrain from," from (2F), we derive:

(3F) *S* can refrain from failing to do *A*; that is, *S* can *A*.

So, assuming that the blameworthiness-requires-wrongness principle (*BO*) is true, Fischer proposes that a proponent of *Kant's Law* is committed to the view that if one is blameworthy for failing to do something, then one can do that thing:

(4F) If *S* is blameworthy for not doing *A*, then *S* can *A*.

But Fischer claims that a subset of Frankfurt examples involving omissions undercuts (4F):

> I believe that there are Frankfurt-type omissions cases that are relevantly similar to Frankfurt-type cases with respect to actions. That is, there are cases in which an agent is morally responsible for not *X*ing, although he cannot in fact *X*. . . . Some of these are cases in which an agent is blameworthy for not *X*ing and yet he cannot *X*. In fact . . . anyone who accepts the Frankfurt-type action cases must accept that there are such omissions-cases. . . . It is then precisely the basic intuitions elicited by the Frankfurt-type cases which show that the most natural justification of the 'ought-implies-can' maxim is faulty. Although this certainly does not decisively refute the maxim, it does suggest that it is not ad hoc for anyone who accepts the 'intended interpretation' of Frankfurt-type cases to reject the 'ought-implies-can' maxim. (Fischer 2003, 248–49.)

All told, Fischer may be construed as arguing that appropriately constructed Frankfurt examples give us reason to reject both the principle of alternative possibilities concerning blameworthiness (*PAP-B*) and *Kant's Law*: he proposes that since blameworthiness does require wrongness (that is, since *BO* is true), and, moreover, since Yasmin is morally to blame for deciding to spend on trifles (and for spending on them) in her Frankfurt situation, we ought to reject *Kant's Law*. We ought not to retain, as Widerker and Copp suggest, the principle of alternative possibilities concerning blameworthiness, or not jettison, as Widerker and Copp seem to recommend, the judgment that it is impermissible for Yasmin to spend on trifles. On

Fischer's view, in Frankfurt cases where the agent is morally *blameworthy* for some omission or commission, the omission or commission is *also* morally *impermissible*, despite the absence of alternatives.

Commenting on the Copp/Widerker argument and Fischer's reply, I agree with Fischer on Frankfurt examples: whether it is an omission or a commission at issue, Fischer in his characteristic elegant way has strongly defended such examples (see, for example, his recent 2010 and 2011). But as I have explained elsewhere, Fischer's rejection of *Kant's Law* is another matter. I summarize key concerns with his rejection.

First, suppose it is agreed that certain Frankfurt examples involving omissions cast doubt on the view that there are no cases in which one is blameworthy for not doing something when one cannot do that thing. However, defenders of *Kant's Law* who *reject* the blameworthiness requires wrongness principle, can accept the view that *Kant's Law* is valid, perhaps on the basis of accepting an analysis of the concept of moral obligation that entails *Kant's Law*, without thereby being committed to accepting the claim that *Kant's Law* is valid because if it were not, there could be cases in which one is blameworthy for failing to do something that one could not do.

Second, (4F), spelled out more fully, is just the principle of alternative possibilities concerning blameworthiness (*PAP-B*) which says that a person is blameworthy for performing some action (or for failing to perform some action) only if she has the power not to perform (or to perform) that action. It appears that Fischer's objection rests on the presupposition that:

> *Kant's Law* is *relevantly just like PAP-B*. So this law stands or falls with *PAP-B*; if Frankfurt examples falsify *PAP-B*, such cases falsify *Kant's Law* as well.

REASON'S DEBT TO FREEDOM

For, if one renounced this presupposition, one might well concede that Frankfurt examples involving omissions call the principle of alternative possibilities concerning blameworthiness (*PAP-B*) into question without conceding that such cases call *Kant's Law* into question.

But *Kant's Law* is *not* relevantly like *PAP-B*. Rather, *Kant's Law*—a "power" or "control" principle for obligation—is pertinently like the following control principle,

> *Control*: One is blameworthy (or, more generally, morally responsible) for performing an action only if one can perform that action.

Control simply affirms the connection between control and blameworthiness or moral responsibility; its gist is that one cannot be responsible for an action unless one has control over it or in doing it. Not only is *Control* true—in the least it has very widespread support—Frankfurt examples involving actions do *not* falsify this principle. Fischer (e.g., 2006) himself has forcefully argued that in such examples, the agent who cannot do otherwise *does* seem morally responsible for his pertinent behavior and evidently does have control ("guidance control") over this behavior. As Zimmerman has indicated, though, the principle of alternative possibilities concerning blameworthiness (*PAP-B*) is a contraction of *Control* and:

> *Action Requires Alternatives*: One can perform [refrain from performing] some action only if one can refrain from performing [perform] that action (Zimmerman 1996, 86).

A Frankfurt example undermines *Action Requires Alternatives*. In such an example, although it is within the pertinent agent's power to perform the relevant action, it is false that it is within his power not to perform that action. But Frankfurt examples leave the principle that "ought not" is equivalent to "wrong" intact. It is this principle and not *Action Requires Alternatives* that preserves the link between obligation and alternative possibilities (Zimmerman 1996, 86–87).

Third, as I have already intimated, the principle that blameworthiness requires wrongness (*BO*) is controversial if not outrightly false. Although they differ on their assessment of Frankfurt cases, Copp, Widerker, and Fischer all accept this principle.[17] *BO*, however, is susceptible to counterexample (Haji 1998; 2002; 2009a). Here's an illustration: Kenzo believes that he can prevent a bomb from going off if and only if he presses a button at 7:00 p.m. Suppose, further, that he inexcusably forgets to press the button at this time (he is too engrossed in the England versus Germany World Cup soccer game). Here, we may assume that he is blameworthy for failing to press the button. But, suppose, in addition, that the button is malfunctioning: even if he had pressed it, the bomb would still have gone off. Arguably, Kenzo's not pressing the button is not wrong but he is, nonetheless, blameworthy for not pressing it.

In addition, the possibility of suberogation presents a serious problem for the blameworthiness requires wrongness principle. Some background on the supererogatory and the suberogatory will help to expose this problem.

Common sense morality recognizes, among other normative statuses, the supererogatory, roughly, permissible action that is beyond the call of duty; and the suberogatory, again, loosely, permissible suboptimality. It also sanctions ascriptions of moral praiseworthiness and moral blameworthiness, respectively, to those who supererogate and to those who suberogate. If this is so, we can draw some revealing conclusions about the principle that blameworthiness requires wrongness.

Stock illustrations of supererogatory behavior include the mailperson's rescuing the child from the inferno at considerable risk to her own life (Feldman 1978, 48), or the soldier's sacrificing his life by throwing himself on the grenade to save his comrades (Urmson 1958). Many advocates of the supererogatory concede that the supererogatory is not confined to the saintly or heroic; unmomentous action, doing small favors, for example, can also qualify as going beyond duty (see, for e.g., Heyd 1982, 142). Although there is controversy on just how the concept of the supererogatory is to be analyzed, there is a fair measure of agreement on these elements: a supererogatory action is morally optional in that it is not overall morally wrong or overall obligatory; it is not morally indifferent and so is morally significant (McNamara 1996, 420–21); indeed, as Zimmerman remarks, it is especially valuable in some way, more so than any morally optional but nonsupererogatory alternative (1996, 234–35); and, lastly, it goes beyond duty's call. Regarding this third feature, McNamara's remarks are especially suggestive. He introduces the idea of doing the minimum morality demands:

> Suppose that in virtue of promising to get in touch with you, I become obligated to do so. Suppose . . . I can fulfill this obligation in two ways: by writing you a letter or by stopping by on the way to the store. (Imagine that you're an eccentric who hates phones.) Add that my other obligations make me too busy permissibly to do both. Finally, suppose that, morally speaking, I put in a better performance if I pay you a visit rather that write you, even though either one is permissible. Then if I *do the minimum morality demands*, I will write rather than visit. . . . The important thing to note is that what is necessitated by *meeting morality's demands in a minimally acceptable way* is not to be confused with doing what I am obligated to do—with doing what

morality demands of me. For morality demands only that I contact you and that I don't both write and visit, whereas doing the minimum that morality demands includes these plus writing you.... [S]ome such notion is vital to the concept of supererogation. For if it is possible for me to discharge my obligations in a supererogatory way (in a better than minimal way), then it ought to be possible for me merely to discharge them in a minimal way—and vice versa. (1996, 425–26)

McNamara proposes that a supererogatory action is a permissible one whose performance is incompatible with doing the minimum (1996, 429). In a more recent piece (2011), he refines the analysis in this way: a supererogatory action is optional, its performance is praiseworthy, its omission is not blameworthy, and it is precluded by doing the minimum.

Suberogatory actions, the roughly symmetric counterparts of supererogatory ones, are morally optional, not morally indifferent, and are offensive or fall short of decency. In one of Julia Driver's putative examples of a suberogatory act, a man who takes a seat on a train, thereby intentionally preventing two other people from sitting together despite availability of another seat, does no wrong but falls short of decency (1992, 286–87). Roderick Chisholm and Ernest Sosa propose that minor discourtesy, such as taking too long in a restaurant when others are waiting, may also be suberogatory (1966, 326). Assuming that there are minimal, better than minimal, and maximal ways of satisfying morality's demands, McNamara recommends that something will be permissibly suboptimal if it is permissible and precluded by doing the maximum (1996, 434). A suberogatory action, he proposes (2011), is morally optional, its performance is blameworthy, it omission is not praiseworthy, and it is precluded by doing the maximum.

Now for our preliminary lesson, assume that though he mistakenly believes he is doing wrong by preventing the lovers from sitting together despite availability of another seat, Grumpy fails to give up his seat. Here, Grumpy may well be blameworthy for not giving up his seat even though, assume, his not giving up his seat is suberogatory and hence morally optional. After all, from his perspective, he is doing wrong: he acts in light of the belief that he is doing wrong. But then Grumpy's case challenges the principle *BO* that one is to blame for an action only if one ought not to perform that action.

As a fuller exposition of this important point, embellish the "contact" case so that I can fulfill the obligation to contact you in these ways: putting in a personal appearance at your store (w1); phoning you (w2); writing you (w3); painting a message on your store window (w4). Suppose, again, that my other obligations make me too busy permissibly to do any two of these things; doing one of them precludes me permissibly from doing any of the others. Finally, imagine that, of these four options, w1 is relatively best, and in the progression from w1 to w4, the pertinent value of each decreases so that w4 is relatively worst; morally, I put in a better performance if I visit than if I phone, or write, or paint a message. Lest one think these rankings arbitrary, we may add some more details. I'm a store owner, too, and you and I are friendly rivals. I'm a few blocks away from you, and during periods when business is very slow—usually early afternoons—I can take a nap, close the store for a bit to attend to other concerns, such as zipping over to the bank, post office, and so on. To nurture our growing friendship, it would be better to put in a personal appearance than to phone you. Writing a note is acceptable but too impersonal; it is something neither one us would do. Finally, painting a message on your store window would cause you a fair bit of trouble; you would have to clean up the window, and so forth. Suppose that I'm aware of these relative rankings. Intuitively, at least, if I deliberately paint, full well knowing that it wouldn't have taken much for me to do significantly better—I could have sauntered over in the afternoon—I'm blameworthy for painting. Similarly, if I deliberately write, well aware that I could have done better by putting in a personal appearance, I am blameworthy (even if to only a minor degree) for writing: I act in light of the nonculpable belief that I could have done far better "deontically."

So far, I haven't said anything about the primary moral statuses of w1–w4. Assume that w1–w3 are permissible ways to fulfill my obligation to contact you whereas w4—painting the message—is not; it is impermissible. Intuitively, it still seems that if I write, I am blameworthy. From my perspective nothing essential has changed: I know that I could have done much better deontically by visiting rather than writing; yet I still deliberately choose to do, and do, what I correctly take to be deontically inferior.

Assume that the "deontic value," so to speak, that differentiates writing (w3) from painting (w4) is minimal in this respect: w4 is just that tad bit deontically worse than w3, the difference being sufficient to render w4 impermissible; but assume, further, that I do not know this. Again, I see little reason to believe that this marginal shift in deontic value, assuming no other changes in the scenario, can underpin the view that whereas I would be morally to blame if I were to paint a message on your store (because doing so would be impermissible), I would not be to blame if I were to write (because writing is permissible).

More fundamentally, we accept the view that one can do moral wrong but not be morally blameworthy for the wrongdoing; we acknowledge that one can have a legitimate excuse. In such cases, the negative deontic assessment of the act is not matched by a negative responsibility appraisal of the agent; agent and act appraisals—or, if one prefers, these two varieties of moral appraisal—come apart. But if this view is accepted, there is little reason to deny that it is possible that a negative responsibility appraisal of the agent not be matched by a negative deontic appraisal of some pertinent act of that agent.

Yet further on the blameworthiness requires wrongness principle (*BO*), for many years partisans of commonsense morality have implored moral theorists not just tacitly to rule out classes of action common sense morality countenances by one's theorizing. Acceptance of *BO* rules out suberogation. The blameworthiness requires wrongness principle is also inconsistent with what Gregory Mellema (1991) calls "quasi-offense." An act is a quasi-offense for an agent if and only if it is morally optional for that agent, its agent is morally blameworthy for performing it, and its agent would be morally praiseworthy for refraining from performing it. (One might want to add to this trio of conditions that an act is a quasi-offense only if it is precluded by doing the maximum.) Here's an example that Mellema advances:

> Begin by considering an act *o* whose performance by an agent *S* is an offence. Perhaps *S* is in a restaurant and *o* consists in walking to the next table and empting the contents of his plate upon a man whose behavior is particularly obnoxious. . . . Assume next that the temptation for *S* to perform *o* is extremely strong. Suppose, for example, that the man at the next table is making loud jokes and mocking gestures about the physical disabilities of *S*'s wife. For this reason *S* is livid with rage, and it requires great effort for *S* to resist the temptation to perform *o*. . . . [Consider a world *w* in which] *S* deliberately chooses not to resist his strong desire to seek revenge, and he ends up causing great anguish to his wife and the restaurant's owner, as well as ruining the man's expensive three-piece suit. Here it seems reasonable to judge that

his refraining from resisting temptation is deserving of blame. It is in his power to resist the temptation in w, and he deliberately chooses not to do so, knowing full well the consequences which will result. . . . One would be justified in having expected better of him, for he could at least have made an effort to resist temptation, and he can justifiably be criticized for his failure to do so. . . . In this example, then, S's resisting the temptation is an act which is praiseworthy and blameworthy to refrain from performing. (1991, 108–09)

Resistance to renouncing *BO* may stem from adherence to the "Traditional Scheme" of deontic logic in which all acts are divided into three jointly exhaustive and mutually exclusive classes: every act is obligatory, optional, or impermissible, but no act falls into more than one of these classes. Roughly, deontic value is that value in virtue of which acts (or states of affairs) have one or more of the moral statuses such as *being obligatory* or *being permissible*. The Traditional Scheme allows for a "non-ranked" range of permissible options when no option is maximally deontically best, two or more options have equal deontic value, and the deontic value of each such option exceeds that of all other options. But our ordinary moral conceptual scheme allows for the notions of permissibly doing the least one can do, and permissibly doing more than one has to do (McNamara 1996a; 2011a). If this is so, then it is possible to have a range of "ranked permissible options," some such options being deontically better than others. The possibility of having such options opens the doors to being blameworthy (or praiseworthy) for doing something permissible that is precluded by doing either the permissibly minimum or the permissibly maximum. When one supererogates, one is praiseworthy for going beyond the call. But one can also be blameworthy for going beyond the call. Suppose Marion sees a baby trapped in a burning building. If she does the minimum morality requires, she pulls the fire alarm which is a block away and directs the fire personnel to the blaze, and doing the minimum (in her circumstances) is incompatible with rescuing the child. Marion, though, goes beyond the call by rushing into the building. Now assume that she rescues the child only to hand him over, for selfish gain, to traffickers in vital organs. Marion goes beyond the call but (given innocuous assumptions) is blameworthy for doing so.

An additional point about the blameworthiness requires wrongness principle, *BO*, is that if it is accepted then, somewhat paradoxically, Fischer's reply to the Copp/Widerker argument calls semi-compatibilism regarding responsibility, something dear to Fischer, in question. We should note that Fischer's argument against *Kant's Law* fails, and on several fronts. In particular, even if we accept the view that blameworthiness requires wrongness (which we should not), *Kant's Law* survives Fischer's criticisms. But I have argued that *Kant's Law* and other principles (*Reason Ought/Can, Reason Ought Not/Can Refrain From*, etc.) confirm that there is an alternative possibilities requirement for moral right, wrong, and obligation. Thus, if we accept the principle that blameworthiness requires wrongness, and wrongness does in fact require alternatives, semi-compatibilism with respect to moral responsibility flies to the wind.

There is a bit of unfinished business to which I wish, if only briefly and in a highly preliminary fashion, to attend. I have favored, as the epistemic condition regarding blameworthiness, the principle that one is culpable for something only if one does it on the basis of the nonculpable belief that one is doing wrong; one is blameworthy only if one willingly does what one nonculpably takes to be wrong (Haji 1998, 2002, 2009b):

B1: *S* is morally blameworthy for doing *A* only if *S* acts in light of the nonculpable belief that *S*'s doing *A* is morally wrong.

The embellished contact case, however, suggests another principle:

B2: *S* is morally blameworthy for doing *A* only if *S* acts in light of the nonculpable belief that *S* could have done something that is morally deontically better than doing *A*.

Ignoring pressure from the direction of determinism or indeterminism, assume that people are blameworthy for at least some of their behavior. Many are blameworthy even though they don't act on the basis of the belief that they could have done something deontically better. They are to blame by virtue of willingly and freely doing what they think is wrong. Similarly, presumably *some* people are blameworthy because they willingly and freely do what they take to be deontically inferior although, when they do some such thing, they don't act in light of the belief that they are doing wrong. We need a single principle that captures the insights of B1 and B2. Here's a preliminary—and I caution only tentative—suggestion:

B3: *S* is morally blameworthy for doing *A* only if *S* does *A* on the basis of the nonculpable belief either that *S*'s doing *A* is morally wrong or that *S*'s doing *A* is morally deontically inferior to something else that *S* could have done instead. (B3 should not, of course, be read as *S*'s having the *disjunctive* belief; rather, when blameworthy, *S* acts in light of the belief expressed by either one but not both of the disjuncts.)

In short, assuming all other conditions of blameworthiness are not in question, if you willingly do what you nonculpably take to be wrong, you're blameworthy; also, if you willingly do what you nonculpably take to be deontically inferior to something else you could have done instead, you're blameworthy. Regarding the latter, some people who are unfamiliar with the technical notion of deontic value might express the point in this way: "I did something that is right but I could easily have done something else that is more right or better."[18]

Finally, I briefly revert to addressing an asymmetry I endorse that many have found puzzling. I believe that Frankfurt examples do exert considerable pressure against the view that responsibility requires alternatives. So, I think there is no requirement of alternative possibilities for responsibility. However, I've also argued that there is such a requirement for moral obligation. Why this asymmetry? One answer the discussion so far suggests is that obligation is essentially associated with objective reasons, the having of which requires alternatives, unlike responsibility that is essentially linked to normative Davidsonian reasons, the having of which does not presuppose our having alternatives.

6.7. OTHER VARIETIES OF SEMI-COMPATIBILISM

As for the viability of other varieties of semi-compatibilism, semi-compatibilism regarding obligation, whether the obligation is prudential or moral, can be thought of as the view that determinism is compatible with obligation quite apart from whether determinism expunges alternatives, strong or weak. Similarly, semi-compatibilism regarding intrinsic value says that determinism is compatible with intrinsic value independently of whether determinism rules out the species of freedom that involves access to alternative possibilities. I suppose there is something such as semi-compatibilism regarding welfare (or happiness): determinism is compatible with personal welfare (or happiness) apart from whether it is compatible with free will. One of the pertinent conclusions from the first part of this work—there is an alternative possibilities requirement for the truth of judgments of moral obligation, prudential obligation, and intrinsic value—together with these semi-compatibilist views implies that semi-compatibilism regarding obligation and semi-compatibilism regarding intrinsic value cannot be sustained. Similarly, on some views of personal well-being and happiness—for example, on a hedonistic view such as *Simple Hedonism*—semi-compatibilism regarding welfare (or happiness) is precluded. One may try to develop a species of semi-compatibilism concerning various aretaic evaluations. If these evaluations, however, are essentially tied to our having objective *pro tanto* reasons, one shouldn't be too optimistic about the prospects of this variety of semi-compatibilism.

Suppose that no world can be intrinsically good (or intrinsically bad or intrinsically neutral) unless anyone who contemplates the atoms, if any, that the world contains has objective *pro tanto* reasons to favor (or to disfavor, or to be indifferent to) these atoms when one contemplates them. If one has an objective *pro tanto* reason to favor something, one has a relevant alternative. If this alternative is weak, then, because obligation supervenes on worldly intrinsic value, we may once again conclude that semi-compatibilism regarding obligation is jeopardized.

Overall, we may conclude that incompatibilists *who favor a strong sense of "can"* should be drawn to the view that living without free will comes with serious costs: determinism imperils various normative appraisals, such as appraisals of obligation, prudence, perhaps personal well-being, and on some views happiness. In addition, determinism endangers pertinent evaluations of intrinsic value, and it may also cast doubt on various aretaic assessments, as well as the rationality of our having certain moral sentiments. Because there is a requirement of alternative possibilities for the truth of judgments of these sorts of appraisal and for the relevant moral sentiments to accommodate these things, compatibilists should opt for a weak sense of "can." A consequence of doing so would be that sundry species of semi-compatibilism, for example, semi-compatibilism regarding moral or prudential obligation, are not sustainable.

NOTES

1. Watson (1998, 138) suggests that a conditional conception of freedom is central in various normative contexts.
2. Clarke (2008) critically discusses these new dispositional views.
3. I further caution the reader that the part of *IV-1* to which I am attracted is the part that implies that if something is intrinsically good, then one has a reason to favor it.
4. Such accounts have been defended or discussed by Dennett 1978; Fischer 1995; Mele 1995; Kane 1996; 1999a; 1999b; and Clarke 2000; 2003.
5. A recent defense of this sort of view is to be found in Kane 1996.
6. Franklin (2011) has recently advanced a powerful criticism of the luck objection. See Haji n.d. for a response to Franklin. More on the luck objection can be found in Waller 1988; Berofsky 2000; Hume 1739/2000, 261–62; van Inwagen 2000; 2011; Clarke 2003; 2011; Mele 1999a; 1999b; 2006; 2007; Nelkin 2007; O'Connor 2007; 2011; Almeida and Bernstein 2011; Ekstrom 2011; Kane 2011.
7. I don't deny that one may perform an akratic action that it is rational for one to perform.
8. See Mele 2006, 60–61 and 125–29 on breakdowns of agency.
9. For the first and third of these explanations, see Mele 1987, chaps. 5–6. For the second of these explanations, see, e.g., Milo 1984, esp. chap. 5.
10. Other concerns are discussed in Haji 2005, sec. 2.
11. I am not ruling out the possibility that if one event causes another, the two may occur simultaneously.
12. These conditions pertain to self-forming decisions.
13. Here I am allowing that an event that is not a decision but is an action can itself be indeterministically caused.

14. A highly informative summary of some of the relevant issues concerning such an impasse can be found in Kane 1996, chap. 4.

15. Both Widerker (1991) and Copp (1997; 2003) accept *BO*. (However, see Widerker 2011, 281, for what appears to be a change of heart regarding *BO*.) It seems Copp accepts the principle that "ought" implies "can"; it is less clear whether Widerker does so (see his 2011). Partly on the basis of accepting these principles, Copp denies that Frankfurt examples undermine the principle that persons are morally blameworthy for what they have done only if they could have done otherwise. More on this in sec. 6.5.

16. John Fischer endorses this position. More carefully, he accepts *BO* and the view that Frankfurt examples undermine *PAP-R* but rejects the "ought" implies "can" principle. See, for e.g., Fischer 1999; 2003.

17. See, however, n. 15.

18. I don't intend to suggest that permissibility comes in degrees.

Chapter 7

Imperiled Compatibilist
Approaches

7.1. INTRODUCTION

In this penultimate chapter, I first examine two prominent semi-compatibilist approaches—the Strawsonian and the "mesh theory" approaches—to moral responsibility. The view that there is an alternative possibilities requirement for a range of normative judgments and for our having various well-founded moral sentiments calls each into doubt. The first approach understands moral responsibility by appealing to some of the moral sentiments. On the second, decisions or actions for which one is morally responsible causally derive from antecedent psychological elements, which harmonize with or relate to each other in some specified way. I conclude with some general remarks on whether reasons-responsiveness accounts of the sort of control that responsibility requires can, in the end, be prized apart from alternative possibilities.

7.2. STRAWSONIAN SEMI-COMPATIBILISM

Peter Strawson is credited for having developed one of the most influential compatibilist perspectives in his 1962/repr. 1982 landmark essay, "Freedom and Resentment." Distinctive of this perspective is the inspiration that moral responsibility is to be understood in terms of susceptibility to the reactive attitudes. Since determinism is, seemingly, no threat to such attitudes, determinism does not imperil moral responsibility. Implicit in the Strawsonian program is a semi-compatibilist strand: being morally responsible does not require having alternatives of any sort. It is this strand of Strawsonian compatibilism that is mistaken, or so I wish to argue.

7.2.1. An Outline of Strawsonian Compatibilism

Strawson develops his compatibilism with the objective of reconciling traditional disputants in the free will debate whom he calls "optimists" and "pessimists" (1962/repr. 1982, 59–60). Optimists are compatibilists who endorse a consequentialist conception of moral responsibility. They hold that responsibility ascriptions provide a means of regulating social behavior, and such regulation, they claim, can be effective even if determinism obtains. According to this social regulation view, overt praise or blame is an appropriate reaction if and only if a reaction of this sort is likely to bring about a desired change in the agent or in the agent's behavior. Regarding blame, one desired change is that the agent refrain from performing germane actions. With praise, among other things, the agent is encouraged to perform actions of the relevant sort. A well-documented, deep problem with this view is that it seems that blame (or praise) can be effective in modifying behavior in the desired way even if the person does not deserve any such negative (or positive) reaction.

Pessimists are incompatibilists who are either libertarians or skeptics about moral responsibility. They insist that being responsible requires the agent to be deserving of, for example, blame or praise, but the social regulation view cannot capture this requirement of desert.

The regulation view, thus, leaves out something vital, and this lacuna, pessimists insist, can be filled only by invoking agent causal freedom, something that some have claimed, mistakenly, it seems, requires the falsity of determinism.[1]

Strawson's "naturalistic turn" draws concessions from these opposed camps. From the optimist, Strawson wants admission that the social regulation view does overlook something pivotal to responsibility. From the pessimist, he desires acknowledgment that the vital element overlooked is not agent causal freedom and the falsity of determinism but the proper role that the reactive attitudes and feelings play in our interpersonal lives.

To understand moral responsibility, Strawson invites his reader to consider the reactive attitudes one has toward another when she recognizes in another's conduct an attitude of ill will. Upon such recognition or perceived recognition, the reactions that issue from one are themselves attitudes directed at the other's intentions or attitudes. For example, suppose someone has intentionally wronged some other person; suppose this other person discerns an attitude of ill will in the conduct of the agent who has wronged her. The wronged party typically has a personal reactive attitude of resentment. A third party, who is witness to this wrongdoing, may naturally express indignation or disapprobation. These are vicarious analogs, Strawson says, of resentment felt on behalf of the wronged party. If you are the agent who has done wrong, when you reflect on the fact or realize that you have done wrong, the typical or natural reactive attitude is guilt. There are, of course, "positive" reactive attitudes that are elicited upon recognition (or perceived recognition) of good will in another's conduct. Gratitude, for instance, is one of them.

Strawson wanted optimists and pessimists to appreciate the following about excuses. An excuse involves more than making a judgment that the person does not deserve a particular reaction or does not deserve to be treated in a certain way because she did not perform the pertinent deed, or she did not intend to do what turned out to be wrong, and so on. Excuses are associated with an emotional dimension: when a person is excused from responsibility, one suspends or withdraws various reactive attitudes.

In Strawson's view, the question about the conditions under which an agent is morally responsible just is the question of the conditions under which it is appropriate to hold an agent morally responsible. These conditions, in turn, are explained in terms of being a fitting candidate for the reactive attitudes. Strawson proposes that holding an agent morally responsible is an expression of certain basic needs and aversions. He says: "It matters to us whether the actions of other people . . . reflect attitudes towards us of good will, affection, or esteem on the one hand or contempt, indifference, or malevolence on the other" (1962/1982, 63). The reactive attitudes are "natural human reactions to the good or ill will or indifference of others towards us as displayed in *their* attitudes and actions" (67); and they express the "demand for the manifestation of a reasonable degree of good will or regard, on the part of others, not simply towards oneself, but towards all those on whose behalf moral indignation may be felt" (71).

On the Strawsonian picture, responsibility is *constituted* by our adopting these attitudes toward one another. The analysis of the concept of responsibility Strawson apparently (or might have) had in mind is this:

Strawsonian Analysis-1: S is morally responsible for A = df. it is fitting to adopt some reactive attitude toward S in respect of A.

The idea here is that, regardless of whether some person is in fact the object of some reactive attitude, if he is morally responsible for something, there is good reason to adopt such an attitude toward this person; he is an appropriate candidate for such a reaction; he deserves or is worthy of such a reaction (see, for e.g., Wallace 1994; Zimmerman 2010).

Strawson proposes that although it is psychologically impossible to suspend or abandon the reactive attitudes altogether, there are two broad sorts of excuses, which call for us to modify or mollify our reactive attitudes or withdraw them altogether. According to the first, contrary to what may be our initial assessment, the agent does not display ill will or disregard toward us in her conduct. An injury, for instance, may be accidental or inadvertent. The second has it that the agent is so incapacitated, perhaps because abnormal or immature, that she is not a suitable target of the reactive attitudes in the first place. Strawson suggests that it may be appropriate to adopt the "objective stance" toward an individual of this sort: we see the person as "an object of social policy; as a subject for what, in a wide range of sense, might be called treatment . . . to be managed or handled or cured or trained; perhaps simply to be avoided" (1962/1982, 66).

Determinism implies neither that no one ever expresses ill will or good will in one's conduct nor that each person never qualifies as an agent who is an apposite candidate for the reactive sentiments. Even if determinism is true, you can, for example, express ill will, or good will, in your conduct; and if you do, you would be a suitable candidate for resentment, indignation, or gratitude. Despite determinism's obtaining (if it does obtain), reacting to your display of ill will, others could adopt these attitudes toward you. But if responsibility is simply *constituted* by our adopting such attitudes toward one another, determinism is no threat to responsibility.

The traditional argument for determinism's incompatibility with moral responsibility proceeds from the premise that determinism expunges all alternatives, and the additional premise that responsibility requires alternatives. To escape this argument, Strawsonian compatibilism implicitly assumes that no element of the Strawsonian project presupposes our having alternatives of any sort. So even if determinism is incompatible with our having free will, it does not rule out the freedom or control that responsibility requires. This is the hallmark of semi-compatibilism.

Finally, in Strawson's estimation, even if theoretical considerations, such as those having to do with our not being ultimate originators of our actions or our not having freedom to do otherwise if determinism were to obtain, give us some reason to abandon wholesale our reactive attitudes, the resulting impoverishment in our lives would give us far stronger reason to retain these attitudes. Consequently, it would, on the whole, be rational to retain rather than suspend our reactive attitudes.

Strawson's rich and highly influential approach has generated a wealth of insightful discussion. I want to focus on one consideration: the implicit Strawsonian view that determinism does not imperil the reactive emotions.

7.2.2. Reactive Attitudes, Obligation, and Alternative Possibilities

As we have read, an important Strawsonian theme is that responsibility is to be understood in terms of our being able to evince certain moral sentiments or emotions or reactive attitudes. If we perceive what we take to be an expression of ill will in somebody's or one's own behavior, typically we react with anger, indignation, resentment, or guilt. Determinism does not preclude us from discerning what we take to be an expression of ill will or good will in our own or someone else's behavior, expressing ill will or good will in our conduct, or evincing the relevant emotions in response to our perception of ill will or good will. It is in this way that moral responsibility is thought to be insulated from determinism.

Another prominent Strawsonian theme is that some of our moral emotions—the reactive attitudes he believes—are intimately associated with involvement or participation in interpersonal relations. In contrast, as Strawson understands it, the objective attitude is associated primarily with "scientific or scholarly inquiry, therapeutic treatment, or social policy" (Wallace 1994, 28). Again, if the reactive attitudes are safe from determinism, then determinism should not threaten interpersonal relations by imperiling these attitudes.

Given these themes, and the interest in assessing whether Strawsonian *semi-compatibilism* is viable, a pressing issue that merits discussion is whether the reactive attitudes presuppose our having alternatives. Here, we can mine the results of chapter 5 on the moral sentiments. Prior to doing so, it is worth digressing somewhat to consider Jay Wallace's views on what distinguishes the *reactive* emotions or attitudes from other emotions. This slight digression will uncover one pathway to the conclusion that Strawsonian semi-compatibilism may well be on slippery footing. Exploiting some of the findings of chapter 5, a second pathway will be discussed in the next section.

Wallace suggests that the reactive attitudes "are not coextensive with the emotions one feels toward people with whom one has interpersonal relationships, rather they constitute a particular category of emotion specially distinguished by its constitutive connection with expectations" (1994. 31). He claims that the central cases of reactive attitudes are the emotions of "resentment, indignation, and guilt; other proposed candidates, such as sympathy, love, hurt feelings, and shame, are simply not counted as reactive attitudes (or at least not as unambiguous cases of such attitudes)" (1994, 30). Wallace explains further that resentment, indignation, and guilt hang together as a class because they are linked by related propositional objects: each is "explained exclusively by beliefs about the violation of moral obligations (construed as strict prohibitions or requirements), whereas other moral sentiments are explained by beliefs about the various modalities of moral value" (1994, 38, note omitted).

Taking our cue from Wallace, we distinguish, first, as we did before, between feeling "legitimate guilt" and feeling guilt. One can feel guilt when one is not in fact guilty; here the guilt is misplaced or not well-founded. Wallace and others have suggested:

Guilt 0: If S feels legitimate guilt at time *t*, then S has a (true) belief that S has violated an overall moral obligation.

To violate an overall moral obligation is to do overall wrong. Thus, *Guilt 0* is equivalent to *Guilt 1*:

Guilt 1: If S feels legitimate guilt at time *t* in respect of *A*, then S has a (true) belief that S's *A*-ing is overall wrong.

I'm unsure about *Guilt 1*. It seems to me that one can feel legitimate guilt if one takes oneself to have done wrong although one has not in fact done any wrong. So rather than *Guilt 1* I would prefer *Guilt 2*:

Guilt 2: If S feels legitimate guilt at time *t* in respect of *A*, then S has a belief that S's *A*-ing is overall wrong. One may want to add that the ground of S's feeling guilt is S's nonculpably believing that S has done wrong, or S's being willing to do what S nonculpably believes is morally wrong.

With legitimate resentment and indignation, it is plausible that the attendant beliefs about the violation of moral obligation are true. If the beliefs are false, the resentment or indignation is not well-founded or not legitimate. We feel legitimate resentment when others have done something wrong. Similarly, we feel legitimate indignation when others have done wrong. I shall use the phrase "S feels legitimate resentment [indignation] toward Y" to signal the view that resentment and indignation are other-directed or other-oriented:

> *Resentment*: If S feels legitimate resentment (or indignation) toward Y in respect of A, then Y's A-ing is overall wrong. Again, one might want to add that the ground of S's resentment (or indignation) is S's nonculpably believing (truly) that Y has done wrong.

Other moral sentiments, fundamental to good interpersonal relationships, that do not qualify as reactive emotions, in Wallace's characterization of such emotions, also presuppose the truth of various morally deontic judgments. A paradigm example, as we have seen, is forgiveness. When you forgive someone for doing something, and the forgiving is well founded, the person has done overall wrong. When forgiveness is well founded, we may say that it is "legitimate." So we have:

> *Forgive*: If S forgives Y for doing something, A, and S's forgiving is legitimate, then it is overall wrong for Y to do A.

Setting guilt aside, we can see that legitimate indignation, resentment, and forgiveness require our having alternatives. Each of these emotions presupposes the truth of the morally deontic judgment that some person has done overall moral wrong. There is an alternative possibilities requirement for overall wrongness (because one does overall moral wrong only if one has an objective *pro tanto* reason, and one has such a reason only if one could have done otherwise).

Guilt is more complicated. If *Guilt o* is true, i.e., if legitimate guilt presupposes wrongness, then again there is an alternative possibilities requirement for this moral sentiment. Assuming *Guilt o* is true, there would be such a requirement for the same reason just exposed as the reason for there being such a requirement regarding legitimate indignation, resentment, and forgiveness: wrongness presupposes our having alternatives by virtue of its association with objective *pro tanto* reasons.

As I have my doubts about *Guilt o* (I'll return to guilt below), what we may initially conclude is to the extent that the Strawsonian project is bound up with our feeling legitimate indignation, resentment, and forgiveness, to this extent Strawsonian semi-compatibilism is imperiled.

7.2.3. Another Pathway to Questioning Strawsonian Semi-Compatibilism

A second pathway that speaks against Strawsonian semi-compatibilism draws on the pertinent results of our previous inquiry regarding moral sentiments implicated in interpersonal relationships, on the one hand, and our having alternatives, on the other. I suggested that the following principles are true:

> *Forgiveness*: Necessarily, if S forgives T for something, then S has an objective *pro tanto* reason—being willing to cease to regard the wrong done to S as a reason to weaken or dissolve the relationship—to forgive T.

Guilt: Necessarily, if S feels (legitimate) guilt for doing something, then S has an objective *pro tanto* reason—taking S's self to have intentionally done wrong—for feeling guilt.

Indignation: Necessarily, if S feels (legitimate) indignation, then S has an objective *pro tanto* reason—S's having been wronged—for feeling indignation.

I argued for these principles by reflecting on the nature of these emotions. I also proposed that other emotions or attitudes intimately associated with interpersonal relationships, such as thankfulness, sorrow, regret, and joy, are customarily associated with objective reasons: typically, when one feels these emotions or adopts these attitudes, one does so for objective reasons. When we express these emotions, at times, for objective *pro tanto* reasons, we have, at those times, pertinent alternatives.

Thus, we may once again conclude that insofar as the Strawsonian project relies upon our adopting attitudes or feeling emotions such as forgiveness, guilt, indignation, and so forth, Strawsonian semi-compatibilism is in jeopardy.

Finally, some remarks on the Strawsonian analysis of responsibility are in order. The analysis was stated in this way:

Strawsonian Analysis-1: S is morally responsible for A = df. it is fitting to adopt some reactive attitude toward S in respect of A.

There is a question about whether this analysis correctly represents *Strawson's* view of the nature of responsibility. I set this query aside and turn to evaluative concerns. Zimmerman (2010, 109–10) argues that the analysis is susceptible to the following sort of objection frequently raised against buck-passing accounts of intrinsic value of this genre: *x* is intrinsically good = df. it would be fitting for anyone who were to contemplate x to favor x for its own sake. Suppose a powerful demon threatens that if you don't express anger toward Ish for performing some act, the demon will torture you. It seems fitting for you to express anger toward Ish for his performing this act. But contrary to what *Strawsonian Analysis-1* implies, Ish need not be morally responsible for this act.

Here is a second concern. *Strawsonian Analysis-1* implies that, necessarily, if S is morally responsible for A-ing, then it is fitting to adopt some (legitimate) reactive attitude toward S in respect of A. Assume, for simplicity, that only persons are or can be morally responsible agents. Suppose—perhaps *per impossibile*—that there are no alternatives for any person at a world. Then, it cannot be fitting or appropriate for anyone in this world to adopt *legitimate* reactive attitudes (the having of which presupposes our having alternatives) toward anyone in this world, in respect of anything anyone in this world does, if no one in this world can have such attitudes. (Compare: It cannot be appropriate for anyone in a world to bring about something it is logically impossible for anyone in this world to bring about. Similarly, it cannot be appropriate for anyone in a world in which no one has alternatives to feel indignation, resentment, or guilt.) This result, in conjunction with the proposition that determinism effaces all alternatives, yields skepticism concerning moral responsibility: no one is morally responsible for anything in a determined world.

But the proposition that determinism rules out all alternatives is false because determinism does not expunge *weak* alternatives. It is open to a proponent of *Strawsonian Analysis-1* to evade this variety of skepticism by calling attention to the fact that weak alternatives survive in a deterministic world. Circumventing such skepticism in this way, however, commits one to renouncing Strawsonian *semicompatibilism*: persons in a world will be morally responsible for at least some of what they do only if they have, at relevant times, at least weak alternatives.

In the wake of these problems, one may want to distinguish "fitting" versions from "having reasons" versions or from "being deserving of" versions of the Strawsonian analysis:

Strawsonian Analysis-2: S is morally responsible for *A* = df. there is a reason to adopt some reactive attitude toward *S* in respect of *A*.
Strawsonian Analysis-3: S is morally responsible for *A* = df. *S* deserves some reactive attitude in respect of *A*.

The example involving the demon, however, seems to undermine *Strawsonian Analysis-2* as well (but not *Strawsonian Analysis-3*). In addition, there is nothing to preclude the relevant reason, in a case such as the demon's, from being an objective *pro tanto* reason. Although you may not have any relevant desires and beliefs that are constituents of a Davidsonian reason of yours to express anger toward Ish, there is a reason for you to express anger. Once, again, Strawsonian semi-compatibilism is endangered because there is an alternative possibilities requirement for our having objective *pro tanto* reasons.

What of the desert version, *Strawsonian Analysis-3*? According to this version, moral responsibility is to be understood in terms of being deserving of some reactive attitude. The ground of responsibility is desert. It is someone's being deserving of a reactive attitude that grounds moral responsibility; the desert comes first, as it were. But it is not clear, as Zimmerman (2010, 110) cautions, that this is true. It might reasonably be claimed that it is moral responsibility that comes first: it is one's responsibility that grounds desert of the reactive attitude; it is because an agent is morally responsible for some action that this agent deserves some reactive attitude with respect to this action.

I want to develop another concern with the desert version. The basic thought is that, necessarily, if someone deserves something, there is a reason to see to it that he or she receives or gets this thing. If Tammy is born with a serious congenital impairment, Tammy deserves sympathy, or help, or comfort. If, in a fit of rage, Jack destroyed the windshield of Bennie's truck, Bennie deserves compensation. If Pam's young daughter unexpectedly died in a car crash, Pam deserves compassion. In each of these examples involving desert, there is a reason someone has to see to it that the person who deserves some thing receives this thing. There is a reason for Tammy to receive sympathy or help; there is a reason for Bennie to receive compensation; there is a reason for Pam to receive compassion. Moreover, someone has a reason to see to it that each of these persons receives what he or she deserves. I think we may safely assume that in many such cases in which there is a reason deriving from considerations of desert—a "desert-based" reason—the reason is an objective *pro tanto* one. Even if Jack, or anyone else for that matter, has no Davidsonian reason to compensate Bennie, at least someone has a reason to compensate Bennie, and this reason, plausibly, is an objective *pro tanto* one.

That there are desert-based reasons threatens Strawsonian semicompatibilism on desert versions of the Strawsonian analysis. If, in at least some cases, desert-based reasons are objective *pro tanto*, then, because there is an alternative possibilities requirement for such reasons, analyses such as *Strawsonian Analysis-3* will be committed to our having alternatives.

Reflection on alternative possibilities associated with at least some desert-based reasons suggests another pathway to the conclusion that moral obligation is tied to alternatives. Here, I merely adumbrate elements of this pathway. Suppose what is obligatory is to be analyzed in terms of what is intrinsically good, and suppose one's axiology or account of intrinsic goodness appeals to desert. Feldman (1992, 182–85; 1997, 160–69), for instance, has advanced an axiology that has it that the better the fit between primary goods, such as intrinsic attitudinal pleasure, which a person receives and such goods which the person deserves to receive, the intrinsically better the state of affairs in which the person receives this good. So, for instance, if you deserve some amount of intrinsic attitudinal pleasure and you receive just this amount, the state of affairs in which you receive this amount is intrinsically better than the one in which you receive this same amount when you do not deserve it (you receive it gratuitously, perhaps). If one deserves some primary good, however, then there is a desert-based reason for one to receive this good. By virtue of there being such a reason that may well be objective *pro tanto*, moral obligation is tied to our having alternatives.[2]

7.3. MESH THEORIES

A highly prominent and attractive idea in the free will literature is that unfree action or lack of free will is to be understood in terms of disharmony among various psychological constituents of an agent. So, for instance, Harry Frankfurt claims that it is in securing conformity of "his will to his second-order volitions . . . that a person exercises freedom of the will. And it is in the discrepancy between his will and his second-order volitions . . . that a person who does not have this freedom feels this lack" (1971, 15). Gary Watson affirms that the "possibility of unfree action consists in the fact that an agent's valuational system and motivational system may not completely coincide" (1975/1986, 91). And Susan Wolf suggests that if there is disparity between what you do and reasons involving the True and the Good that you have for doing what you do, then what you do may well not be free (1980/1986, 234; 1990, 79). Theories of this sort about free action have been called "mesh theories" because each affirms that one's action is free if it nondeviantly and causally issues from various psychological elements that stand in some congruous relation or harmoniously "mesh" together. In this section, I begin with the "hierarchical theory" of freedom whose preeminent exponent is Frankfurt. I show that on what seems to be one of its most credible versions, this theory is committed to the view that the freedom moral responsibility requires is, partly, the freedom to do otherwise. This is somewhat unsettling because Frankfurt has been one of the principal and persistent proponents of the view that being morally responsible does not require having alternatives. I subsequently turn to Wolf's and Watson's mesh theories, and I argue that these theories, too, are committed to free action's requiring our having alternatives.

7.3.1. Hierarchical Control and Reason

In a path-breaking paper in the literature on free will and moral responsibility, Harry Frankfurt asserts that one essential difference between persons and other creatures is to be found in the structure of persons' wills (Frankfurt 1971). *Persons*, unlike simpler animals and young children, are able to form second-order desires, and "have the capacity for reflective self-evaluation that is manifested in the formation of second-order desires" (1971, 7). On Frankfurt's view, an agent has "a desire of the second order either when he wants simply to have a certain desire or when he wants a certain desire to be his will [that is, his motivating desire]" (1971, 10). So unlike a first-order desire, which is not a desire that has some desire as its object, a second-order desire is one whose object is another actual or possible desire of the agent whose desire it is. For instance, a desire that one not have the desire to smoke is a desire of the second order. Or a desire to have a desire that one does not yet have, or a desire to be motivated more often by one sort of desire than another, are second-order desires. Frankfurt distinguishes between mere second-order desires and second-order volitions. A mere second-order desire is a desire to have a particular first-order desire but not to act on this first-order desire. Conducting research on addiction, I may want to have a first-order desire for a drug without having that desire issue in action. In contrast, a second-order volition is a second-order desire that a first-order desire be one's motivating desire, or as Frankfurt says, "one's will" (1971, 9–11).

Relying partly on the difference between first- and second-order desires, and on the distinction between different sorts of second-order desire, Frankfurt differentiates various kinds of freedom. One is supposed to exemplify the type of control moral responsibility requires. Frankfurt contends that one has freedom of action when one is able to do what one wants, and when one has such freedom, one is free do otherwise (1971,14). Even little children and many animals, he claims, have this sort of freedom. As freedom of action entails having genuine alternative options, Frankfurt examples show it is not the kind of freedom or control that moral responsibility demands.

Just as freedom of action is being able to do what we want, freedom of the will, Frankfurt says, is being able to will as we want. More precisely, one has freedom of the will when one has the power to make, as a result or by way of a second-order volition, at least one of one's first-order desires, other than the one that actually motivates one to act when one does, the one that motivates one to act when one does (1971, 15). So, as with freedom of action, one has freedom of the will only if one could have "willed otherwise." And

once again, as freedom of the will entails having genuine options—
this time the option to have willed otherwise (that is, the option to
have made some other first-order desire one's motivating desire)—
appropriately constructed Frankfurt examples show that freedom of
the will is not the right sort of control moral responsibility requires.

Finally, Frankfurt suggests that one *acts freely* when one secures
conformity of one's second-order volition and one's will, where
one's will is one's motivating desire (1971, 15). Apparently, Frankfurt's view is that when one's unopposed second-order volition
causes, in a suitable way, one's action, this suffices for having exercised the appropriate control in performing this action that moral
responsibility requires.

Departing somewhat from this view, a generic account of hierarchical control may be advanced. Introducing some terminology, an
agent, S, identifies with a first-order desire, D, to perform some action, A, if and only if S has a second-order volition, V, (relative to D)
that D be S's motivating desire, and S has no second-order desires
that conflict with V. Thus, when an agent identifies with a first-order
desire, she wants that desire to move her all the way to action; she
wants to be motivated by that desire.

Frankfurt has offered different accounts of identification. For example, in one work, he proposes that one identifies with a first-order
desire when one has an unopposed second-order volition to act in
accordance with it, and one judges that any further deliberation involving other higher-order desires about the matter, would result in
the same decision (1987/1988, 168–69). In recent papers, Frankfurt
appeals to a distinction between being passive and being active with
regard to one's desires in order to explain identification. He says that
the desires with which a person has identified are "wholly internal
to a person's will rather than alien to him; that is, he is not passive
with respect to them" (1992/1999, 99). Moreover, "insofar as a

person's will is affected by considerations that are external to it, the person is being acted upon. To that extent, he is passive. The person is active, on the other hand, insofar as his will determines itself" (1994, 437). In yet other places, Frankfurt draws on *satisfaction* to explain identification. He says that satisfaction requires no adoption of any cognitive, attitudinal, affective, or intentional stance. Nor does it require the performance of any particular act or any deliberate abstention. "Satisfaction is a state of the entire psychic system—a state constituted by the absence of any tendency or inclination to alter its condition" (1992/1999, 104). These differences in how precisely identification is to be conceptualized can, at least initially, be ignored.

Also, let's say that an agent, S, exercises hierarchical control in performing an action A if and only if S does A, and a desire with which S identifies nondeviantly causes A. Finally, the proponent of hierarchical control can be taken to be committed to this principle:

> *Hierarchical Control*: A person is morally responsible for performing an action only if she exercises hierarchical control in performing it.

This sort of theory encounters problems that have invited illuminating and ongoing discussion. Some of the more prominent of these include the following. First, the theory generates certain counterintuitive results. For example, an addict who, assume, has become addicted to a drug through no fault of her own, can identify with an irresistible desire for taking some drug. Supposing other conditions of responsibility, such as epistemic ones, are satisfied, *Hierarchical Control* yields the result that the addict is morally responsible for taking the drug although, it seems, she is a slave to her relevant desire. Another example concerns akratic action, free, intentional action contrary to one's best or better judgment. Assume that Mickey judges it best that he ought not to eat the pie, and he identifies with the desire to refrain from eating the pie. But succumbing to weakness, he akratically eats the pie. Developing the case in a certain fashion, critics have charged that although Mickey is blameworthy for eating the pie, *Hierarchical Control* yields the result that he is not to blame because he does not identify with the desire to eat the pie.[3]

A second sort of worry concerns a possible infinite regress of volitions. For an agent to be morally responsible in virtue of the conformity between his will and a second-order volition, V_1, V_1 must be freely willed. But for V_1 to be freely willed, there must be conformity between V_1 and some higher-order volition, V_2, which must, in turn, be freely willed, and so require a yet higher-order volition, and so forth (Watson 1975/1986; Zimmerman 1981; Shatz 1985; Friedman 1986, Christman 1991; Cuypers 2000). Indeed, the different notions of identification that Frankfurt develops partly reflect his efforts to meet this regress objection.

Third, some critics have claimed that *Hierarchical Control* rests on the unwarranted assumption that the agent's "real self" is to be identified with the cluster of her higher-order volitions and those lower-order elements selected by them (Thalberg 1978; Berofsky 1995).

Finally, there is the so called "wayward source problem" or "manipulation problem" of central interest to us because it motivates a modification of *Hierarchical Control* that introduces an appeal to reason. The problem is simply that identification can be "engineered" in such a fashion that the agent, contrary to the implications of *Hierarchical Control*, is not morally responsible. After all, the very components essential to reasoning, including one's values, desires, and beliefs, so central to identification, can be acquired via means, such as unsolicited, direct electronic stimulation of the brain, that are responsibility-undermining (see, for example, Slote 1980; Watson 1987; Mele 1995; Haji and Cuypers 2007; 2008). The underlying worry here is that hierarchical theories are too "internalist"; they are insufficiently sensitive to how one acquires one's springs of action.

Eleonore Stump (1993a, b) has proposed a revision of Frankfurt's account of freedom of the will that, she believes, enables her revised account to escape the objection that identification can be engineered. She says that an agent's intellect is the computing faculty of the agent. She then proposes that an agent has a "second-order volition V_2 to bring about some first-order volition [or desire] V_1 in himself only if the agent's intellect at the time of the willing represents V_1, under some description, as the good to be pursued. A second-order volition, then, is a volition formed as a result of some reasoning (even when the reasoning is neither rational nor conscious) about one's first-order desires" (1993b, 216).

With regard to the wayward source problem of engineered-in second-order volitions, Stump's seemingly promising solution is this:

> On the revised account, an agent forms a second-order desire by reasoning (rationally or otherwise, consciously or not) about his first-order desires; and a second-order desire is a direct result of an agent's intellect representing a certain first-order desire as the good to be pursued. Given this connection between intellect and second-order desires, an agent cannot be a passive bystander to his second-order volitions. To be a second-order volition, a volition must be the result of reasoning on the agent's part. Even if it were coherent to suppose that one agent, say, Verkhovensky, could directly produce some reasoning in the mind of another, such as Stavrogin, that reasoning would not be Stavrogin's but rather Verkhovensky's. . . . If Verkhovensky continuously

produced thoughts in Stavrogin, then Stavrogin would have ceased to be a person and would instead be something like Verkhovensky's puppet. On the other hand, suppose Verkhovensky produced thoughts in Stavrogin's mind only occasionally, so that Stavrogin remained a person. In the computations leading to an action, Stavrogin's own intellect would take cognizance of the thought Verkhovensky had produced in Stavrogin's mind, and Stavrogin would then either accept or reject Verkhovensky's thought as a result of Stavrogin's own reasoning.... As Stavrogin acts, then, the first-order volition stemming from his reasoning and the accompanying second-order desire will be Stavrogin's and not Verkhovensky's. Either way, Stavrogin would not have any second-order volitions produced by Verkhovensky. So, on the revised Frankfurt account, an agent's second-order volitions cannot be produced by someone else. (1993b, 219–20)

Indeed, it is not unreasonable to develop Frankfurt's own distinction between being passive and being active regarding one's desires along the lines Stump suggests: being active with respect to one's desires involves reasoning, rationally or otherwise, consciously or not, about these desires; being passive involves no such reasoning.

With these suggestions of Stump, a revised hierarchical account of control can be formulated in this way: First, Stump disambiguates the term "second-order desire." She says that an effective desire is a desire to move an agent all the way to action if unimpeded. Stump explains that "when an agent wants to make a certain first-order desire his . . . [effective desire], then he has a second-order desire [or what, following Frankfurt's usage, we have been calling a "second-order volition"]; and when this second-order desire is effective, that is, when . . . [the agent] succeeds in making that first-order desire his . . . [effective desire], then he has a second-order volition" (1993a, 242). So Stump's use of "volition" is more restrictive than Frankfurt's. Second, we reemphasize that according to Stump, a second-order volition is a volition formed as a result of some reasoning, even when the reasoning is neither rational nor conscious, about one's first-order desires. Third, agent, S, identifies as a result of reasoning—"R-identifies"—with a first-order desire D, to perform some action, A, if and only if S has a second-order volition, V, (relative to D) that D be S's effective desire, and S has no second-order desires that conflict with V. Fourth, S exercises hierarchical control in performing A if and only if S does A, and a desire with which S R-identifies nondeviantly causes A. Finally, revised hierarchical theory ($Revised$-HC) says that a person is morally responsible for performing an action only if she exercises hierarchical control in performing it.

7.3.2. Assessment of the Revised Hierarchical View

While there are other problems with the revised account (Haji 1998, 74–75), of interest to us is that this account is not neutral about the basis of second-order volitions. These volitions are formed as a result of some reasoning about one's first-order desires. It is this constraint that provides hope for an answer to the wayward source concern. Consider the following case involving manipulation that is meant to signal a problem for the original, unrevised theory. A bunch of evil neurosurgeons can, without Sara's being aware of it, directly stimulate her brain, thereby causing her to have various desires and losing others. Suppose, using their technique of brain stimulation, they succeed in implanting in Sara a desire to take a drug and a second-order volition concerning that desire. Suppose they also succeed in eradicating all second-order desires that conflict with the implanted second-order volition. In other words, they orchestrate identification; they manipulate Sara in such a way that she not only finds herself with a desire for the drug, but she also identifies with it. Since the implanted first-order desire for the drug is irresistible, Sara acts on it. In this case, it seems that Sara is not morally responsible for taking the drug because she is a marionette of her manipulators. According to the unrevised theory (*Hierarchical Control*), however, Sara *would* be morally responsible for taking the drug, assuming other conditions of moral responsibility, such as epistemic ones, are satisfied because she exercised hierarchical control in taking the drug.

On the revised theory, however, Sara is *not* morally responsible for taking the drug owing to her taking the drug's not being an action that issues from a second-order volition that is appropriately formed. The volition concerning the desire which gives rise to Sara's action is not the product of Sara's reflecting on her first-order desires. Rather, it is an engineered-in second-order desire.

If, as the revised theory has it, the volitions implicated in free action are ones that are formed as a result of reasoning concerning one's first-order desires, we may ask about the sorts of reason— objective, subjective, or Davidsonian—one brings to bear on one's first-order desires when one acts freely by the lights of this theory. I said that objective reasons are, roughly, facts that are not, even in part, about any motivating desire of the agent who has this reason; in this sense, they are "agent external." Davidsonian reasons are typically, desire/belief pairs. Subjective reasons are beliefs concerning objective reasons: an agent has such a reason to do something if and only if the agent believes (truly or falsely) that she has an objective *pro tanto* reason to do that thing. We said that on one view, subjective reasons are not "stand alone" reasons independent of being affiliated with desires or having a desire-like component. Rather, on this view, they are either the belief components of Davidsonian reasons or they have a "built-in" desire-like or motivational constituent. On an opposed view, subjective reasons are "stand alone."

Imagine that you have a pair of competing first-order desires: satisfaction of either one precludes satisfaction of the other. You reflect on them; you assess their objects. Suppose your reasons favor one of these desires. On the basis of these reflections as *Revised-HC* has it, you form a second-order volition concerning this desire. We may then say that this first-order desire has the sanction or support of your reasons; your reasons to favor this desire over its first-order rival constitute this desire's "justifying reasons."

It appears that the justifying reasons, on pain of an undesirable regress, cannot be Davidsonian (normative or otherwise): Suppose you have a first-order desire to take some medicine because you want to get well, and you believe that taking the medicine will contribute to your getting well. Call the former desire "D." What would it be for the object of D to have the support of your reasons when the reasons in question are Davidsonian? Since these putatively supporting reasons are Davidsonian, a constituent of each of these supporting reasons will itself be a desire. Focus on one such reason and its constituent desire "D_1." Either this desire—D_1—is itself supported or it is not. If it lacks any support—that is, if Davidsonian reasons you have do not support this desire (D_1) itself—then it is hard to see how D—your desire to get well—could, in turn, be supported. Suppose, then, that D_1 is itself supported. If D_1 is supported, either it is by some other desire/belief pair whose desire constituent is D_2, or it is self-supporting. It is not clear how the latter is possible. If the former is true, then we commit to an undesirable regress. It would seem that for these reasons, the justifying reasons for your desire to get well—desire D—cannot be Davidsonian.

For similar reasons, the justifying reasons for desire D cannot be subjective if subjective reasons are not "stand alone" and are essentially linked to desires or have a desire-like constituent. If, on the one hand, your belief that taking the medicine is the belief constituent of a Davidsonian reason, the desire component of this reason will require support. But if the supporting reasons are themselves Davidsonian, the desire components of these Davidsonian reasons, in turn, will require support. Once, again, an ugly regress seems inevitable. If, on the other hand, the subjective reason itself has a built-in desirelike component, this desirelike component, just like the desire component of a typical Davidsonian reason, would need support. Moreover, if this support is itself by way of another subjective reason with a built-in desirelike component (or a standard Davidsonian reason), the desirelike component (or the relevant desire) will itself require support. Again, a regress threatens.

Nor can it plausibly be the case that the justifying reasons for a first-order desire D^* are subjective if subjective reasons are "stand alone." For suppose you believe, on highly dubious grounds you realize (at least at some level) are suspect, that desire D^* has the support of objective *pro tanto* reasons. Or suppose such a belief (the belief that the object of D^* is reasons-wise permissible or obligatory) is surreptitiously implanted in you. Or, yet, suppose you are self-deceived regarding this belief or this belief is an akratically held one. It would not be credible to propose that in virtue of D^*'s being "supported" by *such* subjective reasons, it is this first-order desire as opposed to some other competing first-order desire that is "truly your own."

It would seem that a defensible version of the revised hierarchical theory, then, should be wedded to a view of justifying reasons that are objective. However, there is an alternative possibilities requirement for having objective reasons. Consequently, the revised theory is committed to our having access to alternatives.

7.4. WOLF'S REASON VIEW

Wolf's theory is a variant of what can be called the "Values View of Free Action." On these views, an agent's action expresses what she values only if what she values plays a nondeviant, causal role in the production of that action. At the core of the Values View lies this principle:

Free Action: An action is free only if it expresses what one values.

Toward clarifying *Free Action*, "value," as a noun, is richly ambiguous. In the present context of formulating and assessing Wolf's development of the Values View, I take values, most fundamentally, to be (1) states of affairs, that (2) are the objects of desires, and (3) have the support of practical reason.

I offer little on (1) and (2) with the exception of the following. A person can desire *that 2 + 2 = 4*, or *that the sun shines*. But these objects cannot have the support of *practical* reason; they are not the right sorts of object that practical reason can favor or disfavor. The right sorts of object, broadly conceptualized, are "actional states of affairs"; these are states of affairs regarding which there can be practical reasons for or against them. Pretty clearly, the final clause in the last sentence would render an analysis of something's being the right sort of object circular were this clause to occur in the relevant analysans; but here, it seems, the characterization is not entirely empty.

We need to say more on (3), on what it is for an object of a desire, a state of affairs, to have the support of practical reason. I limit discussion to one aspect of (3): whether the supporting reasons are objective or Davidsonian.

It appears that in Wolf's estimation the reasons are objective. She explains that according to her version of the Values View that she dubs the "Reason View," "responsibility depends on the ability to act in accordance with the True and the Good" (1990, 91). In an example she advances, Wolf assumes that it is literally impossible for a woman to refrain from saving a child who is drowning "because her understanding of the situation is so good and her moral commitment so strong" (1990, 82). Wolf concludes that even though the woman is not free to do otherwise, she is praiseworthy for saving the child, because her action accords with the True and the Good.[4] It is not simply that the woman believes that her action accords with the True and the Good; rather, the object of her desire that moves her to action has the support of practical reason. In a range of cases involving kleptomania, drug addiction, hypnosis, and deprived childhoods in which agents are apparently not responsible for performing seemingly wrong or bad actions even though they could not have done otherwise, Wolf affirms that the judgment that they are not responsible derives from the fact that the agents could not do the right thing for the right reasons; their actions issued from desires whose objects were not supported by practical reason (1980/1986).

Additional considerations shore up the proposal that the supporting reasons are neither Davidsonian nor subjective on the Reason View; rather, they are objective. First, were the reasons Davidsonian, Wolf's theory would run afoul of the regress problem we discussed in connection with Frankfurt's hierarchical view: Suppose a Davidsonian reason whose desire component is desire D putatively supported the object of some desire. Then, again, either D is self-supporting or some other Davidsonian reason supports D. The first option is untenable; the second runs up against the regress problem.

Nor, second, does it seem that on the Reason View the supporting reasons could be subjective. An insane person may believe that killing an innocent child on a Friday has the backing of objective *pro tanto* reasons. But surely, we would not, for this reason, concur that her desire to kill an innocent child on a Friday has the sanction of reason. We would want to claim that if she did kill the child on the basis of this subjective reason, her action failed to accord with the True and the Good.

It would thus seem that on Wolf's theory the supporting reasons for the objects of desires are objective. Then, however, the Reason View is also committed to our having alternatives because there is an alternative possibilities requirement for the truth of objective reasons.

Before leaving the Reason View, it is worth registering that Wolf's "Asymmetry Thesis," on at least one construal of this thesis that Wolf proposes, is questionable. This thesis says that whereas there is a requirement of alternative possibilities for moral blame-worthiness—one cannot be blameworthy unless one could have done otherwise—there is no such requirement for moral praise-worthiness. Elaborating, Wolf explains that on her view praisewor-thiness does not require having alternatives: you could have been morally praiseworthy even if you could not have done otherwise because not being able to do otherwise does *not* preclude you from acting in accordance with the True and the Good. In contrast, blameworthiness does call for your having alternatives because if you cannot act in accord with the True and the Good, you lack the control that responsibility requires. On a morally deontic interpre-tation of Wolf's Reason View, the clause concerning moral praise-worthiness is mistaken. On this interpretation, necessarily, if one is morally praiseworthy for something, one is able to act in accordance with what is morally obligatory (or permissible). Furthermore, nec-essarily, to be able to act in accordance with what is morally obliga-tory (or morally permissible), one is able to *do* what is morally obligatory (or morally permissible) in this sense: one is able to fulfill or execute one's moral obligations. But one cannot do so—one can't discharge one's moral obligations—without having alternatives simply because one cannot *have* an obligation to do something if one cannot refrain from doing it. Similar considerations apply to doing moral wrong. So Wolf's Asymmetry Thesis, on its deontic reading, is false.[5]

7.5. WATSON'S MESH THEORY

Watson's mesh account (1975/1986; 1986) is another variation of the Values View. At least in its initial development, this account assumes that responsibility requires a suitable connection between the agent's behavior and her values. Watson takes values to be a subset of desires (1975/1986, 91). Reviving certain Platonic themes, he claims that our desires have different sources. Our valuational desires have their source in reason and express what reason recommends. Mere motivational desires, in contrast, have their source in "appetite." Watson believes that values and desires can diverge in the following fashion that is significant for free action: the motivational strength of a desire may be misaligned with its agent's assessment of the object of the desire. For instance, it is possible for an agent to judge that the object of his desire—an "actional" state of affairs—is not good; alternatively, the agent believes that the object of his desire does not have the support of practical reason, and yet he is strongly motivated to bring about this state of affairs. Having suffered an ignominious defeat, the squash player has a motivationally strong desire to smash the face of his opponent with his racquet; still, he believes that he reasons-wise ought not to do so. Watson claims that there seem to be two ways in which, in principle, the relevant discrepancy may arise. First, "what one desires is not to any degree valued, held to be worth while, or thought good" (1975/1986, 86). Second, although one may value what is desired, "the strength of one's desire may not properly reflect the degree to which one values its object" (1975/1986, 86). Watson writes:

> *The valuational system* of an agent is that set of considerations which, when combined with his factual beliefs (and probability estimates), yields judgments of the form: the thing for me to do in these circumstances, all things considered, is *a*. To ascribe free agency to a being presupposes it to be a being that makes judgments of this sort. To be this sort of being, one must assign values to alternative states of affairs, that is, rank them in terms of worth. (91)
>
> *The motivational system* of an agent is that set of considerations which move him to action. We identify his motivational system by identifying what motivates him. The possibility of unfree action consists in the fact that an agent's valuational system and motivational system may not completely coincide. Those systems harmonize to the extent that what determines the agent's all-things-considered judgments also determines his actions. (91)

Watson adds:

> The free agent has the capacity to translate his values into action; his actions flow from his evaluational system. (91)
>
> This distinction [between wanting and valuing] is important to the adherent of the familiar view—that talk about free action and free agency can be understood in terms of the idea of being able to get what one wants—because it gives sense to the claim

that in unfree actions the agents do not get what they really or
most want. (92)

There is some question about how to interpret Watson's theory.
We may distinguish between an objective and a subjective version
of the theory. Briefly, on the subjective variant, one's values are one's
desires whose objects one believes, even if falsely, have the support
of objective *pro tanto* reasons. On the objective variant, one's values
are one's desires that do in fact have the support of such reasons.

Elaborating, on the subjective view, suppose agent, S, desires to
do A. Suppose, further, S believes that S's doing A is reasons-wise
permissible for S (or, in a slightly amended case, reasons-wise obligatory for S); in, short, S believes that practical reasons support S's
doing A. Then, assuming other conditions of free action are met, the
subjective view implies, in conjunction with these facts, that S's
doing A, if S were to do A, is free. According to this view, states of
affairs that have the support of what an agent takes to be, or believes,
are practical reasons may be called "derivative subjective values";
and a desire whose object is a derivative subjective value is a subjective value of its agent. A Watsonian subjective theory, then, has it
that an agent's action is free only if this action expresses a desire
whose object is a derivative subjective value—a state of affairs that
the agent takes to be reasons-wise obligatory or permissible; in
short, an agent's action is free only if it expresses a subjective value
of that agent.

On the objective view, if an agent's action is free, then that action
expresses a value of that agent. On such a view, an agent's action
expresses what an agent values only if a desire of that agent whose
object is reasons-wise obligatory or reasons-wise permissible for
that agent, plays a nondeviant, causal role in the production of that
action. Alternatively, on the objective view, an agent's action is free

only if it is nondeviantly caused by a desire of that agent whose object has the support of practical reason. As an example, suppose that it is reasons-wise obligatory for you to do A, and, thus, reasons-wise wrong for you to do either B or C. Assuming all other conditions of free action are satisfied, it would follow, on the objective view, that whereas your doing A is free, doing B (or doing C) is not free. More simply, we may say that because doing A is reasons-wise obligatory for you, objective practical reasons support your doing A, and so doing A is free. In contrast, objective practical reasons do not support your doing B, and so doing it is not free. States of affairs that are the objects of an agent's desires, and have the support of practical reason, may be called "derivative objective values" of this agent; and a desire whose object is a derivative objective value is an objective value of its agent. On the objective view, then, an agent's action is free only if it expresses a desire whose object is a derivative objective value of this agent—the object of this desire is a state of affairs that is reasons-wise obligatory or reasons-wise permissible for this agent. In brief, on this view, an agent's action is free only if it expresses an objective value of that agent.

Is Watson's view to be identified with the subjective view or the objective view? On the one hand, there is Watson's appeal to Platonic reason. This strongly suggests that one's values are members of the subset of one's desires that do in fact have the support of reason; there are objective *pro tanto* reasons that favor these desires. There is another reason to believe that Watsonian values are desires that have the support of such reasons. Suppose agent S has no idea whether the objects of his two conflicting desires have the support or condemnation of practical reason; S simply cannot tell whether the desire to do A or the desire to do B is so supported or condemned. It is unclear why S could not be in this sort of epistemic position of ignorance. Suppose S flips a coin about what to do; and suppose the results of the coin flip indicate, in accordance with what S has decided, that S do A. On the subjective view, whatever S does S does not do freely: if S does not have any beliefs concerning which desire is supported by practical reasons, neither desire is a value for him. If neither desire is a value for him, in this case there is neither conformity nor disconformity between his desires and relevant values. So it appears he does not exercise responsibility-level control in doing whatever it is that he does. This just seems wrong. The objective view evades this troubling consequence.

On the other hand, however, I see no definitive textual evidence to rule out the subjective interpretation of Watson's theory; moreover, there is some textual support for this interpretation. For instance, as previously noted, Watson says "what one desires is not to any degree valued, *held* to be worthwhile, or *thought* good" (emphasis added, 1975/1986, 86). In a later paper (1987), reflecting on the concern that it is not clear what confers a special, "authoritative" status to second-order volitions in Frankfurt's hierarchical account, Watson writes:

> In the past, I believed that the notion of an evaluational standpoint could do this job; that the hierarchy must be grounded in the subject's evaluations, or conceptions of the good, and this notion would suffice to define the relevant (necessarily internal) standpoint. To be alienated from one's conduct or desires is to *see* them as unworthy or in some way bad. What gives the appeal to higher-order volitions whatever plausibility it has is that higher-order volitions characteristically are grounded in one's conception of a worthwhile way to live. (1987, 149, emphasis added)

Owing to this uncertainty of how precisely to interpret Watson's theory, let's consider each variant of the theory independently. On the objective value theory, because one's values are desires whose objects have the support of objective *pro tanto* reasons one has, and because there is an alternative possibilities requirement for having such reasons, Watsonian objective value theory is committed to our having alternatives.

What, then, of the subjective value theory according to which if an action expresses a subjective value—if this action nondeviantly arises from a desire whose object the agent believes has the support of practical reason—then it is free? Since this theory is divorced from there being practical reasons for an agent—the theory requires merely belief that there are practical reasons and not also that this belief is true—it would seem that the theory would accommodate free action even if one lacks alternatives. So if one is a compatibilist who is attracted to a reasons-like view of free action, one *may* be tempted to move from the objective theory to the subjective theory.

There, are however, concerns with this sort of theory as well. Watson, in a candid assessment of his own view, summarizes the first:

> In "Free Agency" I wished to reject a Humean conception of desire, reason, and evaluation that was common to the hierarchical view and classical compatibilism: valuing cannot be reduced to desiring (at any level). While I still wish to maintain a non-Humean view, it now seems to me that the picture presented there is altogether too rationalistic. For one thing, it conflates valuing with judging good. Notoriously, judging good has no invariable connection with motivation, and one can fail to 'identify' with one's evaluational judgements. One can in an important sense fail to value what one judges valuable. But even if this conflation is rectified by construing valuing as caring about something because (in as much as) it is deemed to be valuable,

what one values in a particular case may not be sanctioned by a more general evaluational standpoint that one would be prepared to accept. When it comes right down to it, I might fully 'embrace' a course of action I do not judge best; it may not be thought best, but is fun, or thrilling; one loves doing it, and it's too bad it's not also the best thing to do, but one goes for it without compunction. Perhaps in such a case one must see this thrilling thing as good, must value it; but, again, one needn't see it as expressing or even conforming to a general standpoint one would be prepared to defend. . . . Call such cases, if you like, perverse cases. The point is that perverse cases are plainly neither cases of compulsion nor weakness of will. There is no estrangement here. One's will is fully behind what one does. (1987, 150.)

A second concern has to do with discordance. Suppose some agent performs some action, *A*. Suppose a desire whose object is not a derivative subjective value of its agent nondeviantly causes *A*; the agent, like our akrates, believes that her doing *A* is reasons-wise forbidden. Despite this belief, desiring to do *A*, she does *A*. Ignoring the problem just recorded of fully embracing a course of action one does not judge best, on the Watsonian subjective theory, this discrepancy between, as we may roughly put it, motivational strength and subjective value, renders her doing *A* not free. So this theory, it seems, entails the following:

Principle-1: If one does something, *A*, one desires to do and which one believes (falsely) reason does not recommend, then one does *A* unfreely.

Suppose, now, that we are in an indeterministic world. Suppose, for the sake of argument, that such a world is hospitable to the truth of judgments of practical reason. Suppose, further, that in this world, the agent desires to do B, judges it is reasons-wise obligatory or best for her to do B, but indeed has no reason at all to do B. Why should *this* discrepancy between what the agent believes she has reason to do or what the agent desires to do and practical reason not render her doing B unfree, *if* (as in the former case) a discrepancy between motivational strength and subjective value renders her doing A unfree? Alternatively, *if Principle-1 is true*, what is there to recommend the following principle?

> Principle-2: If one does something, A, one desires to do and which one believes (falsely) reason recommends, then one does A freely.

Again, if *Principle-1* is true, shouldn't *Principle-2* be renounced in favor of the following principle?

> Principle-3: If one does something, A, one desires to do and which one believes (falsely) reason recommends, then one does A unfreely.

Imagine it being proposed that disharmony between S's desire to do A and A's not being a derivative subjective value of S is sufficient to render unfree S's doing A; but it is *not* also the case that disharmony between S's desire to do B and B's not being a derivative objective value of S is sufficient to render unfree S's doing B. It appears that a proponent of this asymmetrical thesis believes that there is a sense in which subjective value is privileged over objective value; relevant disharmony involving subjective value erodes the control moral responsibility requires while germane disharmony involving objective value does not. But I see little reason to support the view that belief, especially false belief, regarding what reason recommends has this sort of "undermining power" over responsibility-level control whereas what reason itself recommends does not.

We may conclude that neither the subjective nor the objective Watsonian view escapes serious difficulty associated with our having practical reasons.

7.6. CONCLUDING REMARKS ON REASONS-RESPONSIVENESS ACCOUNTS OF CONTROL

We may think of Wolf's Reason View and Watson's "value-sensitive" theory as two variations of a reasons-responsiveness account of the control that moral responsibility requires: such control demands that we be able both to recognize moral reasons for action and to act on the basis of such reasons.[6] Recently, Fischer and Ravizza (1998) have developed another, distinguished, highly influential reasons-responsiveness account of control. I want, briefly, to examine this account to draw some general lessons concerning whether these sorts of account can be entirely divorced from our having access to genuine alternatives.

According to Fischer and Ravizza, to be morally responsible for an action, the agent must act from a mechanism that is his own reasons-responsive mechanism. Setting aside the ownership constituent, reasons-responsiveness has two components, receptivity to reasons or the capacity to recognize reasons that exist, and reactivity to reasons or the capacity to translate reasons into choices, and then subsequent behavior (1998, 69). Imagine that in the actual world some agent, Brown, performs an action, A, and Brown's relevant antecedent reasons states (or their neural realizers) cause A in a suitable way. Refer to the process that culminates in Brown's intentionally doing A as the actual kind of mechanism—ordinary practical deliberation in this instance—that is operative in Brown's doing A. This mechanism may be strongly, weakly, or moderately responsive to reasons. Fischer and Ravizza favor the third, which together with the ownership component, constitutes the control requirement—"guidance control"—for moral responsibility.

Suppose that a certain kind K of mechanism actually issues in an action. Fischer and Ravizza explain that a mechanism is *strongly reasons-responsive* if, when it operates, an agent will react differently to sufficient reasons to do otherwise (41):

(SRR): Strong-reasons-responsiveness obtains under the following conditions: if K were to operate and there were sufficient reason to do otherwise, the agent would *recognize* the sufficient reason to do otherwise and thus *choose* to do otherwise and *do* otherwise. (1998, 63)

In contrast, a mechanism is *weakly reasons-responsive* if, when it operates, the agent will respond differently to at least some reasons to do otherwise:

(WRR): As with strong reasons-responsiveness, we hold fixed the operation of the actual kind of mechanism, and we then simply require that there exist *some* possible scenario (or possible world)—with the same laws as the actual world—in which there is a sufficient reason to do otherwise, the agent recognizes this reason, and the agent does otherwise. (1998, 63)

On the one hand, strong reasons-responsiveness is too strong for moral responsibility. It would, for instance, preclude agents from being morally responsible for their akratic actions. On the other hand, weak reasons-responsiveness is too weak. An agent who goes to some football game may think a sufficient reason for her not to go to the game is that the ticket costs $1000, but yet not believe that such a reason for her not to go is that the ticket costs $2000 or more. The actual kind of mechanism that operates in her going to the game is weakly reasons-responsive. But, intuitively, such an agent does not exhibit the control in going to the game that moral responsibility demands (1998, 65–68).

Moderate reasons-responsiveness requires *regular* receptivity to reasons. A person who acts on a regularly receptive mechanism must exhibit a certain sort of pattern of reasons recognition. Fischer and Ravizza claim that "it is a defining characteristic of regular reasons-receptivity that it involves an *understandable pattern* of (actual and hypothetical) reasons-receptivity" (1998, 71). When acting on the kind of mechanism that is actually operative, we want to know if the agent recognizes "how reasons fit together, sees why one reason is stronger than another, and understands how the acceptance of one reason as sufficient implies that a stronger reason must also be sufficient" (1998, 71). So, for a mechanism to be regularly receptive, Fischer and Ravizza require that the array of sufficient reasons to do otherwise the agent recognizes exhibit a pattern of rational stability (1998, 70–71); a third-party inquirer could come to understand the pattern of reasons the agent would accept (1998, 71–72). A comprehensive pattern of reasons-recognitions, however, may be utterly divorced from reality. Thus, Fischer and Ravizza add that regular receptivity to reasons requires an understandable pattern of reasons recognition "minimally grounded in reality" (1998, 73).

Regarding reactivity to reasons, Fischer and Ravizza propose that the mechanism that is actually operative and reacts differently to a sufficient reason to do otherwise in some other possible world shows that this kind of mechanism can react differently to the actual reason to do otherwise (1998, 73). On their view, holding fixed the actual kind of mechanism that is operative, "reactivity is all of a piece" in that if the mechanism can react to any reason to do otherwise, it can react to all such reasons (1998, 74). In sum, Fischer and Ravizza propose an interesting asymmetry. Guidance control requires *regular receptivity* to reasons but only *weak reactivity* to reasons.

Finally, Fischer and Ravizza stress that reasons-responsiveness requires an appropriate connection between reasons and action. In particular, when we test for reasons-responsiveness by considering possible scenarios in which there is sufficient reason to do otherwise, the actual kind of mechanism operates, and the agent does otherwise, the actual kind of mechanism is reasons-responsive only if the agent does otherwise *for* these sufficient reasons. Furthermore, to be morally responsible, the kind of responsiveness must be characterized not merely as responsiveness to reasons, but rather as "responsiveness to a range of reasons that include moral reasons" (1998, 81); the relevant sort of responsiveness must embrace receptivity to an appropriate range of *moral* reasons.

Fischer and Ravizza underscore something else: guidance control is "one-way" control; responsibility does not require alternative possibilities. Reasons-responsiveness is analyzed in terms of whether and how an agent would respond to sufficient reasons in worlds other than the actual world. But it is not a requirement of moderate reasons-responsiveness that these worlds or a subset of them be genuinely accessible to the agent, as Frankfurt examples, they claim, confirm (1998, 52–53).

We note the following: moderate reasons-responsiveness requires recognizing moral reasons and acting on at least some of these reasons if the agent is to be *morally* responsible (Tod and Tognazzini 2008). If some reason of an agent nondeviantly gives rise to an action, the agent has that reason. If all reasons are objective, and there is an alternative possibilities requirement for having such reasons, then contrary to Fischer and Ravizza, responsibility would require alternative possibilities. The general moral is that moderate reasons-responsiveness is *not* neutral among competing accounts of reasons in this respect: if moderate reasons-responsiveness is to be divorced from agents being committed to having alternatives, it must not be the case that all moral reasons are objective.

Moral reasons, however, may be a mixed bag: some may be objective, others subjective, and yet others Davidsonian. Suppose blameworthiness requires wrongness, that is, suppose principle *BO* is true, as Fischer thinks it is. Then it would be highly implausible to suppose that whenever an agent is morally blameworthy for something, the agent has exercised her capacity to translate appropriate moral reasons into choices and subsequent behavior, and, *moreover*, the reasons so translated *never* can turn out to be objective. There is no reason whatsoever for a theorist who accepts the view that blameworthiness requires wrongness to think that, necessarily, or coincidentally, or nomically, responsibility is wedded to translating "non-objective" reasons into choices (and then conduct). A reasons-responsive theorist, who also endorses the view that blameworthiness requires wrongness, would presumably grant that there are occasions when an agent who is blameworthy for doing something recognizes that that thing is wrong and is weakly reactive to this reason. But the fact that something is wrong for one is a paradigmatic example of some fact's being an objective reason for one. So if moral reasons are a mixed bag, and if one accepts the view that blameworthiness requires wrongness, then it seems that a reasons-responsiveness account, such as Fischer and Ravizza's, will in the end have to appeal to agents' having, on at least some occasions when they are blameworthy, alternatives.

The possibility is still left open, however, that a reasons-responsiveness theory *not* wedded to the principle that blameworthiness requires wrongness can be developed independently of committing to alternative possibilities. Semi-compatibilism regarding responsibility has resilience.

In conclusion, I have proposed that a number of compatibilist approaches seem to rely, at least implicitly, on this sort of principle: one exercises responsibility-level control in performing an action only if some objective reason one has nondeviantly causes that action. But because there is an alternative possibilities requirement for our having objective reasons, these compatibilist approaches cannot escape our having alternatives.

NOTES

1. Strawson speaks of "contra-causal freedom" rather than agent causal freedom. There is little to be said in support of the view that it is not possible for an event to be both agent caused and deterministically (or indeterministically caused). See, for example, Clarke 2003, 148, 182.
2. In *Moral Dimensions* Thomas Scanlon (2008) defends a novel analysis of the concept of blameworthiness that, like the Strawsonian one, appeals to persons' attitudes and their relations with others. The analysis suggests both an interesting species of semi-compatibilism and exposes what Scanlon sees as close links between blameworthiness and reasons. I believe that on its most credible reading, however, the analysis implies that blameworthiness is frequently associated with our having objective *pro tanto* reasons. If this is correct, Scanlon's view implies that blameworthiness requires our having alternatives. See Haji (n.d.) for further discussion of this issue.
3. See Mele 1995, 65–80 for an illuminating, critical discussion on akratic action and hierarchical motivation. See also Vihvelin 1994.
4. Action in accord with the True and the Good is suggestive of the principle (*PO*) that praiseworthiness requires obligation or permissibility.

5. Dana Nelkin (2008) develops a variation of Wolf's Reason View, which she calls the "rational abilities view" (2008, 497). It says that "people are responsible when they act with the ability to do the right thing for the right reasons, or a good thing for good reasons" (497). I believe her view is susceptible to problems analogous to the ones I have raised for Wolf's views.

6. Wallace (1994) accepts such a view as well. He says that normative competence should be understood in terms of the power to grasp and apply moral reasons, and the power to regulate behavior in light of such reasons (1994, 86, 157).

Chapter 8

Conclusion

8.1. SUMMARY OF THE ARGUMENT

It has long been thought that moral responsibility requires control. In addition, in a venerable tradition, this control is the freedom to do otherwise; the freedom to actualize one of alternative pathways into the future. Recently, we have seen that pressure from, for instance, Frankfurt examples, has challenged this age-old view about the control that responsibility demands; Frankfurt examples attempt to sever the connection between responsibility, on the one hand, and free will, on the other.

If responsibility requires control—if the truth of judgments of moral praiseworthiness and blameworthiness presupposes freedom—then it is not implausible to suppose that the truth of other varieties of normative appraisal also requires that we have control. Judgments of moral or prudential obligation are especially instructive in this respect. I have viewed *Kant's Law*—the moral "ought" implies "can" principle—as a control condition for obligation: no action, for instance, can be morally obligatory for one unless one has control in doing it, and one element of this control is the ability to do it. I have argued that if we accept *Kant's Law*, we should also accept the principles that "wrong" implies "can" and "right" implies "can." Assuming it is unproblematic that something is obligatory for one if and *only* if it is not wrong for one, then through some simple logical maneuvering we can derive the result that obligation, right, and wrong require alternatives. No action, for example, can be wrong for one unless one *could* have done otherwise. The sequence of reasoning leading to this conclusion regarding impermissibility is straightforward: If it is wrong for one to do something, one ought not to do it; if one ought not to do something, one can refrain from doing it; so, if it is wrong for one to do something, one can refrain from doing it. But "wrong" also implies "can." This first route to the conclusion that there is an alternative possibilities requirement for obligation, right, and wrong should strike us as significant, especially if lingering in our mind is the concern about whether determinism is compatible with obligation.

Further reflection on obligation reveals something that should dawn on many as even more engaging. Obligation is conceptually tied to reasons. If an agent has a moral obligation to do something, then she has a reason to do it. Similarly, it seems that an act's being morally wrong just is its being such that there is a moral reason not to do it. I proposed that the reasons in question are objective *pro tanto* reasons. I also suggested that *Kant's Law* just is a special instance of the more general principle that if something is obligatory for one from the perspective of objective reasons, then one can do it. This reason-wise "ought" implies "can" principle, in conjunction with some other highly reasonable principles, generates the result that there is a requirement of alternative possibilities for objective *pro tanto* reasons: no one can have such a reason to do something unless one could have done otherwise. I've called this "reason's debt to free will" (or, simply, "reason's debt to freedom"). So if obligation is conceptually tied to objective *pro tanto* reasons, and such reasons are logically tied to our having alternatives, then we derive, again, the result that obligation requires alternatives. This second route to the conclusion that the truth of judgments of moral and prudential obligation presupposes our having alternatives serves to bolster confidence in this same conclusion derived via the first route outlined earlier.

Once we recognize that obligation is essentially associated with objective *pro tanto* reasons, and we appreciate reason's debt to freedom, then it seems natural to inquire whether other normative appraisals are also essentially tied to such reasons. For if they are, we may well be able to show that such normative appraisals also require alternatives. In chapter 4, I argued that judgments of intrinsic value are essentially linked to objective *pro tanto* reasons: if something is intrinsically good (or bad or neutral), then anyone who contemplates it has such reasons to favor (or disfavor or be indifferent to) it for its own sake. It follows that because of reason's debt to freedom, the truth of pertinent judgments of intrinsic value presupposes our having access to alternatives.

Responsibility appraisals are also tied to reasons: if one is morally praiseworthy or blameworthy for something, one has a reason to do it. But I have left it open whether these reasons are objective *pro tanto*. (I suspect they are not.) Hence, one cannot exploit the line of reasoning for the view that the truth of germane judgments of intrinsic value, or the truth of judgments of moral obligation, presupposes our having alternatives to sustain the view that the truth of judgments of responsibility also requires that we have alternatives. I have also said that I do not have an account of reasons. Theorists who think that all reasons are, in the end, objective should conclude that responsibility requires our having alternatives.

8.2. PRIMARY RAMIFICATIONS

Whether determinism is compatible with the truth of judgments of moral responsibility, and indeed with the truth of judgments of other sorts of normative appraisal, is an issue of perennial interest. A well-entrenched line of argument for the view that determinism rules out responsibility is this: responsibility requires that we have access to alternatives; determinism effaces alternatives; so, determinism and responsibility are not friendly mates. One complication with this argument is whether the alternatives it's alleged responsibility requires are strong alternatives that are incompatible with determinism, or weak alternatives that can co-exist with determinism.

I have explored whether this sort of argument can be marshaled to show whether determinism is incompatible with obligation and intrinsic value. My approach was guarded, having proposed that if one is convinced that the alternatives obligation and intrinsic value require are strong, determinism may well undermine these things by virtue of effacing strong alternatives. If, however, obligation and intrinsic value require only weak alternatives, determinism won't preclude these things as a result of precluding strong alternatives. But then semi-compatibilism concerning obligation or intrinsic value cannot be sustained: one cannot reasonably subscribe to the view that quite independently of whether determinism is compatible with our having alternatives no matter weak or strong, determinism is compatible with obligation and intrinsic value.

If we accept reason's debt to freedom—our having objective *pro tanto* reasons requires that we have alternatives—then we can tease out some other results that should be of interest to those concerned about the costs of living without free will. The strategy here, again, is to show that some things of value to us are essentially tied to our having objective *pro tanto* reasons, but by virtue of reason's debt to freedom, determinism may well imperil these things. For instance, I argued that many moral sentiments, such as forgiveness and guilt, which figure prominently in interpersonal relationships, are essentially associated with objective *pro tanto* reasons, as are judgments about being intrinsically pleased or displeased about something. In some views, such judgments concerning intrinsic pleasure and intrinsic displeasure lie at the heart of personal welfare or even happiness. In addition, some approaches to virtue ethics imply that the truth of at least some aretaic judgments are also essentially linked to objective *pro tanto* reasons. Suppose, again, one thinks that judgments of objective *pro tanto* reasons are tied to our having strong alternatives. Then it is not evident that a range of moral sentiments, or interpersonal relationships, or personal welfare, or happiness, or certain aretaic assessments do not fall victim to determinism. If the alternatives in question are weak, then again, various varieties of semi-compatibilism are ruled out. For instance, one cannot credibly endorse the view that independently of whether determinism is compatible with our having alternatives, determinism is compatible with the truth of judgments concerning our being intrinsically pleased or displeased about things.

Of course, one might take issue with the considerations I have advanced for the view that various axiological judgments, or obligation judgments, or aretaic judgments are essentially associated with objective *pro tanto* reasons. Still, it may be well worth keeping in mind the following template: various things we value are essentially associated with objective *pro tanto* reasons. There is an alternative possibilities requirement for these things because there is such a requirement for having such reasons. One is invited to plug into this template those things one thinks are suitable candidates for what we value.

Finally, reason's debt to freedom casts a dark shadow on several compatibilist accounts of responsibility. On Wolf's in many ways attractive reasons-responsiveness view, for instance, the freedom moral responsibility requires is the freedom to act in accordance with the True and the Good—the freedom to do the right thing for the right reasons. Since doing the morally right thing is essentially tied to our having objective *pro tanto* reasons and because of reason's debt to freedom, doing the right thing for the right reasons is essentially connected to our having alternatives. So such approaches to responsibility cannot be unhitched completely from our having alternatives. As compatibilists, advocates of this sort of position would take on the burden of developing and defending a compatibilist account of weak alternatives.

I have been a fairly staunch advocate of semi-compatibilism regarding responsibility. Having compatibilist leanings, it has been my wish to defend semi-compatibilism concerning both obligation and intrinsic value. But, because reason is indebted to freedom and because judgments of obligation and pertinent judgments of intrinsic value are essentially tied to our having objective *pro tanto* reasons, it seems this is a wish that will elude fulfillment.

APPENDIX

Agent Causation and Luck

In this appendix, I argue that agent causalists of a certain sort countenance a problem of luck analogous to the problem event causalists countenance.

There is some thought that supplementing the agent's freedom-level control in making a decision (or performing an overt action), which the agent exercises in virtue of the decision's being nondeviantly and indeterministically caused by prior agent-involving events with the agent's *agent* causing that decision, can evade the problem of luck. With agent causation, the *agent's* control in making a decision is not exercised (perhaps solely) via the control that is exercised as a result of agent-involving events causing the decision, but is exercised directly in the making of the decision itself. It is, literally, then, the agent who contributes to generating the decision, and if this is so, it is hard to see how the outcome of the decision's being made can be a matter of luck.

Developing this point further, Randolph Clarke proposes that the sole difference between agent causation and event causation is this: with the former, the first relatum of the causal relation is a substance; with the latter, the first relatum is an event, and the causal relation is exactly the same with either relatum. As Clarke himself notes, explaining agent causation along these lines is tenable only if certain accounts of causation in general prove correct. A reductive analysis of causation that explains causation in terms of noncausal phenomena, such as a regularity or counterfactual account, would not be amenable to Clarke's approach. Clarke suggests, instead, that a realist or nonreductive account of causation, according to which the causal relation is among the basic constituents of the universe, and causation just is producing, bringing about, or making happen, is much more promising (Clarke 1996, 21–23).

Clarke's proposes that a free decision is indeterministically caused by apt agent-involving events *and* co-produced by the agent's causing it. He further proposes that as a matter of nomological necessity, whichever of the "open" decisions the agent makes, that decision will be made and caused by the agent's having the reasons that favor it (together with other mental events) only if the agent herself causes that decision. Augmentation of the indeterministic causation of the decision with the agent causation of it by its agent, secures for the agent the exercise of further positive powers. These powers influence causally which of the open alternative courses of action (mental or otherwise) that a modest libertarian view permits will become actual (Clarke 1996, 25–26; 2003, chaps. 7–9).[1] An agent who is, in this way, a co-determinant of her action will, thus, exercise "determining control" in its production.

Assume that an agent has prior motivational (or reason) states $r1 \ldots rn$ having nonzero probabilities of causing decisions $D1 \ldots Dn$. In Clarke's view, it is a law of nature—"Clarke's Law"—that (1) whatever action is performed will be (agent) caused by the agent; (2) a reason $r1$ will (event) cause a decision $D1$ only if the agent causes $D1$; and (3) the agent will cause a decision, $D1$, only if a corresponding reason, $r1$, causes $D1$ (Clarke 2003, 145).

Let us suppose that Peg in the actual world has a desire to do $A1$ and an opposed desire to do $A2$ (where doing $A1$, again, may be making the decision to do $A1$). Suppose, also, that her desire to do the former is stronger than her desire to do the latter, and that after deliberation she forms the best judgment that she ought to do $A1$, and she does $A1$. Finally, assume that Clarke's Law is satisfied in this case: Peg agent causes $A1$; her prior reason states, $r1$, appropriately (indeterministically) cause $A1$ only if she agent causes $A1$, and she will agent cause $A1$ only if $r1$ causes $A1$. We note that Peg's desire to do $A1$, her motivationally stronger desire, is aligned with her best judgment to do $A1$; it is aligned with her evaluation of the object of her desire to do $A1$. Turn to the relevant non-actual world (or worlds) in which she (Peg*) putatively freely does $A2$. As this world has the same past up to the time at which she makes her decision in either (and the same laws as does the actual world), we assume (initially) that Peg*'s desire to do $A1$ remains stronger than her competing desire to do $A2$, and that Peg* retains the judgment that it is best for her to do $A1$. Her doing of $A2$, then, with the sorts of familiar stipulations—no new information is introduced, she does not continue to deliberate, she is not hostage to surreptitious manipulation, etc.—is akratic. Is the agent causalist of Clarke's variety in any better position than the modest libertarian to give a reasonable account of Peg*'s akratic action? If Peg*'s $A2$-ing is free, then Clarke's Law is satisfied: Peg* agent causes $A2$; her prior reason states, $r2$, appropriately (indeterministically) cause $A2$ only if she agent causes $A2$, and she will agent cause $A2$ only if $r2$ causes $A2$. With these details laid out, there is a concern here not difficult to discern: with Peg in the actual world, the agent causal contribution she makes to doing $A1$ complements the contribution to her doing $A1$ that her reason state $r1$ makes. If we were to "subtract" agent causation from the scenario, Peg's reason states would favor her doing $A1$. But we have supposed that Peg also agent causes $A1$. In this scenario agent causation and event causation are in harmony. With Peg*, however, the contribution of her reason states to doing what she does, *assuming that the past and the laws are fixed*, remains, or so it seems, what it is in the actual world. Her reason states favor her doing A_1, yet she agent causes A_2. If we suppose that in the production of her A_2-ing, Peg*'s agent causing A_2 had "veto power" over reason states that (event-) cause A_2 (something whose possibility remains unclear by the lights of Clarke's Law), it would seem that the problem of explaining her akratic action of A_2-ing would remain. There is, apparently, no mis-alignment between Peg*'s best judgment that she ought to do A_1 and her stronger desire to do A_1 which is a constituent of her reason state r_1; yet she does A_2. With akratic action, one would expect to find that although Peg* judges that it is best for her to do A_1, her desire to do A_2 is stronger than her desire to do A_1.

Perhaps the agent causalist will propose that to account for the relevant mis-alignment, Peg*'s agent causal contribution to do A_2 augments the motivational strength of her desire to do A_2 (which is a constituent of her reason state r_2), and, as a result, its motivational strength is relatively higher than the motivational strength of her competing desire to do A_1.[2] The primary concern with this proposal is that Peg*'s agent causal contribution, it seems, is not "informed" by her prior reason states: she does not entertain any considerations different from those that Peg entertains, no new information comes to her mind, she does not selectively focus on various out-comes, and so on. Why, then, does Peg* agent cause A_2 when, given the same past and the laws, Peg agent causes A_1? Even if we entertain the (unpromising) supposi-tion that Peg* *did* selectively focus, etc. at the time at which she agent causes A_2, what would explain this radical shift in her psychology, assuming that Peg exercises self-control in A-ing in the actual world?

It remains problematic whether this sort of hybrid agent causal account can escape the problem of luck.

NOTES

1. Clarke argues that the notion of agent causation is intelligible, but he doubts whether it is possible for persons to agent cause events (2003, chap. 10).
2. This is not Clarke's view. In his view, "when an agent acts with direct freedom, she directly causes her action. Her causing the action, if that is an event, occurs when the action occurs, and not before. She does not, in causing that action, produce any changes before the action begins" (2003, 144, note omitted).

BIBLIOGRAPHY

Adams, Robert. 1994. "Involuntary Sins." *Philosophical Review* 85:3–31.

Alemeida, Michael, and Mark Bernstein. 2011. "Rollbacks, Endorsements, and Indeterminism." In Robert Kane, ed., *The Oxford Handbook of Free Will*, 2nd ed. New York: Oxford University Press, 484–95.

Aristotle. 1941. *Rhetoric*. In Richard McKeon, ed., *The Basic Works of Aristotle*. New York: Random House.

Arpaly, Nomy. 2003. *Unprincipled Virtue*. New York: Oxford University Press.

———. 2006. *Merit, Meaning, and Human Bondage: An Essay on Free Will*. Princeton, NJ: Princeton University Press.

Austin, J. L. 1961. "Ifs and Cans." In J. O. Urmson and G. Warnock, eds., *Philosophical Papers*. Oxford: Clarendon Press, 153–80.

Ayer, A. J. 1954. "Freedom and Necessity." In *Philosophical Essays*. New York: St. Martin's Press, 3–20.

Berofsky, Bernard. 1995. *Liberation from Self*. Cambridge: Cambridge University Press.

———. 2000. "Ultimate Responsibility in a Deterministic World." *Philosophy and Phenomenological Research* 60:135–40.

———. 2003. "Classical Compatibilism: Not Dead Yet." In David Widerker and Michael McKenna, eds., *Moral Responsibility and Alternative Possibilities: Essays on the Importance of Alternative Possibilities*. Aldershot, UK: Ashgate Press, 107–26.

———. 2011. "Compatibilism Without Frankfurt: Dispositional Analysis of Free Will." In Kane, *Oxford Handbook of Free Will*, 153–74.

Blanshard, Brand. 1961. *Reason and Goodness*. London: George Allen and Unwin.

Brentano, F. 1969. *The Origin of Our Knowledge of Right and Wrong*. London: Routledge and Kegan Paul. (Original publication date, 1889.)

Broad, C. D. 1930. *Five Types of Ethical Theory*. London: Kegan Paul, Trench, Trubner.

Broome, J. 2004. "Reasons." In P. Pettit, S. Scheffler, M. Smith, and R. J. Wallace, eds., *Reason and Value: Essays on the Moral Philosophy of Joseph Raz*. Oxford: Oxford University Press, 28–55.

Bykvist, Krister. 2009. "No Good Fit: Why the Fitting Attitude Analysis of Value Fails." *Mind* 118:1–30.

Chisholm, Roderick M. 1986. *Brentano and Intrinsic Value*. Cambridge: Cambridge University Press.

Chisholm, Roderick, and E. Sosa. 1966. "Intrinsic Preferability and the Problem of Supererogation." *Synthese* 16:321–31.

Christman, John. 1991. "Autonomy and Personal History." *Canadian Journal of Philosophy* 21:1–24.

Clarke, Randolph. 1996. "Agent Causation and Event Causation in the Production of Free Action." *Philosophical Topics* 24:19–48.

———. 2000. "Modest Libertarianism." *Philosophical Perspectives* 14:21–45.

———. 2003. *Libertarian Accounts of Free Will*. New York: Oxford University.

———. 2008. "Dispositions, Abilities to Act, and Free Will: The New Dispositionalism." *Mind* 118:323–51.

———. 2011. "Alternatives for Libertarians." In Kane, *Oxford Handbook of Free Will*, 329–48.

Copp, David. 1997. "Defending the Principle of Alternative Possibilities: Blameworthiness and Moral Responsibility." *Nous* 31:441–56.

———. 2003. "'Ought' Implies 'Can,' Blameworthiness, and the Principle of Alternative Possibilities." In David Widerker and Michael McKenna eds., *Moral Responsibility and Alternative Possibilities: Essays on the Importance of Alternative Possibilities*. Aldershot, UK: Ashgate Press, 265–99.

Crisp, Roger. 2006. *Reasons and the Good*. Oxford: Clarendon Press.

Cuneo, Terence. 2001. "Are Moral Qualities Response-dependent?" *Nous* 35:569–91.

Cuypers, Stefaan E. 2000. "Autonomy Beyond Voluntarism: In Defense of Hierarchy." *Canadian Journal of Philosophy* 30:225–56.

Dancy, Jonathan. 2005. "Should We Pass the Buck?" In Toni Rønnow-Rasmussen and Michael J. Zimmerman, eds., *Recent Work in Intrinsic Value*. Dordrecht, Netherlands: Springer, 33–44.

Davidson, Donald. 1963. "Actions, Reasons, and Causes." *Journal of Philosophy* 60:685–700.

Dennett, Daniel. 1978. "On Giving Libertarians What They Say They Want." In *Brainstorms: Philosophical Essays on Mind and Psychology*. Montgomery, VT: Bradford, 286–99.

Double, Richard. 1991. *The Non-Reality of Free Will*. Oxford: Oxford University Press.

———. 2004. "The Ethical Advantages of Free Will Subjectivism." *Philosophy and Phenomenological Research* 69:411–22.

Driver, Julia. 1992. "The Suberogatory." *Australasian Journal of Philosophy* 70:286–95.

Ekstrom, Laura W. 2011. "Free Will is not a Mystery." In Kane, *Oxford Handbook of Free Will*, 366–80.

Ewing, A. C. 1948. *The Definition of Good*. New York: Macmillan and Co.

———. 1939. "A Suggested Non-naturalistic Analysis of Good." *Mind* 39:1–22

Feldman, Fred. 1978. *Introductory Ethics*. Englewood Cliffs: Prentice Hall.

———. 1986. *Doing the Best We Can*. Dordrecht, Netherlands: D. Reidel Publishing Company.

———. 1988. "On the Advantages of Cooperativeness." *Midwest Studies in Philosophy* 13:308–23.

———. 1990. "A Simpler Solution to the Paradoxes of Deontic Logic." *Philosophical Perspectives* 4:309–41.

———. 1992. *Confrontations with the Reaper: A Philosophical Study of the Nature and Value of Death*. New York: Oxford University Press.

———. 1997. *Utilitarianism, Hedonism, and Desert*. Cambridge: Cambridge University Press.

———. 2000. "Basic Intrinsic Value." *Philosophical Studies* 99:319–46.

———. 2004. *Pleasure and the Good Life. Concerning the Nature, Varieties, and Plausibility of Hedonism*. Oxford: Clarendon Press.

———. 2010. *What Is This Thing Called HAPPINESS?* New York: Oxford University Press.

Fields, Lloyd. 1994. "Moral Beliefs and Blameworthiness." *Philosophy* 69:397–415.

Fischer, John M., ed. 1986. *Moral Responsibility*. Ithaca, NY: Cornell University Press.

———. 1995. "Libertarianism and Avoidability: A Reply to Widerker." *Faith and Philosophy* 12:11–25.

———. 1999. "Recent Work on Moral Responsibility." *Ethics* 110:93–139.

———. 2003. "'Ought-Implies-Can,' Causal Determinism, and Moral Responsibility." *Analysis* 63:244–50.

———. 2005. "Free Will and Moral Responsibility." In David Copp, ed., *The Oxford Handbook of Ethics*. New York: Oxford University Press, 321–54.

———. 2006. *My Way: Essays on Moral Responsibility*. New York: Oxford University Press.

———. 2008a. "Freedom, Foreknowledge, and Frankfurt: A Reply to Vihvelin." *Canadian Journal of Philosophy* 38:327–42.

———. 2008b. "Responsibility and the Kinds of Freedom." *Journal of Ethics* 12:203–28.

———. 2010. "The Frankfurt Cases: The Moral of the Stories." *Philosophical Review* 119:315–36.

———. 2011. "Frankfurt-Type Examples and Semi-Compatibilism." In Kane, *Oxford Handbook of Free Will*, 243–65.

Fischer, John M., and Mark Ravizza. 1998. *Responsibility and Control: A Theory of Moral Responsibility.* Cambridge: Cambridge University Press.

Frankfurt, Harry. 1969. "Alternative Possibilities and Moral Responsibility." *Journal of Philosophy* 66:829–39.

————. 1971. "Freedom of the Will and the Concept of a Person." *Journal of Philosophy* 68:5–20.

————. 1987. "Identification and Wholeheartedness." In F. D. Schoeman, ed., *Responsibility, Character, and the Emotions: New Essays in Moral Psychology.* New York: Cambridge University Press, 27–45. Repr. in and cited from Frankfurt 1988:159–76.

————. 1988. *The Importance of What We Care About.* Cambridge: Cambridge University Press

————. 1992. "The Faintest Passion." Presidential address. *Proceedings of the American Philosophical Association* 66:5–16. Repr. in and cited from Frankfurt 1999: 95–107.

————. 1994. "Autonomy, Necessity, and Love." In Hans Friedrich Fulda and Rolf-Peter Horstmann, eds., *Vernunftbegriffe in der Moderne.* Stuttgart: Klett-Cotta, 433–47. Repr. in Frankfurt 1999: 129–41.

————. 1999. *Necessity, Volition, and Love.* Cambridge: Cambridge University Press.

Franklin, Chris. 2011. "Farewell to the Luck (and Mind) Argument." *Philosophical Studies* 156:199–230.

Friedman, Marilyn. 1986. "Autonomy and the Split-Level Self." *Southern Journal of Philosophy* 24:19–35.

Ginet, Carl. 2003. "Libertarianism." In M. J. Loux and D. W. Zimmerman, eds., *The Oxford Handbook of Metaphysics.* New York: Oxford University Press, 587–612.

Ginet, C. 1990. *On Action.* Cambridge: Cambridge University Press.

Goetz, Stewart. 1998. "A Noncausal Theory of Agency." *Philosophy and Phenomenological Research* 49:303–16.

Haji, Ishtiyaque. 1998. *Moral Appraisability.* New York: Oxford University Press.

————. 2002. *Deontic Morality and Control.* Cambridge: Cambridge University Press.

————. 2005. "Libertarianism, Luck, and Action Explanation." *Journal of Philosophical Research* 30:321–40.

————. 2006. "Frankfurt-Type Examples, Obligation, and Responsibility." *Journal of Ethics* 10:255–81.

————. 2009a. *Incompatibilism's Allure: Principal Arguments for Incompatibilism.* Peterbrough, Ontario: Broadview Press.

————. 2009b. *Freedom and Value: Freedom's Influence on Welfare and Worldly Value.* New York: Springer.

————. 2010. "Incompatibilism and Prudential Obligation." *Canadian Journal of Philosophy* 40:385–410.

————. 2011. "Obligation, Reason, and Frankfurt Examples." In Kane, *Oxford Handbook of Free Will,* 288–305.

————. n.d. "Reason, Responsibility, and Free Will: Reply to my Critics." *Journal of Ethics.*

Haji, Ishtiyaque, and Stefaan Cuypers. 2007. "Magical Agents, Global Induction, and the Internalism/Externalism Debate." *Australasian Journal of Philosophy* 85:343–71.

————. 2008. *Moral Responsibility, Authenticity, and Education.* New York: Routledge.

Haji, Ishtiyaque, and Michael McKenna. 2004. "Dialectical Delicacies in the Debate about Freedom and Alternative Possibilities." *Journal of Philosophy* 101:299–314.

————. 2006. "Defending Frankfurt's Argument in Deterministic Contexts: A Reply to Palmer." *Journal of Philosophy* 103:363–72.

Harman, Gilbert. 1967. "Toward a Theory of Intrinsic Value." *Journal of Philosophy* 64:792–804.

Heyd, David. 1982. *Supererogation.* Cambridge: Cambridge University Press.

Hobart, R. E. 1934. "Free Will as Involving Indeterminism and Inconceivable Without It." *Mind* 43:1–27.

Honderich, Ted. 1993. *How Free Are You?* Oxford: Oxford University Press.

Hooker, Brad, and Bart Streumer. 2004. "Procedural and Substantive Practical Rationality." In Alfred Mele and Piers Rawling, eds., *The Oxford Handbook of Rationality.* New York: Oxford University Press, 57–74.

Hume, David. 1739. *A Treatise of Human Nature.* Edited by D. F. Norton and M. J. Norton. New York: Oxford University Press (2000).

Kagan, Shelly. 1998. "Rethinking Intrinsic Value." *Journal of Ethics* 2:277–97.

Kane, Robert. 1996. *The Significance of Free Will.* Oxford: Oxford University Press.

————. 1999a. "On Free Will, Responsibility, and Indeterminism: Responses to Clarke, Haji, and Mele." *Philosophical Explorations* 2:105–21.

————. 1999b. "Responsibility, Luck, and Chance: Reflections on Free Will and Indeterminism." *Journal of Philosophy* 96:217–40.

————. 2005. *A Contemporary Introduction to Free Will.* New York: Oxford University Press.

————. 2011. "Rethinking Free Will: New Perspectives on an Ancient Problem." In *The Oxford Handbook of Free Will,* 2nd ed. New York: Oxford University Press, 381–404.

Kim, Jaegwon. 1976. "Events as Property Exemplifications." In M. Brand and D. Walton, eds., *Action Theory.* Dordrecht, Netherlands: D. Reidel, 159–77.

Lemos, Noah. 1994. *Intrinsic Value.* Cambridge: Cambridge University Press.

Lewis, David. 1997. "Finkish Dispositions." *Philosophical Quarterly* 47:143–58.

Mann, William. 1983. "Dreams of Immorality." *Philosophy* 58:378–85.

McCann, Hugh. 1998. *The Works of Agency: On Human Action, Will, and Freedom.* Ithaca, NY: Cornell University Press.

McNamara, Paul. 1996. "Making Room for Going Beyond the Call." *Mind* 105:415–50.

————. 2008 "Praise, Blame, Obligation, and Beyond: Toward a Framework for the Classical Conception of Supererogation and Kin." In Ron van der Meyden and

Leendert van der Torre, eds., *Deontic Logic in Computer Science*. Berlin: Springer Verlag, 233–47.

———. 2011. "Praise, Blame, Obligation, and DWE: Toward a Comprehensive Framework for the Classical Conception of Supererogation and Kin." *Journal of Applied Logic*:153–70.

Mele, Alfred. 1987. *An Essay on Akrasia, Self-Deception, and Self-Control*. New York: Oxford University Press.

———. 1995. *Autonomous Agents*. New York: Oxford University Press.

———. 1999a. "Ultimate Responsibility and Dumb Luck." *Social Philosophy and Policy* 16: 274–93.

———. 1999b. "Kane, Luck, and the Significance of Free Will." *Philosophical Explorations* 2: 96–104.

———. 2003. *Motivation and Agency*. New York: Oxford University Press.

———. 2006. *Free Will and Luck*. New York: Oxford University Press.

———. 2007. "Free Will and Luck: Reply to Critics." *Philosophical Explorations* 10:195–210.

Mellema, Gregory. 1991. *Supererogation, Obligation, and Offence*. Albany, NY: State University Press of New York.

Milo, R. 1984. *Immorality*. Princeton, NJ: Princeton University Press.

Moore, G. E. 1903. *Principia Ethica*. Cambridge: Cambridge University Press.

Nelkin, Dana K. 2007. "Good Luck to Libertarians: Reflections on Al Mele's *Free Will and Luck*." *Philosophical Explorations* 10:173–84.

———. 2008. "Responsibility and Rational Abilities: Defending An Asymmetrical View." *Pacific Philosophical Quarterly* 89:497–515.

O'Connor, Timothy. 2007. "Is it all Just a Matter of Luck?" *Philosophical Explorations* 10:157–61.

———. 2011. "Agent-Causal Theories of Freedom." In Kane, *Oxford Handbook of Free Will*, 309–28.

Olson, Jonas. 2009. "Fitting Attitude Analyses of Value and the Partiality Challenge." *Ethical Theory and Moral Practice* 12:365–78.

Parfit, Derek. 2001. "Rationality and Reasons." In D. Egonsson, B. Peterson, J. Josefsson, and T. Rønnow-Rasmussen, eds., *Exploring Practical Philosophy: From Action to Values*. Aldershot: Ashgate, 17–39.

Parfit, Derek. 1997. "Reasons and Motivation." *Proceedings of the Aristotelian Society* S71:99–130.

Pereboom, Derk. 2001. *Living Without Free Will*. Cambridge: Cambridge University Press.

———. 2002. "Living Without Free Will: The Case For Hard Incompatibilism." In Kane, *Oxford Handbook of Free Will*. New York: Oxford University Press: 477–88.

———. 2007. "Hard Incompatibilism." In J. M. Fischer, R. Kane, D. Pereboom, and M. Vargas, *Four Views on Free Will*. Oxford: Blackwell Publishing: 85–125.

Rabinowicz, Wlodek, and Toni Rønnow-Rasmussen. 1999. "A Distinction in Value: Intrinsic and For Its Own Sake." *Proceedings of the Aristotelian Society* 100:33–52.

Rønnow-Rasmussen, Toni. 2009. "Normative Reasons and the Agent-Neutral/Relative Dichotomy." *Philosophia* 37:27–43.

Ross, W. D. 1939. *Foundations of Ethics*. Oxford: Oxford University Press.

Scanlon, Thomas M. 1998. *What We Owe to Each Other*. Cambridge, MA: Harvard University Press.

———. 2008. *Moral Dimensions*. Princeton, NJ: Princeton University Press.

Schlossberger, E. 1992. *Moral Responsibility and Persons*. Philadelphia: Temple University Press.

Schroeder, M. 2007. "Reasons and Agent-Neutrality." *Philosophical Studies* 135:279–306.

Shatz, David. 1985. "Free Will and the Structure of Motivation." *Midwest Studies in Philosophy* 10:451–82.

Slote, Michael. 1980. "Understanding Free Will." *Journal of Philosophy* 77:136–51.

———. 1992. *From Morality To Virtue*. New York: Oxford University Press.

Smart, J. J. C. 1961. "Free Will, Praise and Blame." *Mind* 70:291–306.

Smith, Angela M. 2005. "Responsibility for Attitudes: Activity and Passivity in Mental Life." *Ethics* 115:236–71.

———. 2008. "Control, Responsibility, and Moral Assessment." *Philosophical Studies* 138:367–92.

Smith, Holly. 1991. "Varieties of Moral Worth and Moral Credit." *Ethics* 101:279–303.

Smith, Michael. 1994. *The Moral Problem*. Oxford: Blackwell.

———. 2003. "Rational Capacities, or: How to Distinguish Recklessness, Weakness, and Compulsion." In Sarah Stroud and Christine Tappolet, eds., *Weakness of Will and Practical Irrationality*. Oxford: Clarendon Press, 17–38.

Speak, Daniel. 2011. "The Consequence Argument Revisited." In Kane, *Oxford Handbook of Free Will*, 115–30.

Strawson, Peter. 1962. "Freedom and Resentment." *Proceedings of the British Academy* 48:1–25. Repr. in and cited from Watson 1982:59–80.

Streumer, Bart. 2007a. "Reasons and Impossibility." *Philosophical Studies* 136:351–84.

———. 2007b. "Does 'Ought' Conversationally Implicate 'Can?'" *European Journal of Philosophy* 11:219–28.

———. 2010. "Reasons, Impossibility, and Efficient Steps: Reply to Heuer." *Philosophical Studies* 151:78–86.

Stump, Eleonore. 1993a. "Intellect, Will, and the Principle of Alternative Possibilities." In John M. Fischer and Mark Ravizza, eds., *Perspectives on Moral Responsibility*. Ithaca, NY: Cornell University Press, 237–62.

———. 1993b. "Sanctification, Hardening of the Heart, and Frankfurt's Concept of the Will." In Fischer and Ravizza, *Perspectives on Moral Responsibility*, 211–34.

Thalberg, Irving. 1978. "Hierarchical Analyses of Unfree Action." *Canadian Journal of Philosophy* 8:211–26.

Tod, Patrick, and Neal Tognazzini. 2008. "A Problem for Guidance Control." *Philosophical Quarterly* 58:686–92.

Trakakis, Nick. 2008. "Whither Morality in a Hard Determinist World?" In N. Trakakis and D. Cohen, eds., *Essays on Free Will and Moral Responsibility*. Newcastle upon Tyne: Cambridge Scholars Press: 34–70.

Urmson, J. O. 1958. "Saints and Heroes." In A. I. Meldin, ed., *Essays in Moral Philosophy*. Seattle: University of Washington Press, 198–216.

van Inwagen, Peter. 1983. *An Essay on Free Will*. Oxford: Clarendon Press.

———. 2000. "Free Will Remains a Mystery." *Philosophical Perspectives* 14:1–19.

———. 2008. "How to Think about the Problem of Free Will." *Journal of Ethics* 12:327–41.

———. 2011. "A Promising Argument." In Kane, *Oxford Handbook of Free Will*, 475–83.

Vihvelin, Kadri. 1994. "Are Drug Addicts Unfree?" In Steven Luper-Foy and Curtis Brown, eds., *Drugs, Morality, and the Law*. New York: Garland, 51–78.

———. 2004. "Free Will Demystified: A Dispositional Account." *Philosophical Topics* 32:427–50.

———. 2008a. "Compatibilism, Incompatibilism, and Impossibilism." In John Hawthorne, Theodore Sider, and Dean Zimmerman, eds., *Contemporary Debates in Metaphysics*. Malden, MA: Blackwell Publishing, 303–18.

———. 2008b. "Foreknowledge, Frankfurt, and Ability to Do Otherwise: A Reply to Fischer." *Canadian Journal of Philosophy* 38:343–72.

Vranas, Peter B. M. 2007. "I Ought, Therefore I Can." *Philosophical Studies* 136:167–216.

Wallace, Jay R. 1994. *Responsibility and the Moral Sentiments*. Cambridge, MA: Harvard University Press.

Waller, Bruce. 1988. "Free Will Gone Out of Control." *Behaviorism* 16:149–67.

———. 1990. *Freedom Without Responsibility*. Philadelphia: Temple University Press.

Watson, Gary. 1975. "Free Agency." *Journal of Philosophy* 72:205–20. Repr. in and cited from Fischer 1986: 81–96.

———, ed. 1982. *Free Will*, 1st ed. Oxford: Oxford University Press.

———. 1986. Review of Dennett's *Elbow Room*. *Journal of Philosophy* 83:517–22.

———. 1987. "Free Action and Free Will." *Mind* 96:145–72.

———. 1993. "On the Primacy of Character." In Owen Flanagan and Amelie Oksenberg Rorty, eds., *Identity, Character, and Morality: Essays in Moral Psychology*. Cambridge, MA: MIT Press: 449–69.

———. 1998. "Some Worries about Semi-Compatibilism: Remarks on John Fischer's *The Metaphysics of Free Will*." *Journal of Social Philosophy* 29:135–43.

Widerker, David. 1991. "Frankfurt on 'Ought Implies Can' and Alternative Possibilities." *Analysis* 51:222–24.

———. 2009. "A Defense of Frankfurt-friendly Libertarianism." *Philosophical Explorations* 12:87–108.

————. 2011. "Frankfurt-Friendly Libertarianism." In Kane, *Oxford Handbook of Free Will*, 266–87.

Wiggins, David. 1973. "Towards a Reasonable Libertarianism." In Ted Honderich, ed., *Essays on Freedom and Action*. London: Routledge and Kegan Paul, 31–62.

Williams, Bernard. 1981. *Moral Luck*. New York: Cambridge University Press.

————. 1995a. "Internal Reasons and the Obscurity of Blame." In *Making Sense of Humanity*. Cambridge: Cambridge University Press, 35–44.

————. 1995b. "Replies." In J. E. J. Altham and R. Harrison, eds., *World, Mind, and Ethics*. Cambridge: Cambridge University Press, 185–224.

Wolf, Susan. 1980. "Asymmetrical Freedom." *Journal of Philosophy* 77:151–66. Repr. in and cited from Fischer 1986, 225–40.

————.1990. *Freedom Within Reason*. New York: Oxford University Press.

Zimmerman, David. 1981. "Hierarchical Motivation and the Freedom of the Will." *Pacific Philosophical Quarterly* 62:354–68.

Zimmerman, Michael J. 1988. *An Essay on Moral Responsibility*. Totowa, NJ: Rowman and Littlefield.

————. 1996. *The Concept of Moral Obligation*. Cambridge: Cambridge University Press.

————. 2001. *The Nature of Intrinsic Value*. Lanham, MD: Rowman and Littlefield.

————. 2006. "Moral Luck: A Partial Map." *Canadian Journal of Philosophy* 36:585–608.

————. 2007. "The Good and the Right." *Utilitas* 19:326–53.

————. 2008. *Living with Uncertainty*. Cambridge: Cambridge University Press.

————. 2010. "Responsibility, Reaction, and Value." *Journal of Ethics* 14:103–15.

————. 2011. "Partiality and Intrinsic Value." *Mind* 120:447–83.

INDEX